An Introduction to
CHINESE
CULTURE

中国
文化概况

主编◎罗晓黎

编者◎欧秋耘 洪 琪 华丹丹 鲁维佳

金 汤 王文明 刘 晖 黎闯进

U0360641

清华大学出版社
北 京

内 容 简 介

本教材依据文化主题进行分类，共设 12 章，依次为中国文化起源、中国概况、中国语言、中国哲学、中国传统教育、中国文学、中国表演艺术、中国建筑、中国节日、中国饮食、中国工艺品和中国传统医学。每章包括三篇主体课文、两篇拓展阅读文章和相关课后练习。本教材旨在帮助学生构建对中国文化的立体认知，引导学生深刻理解文化现象背后的文化内核，有利于提升学生的思辨能力及思政素养。

本教材适用于英语专业核心课程教学，也适用于高校人文素养类通识选修课程教学，还可供希望了解中国文化的读者参考使用。

图书在版编目（CIP）数据

中国文化概况：英文 / 罗晓黎主编. —北京：清华大学出版社，2025.2
ISBN 978–7–302–64670–9

Ⅰ. ①中… Ⅱ. ①罗… Ⅲ. ①中华文化—概况—英文 Ⅳ. ①K203

中国国家版本馆 CIP 数据核字（2023）第 182377 号

责任编辑：刘细珍
封面设计：李伯骥
责任校对：王荣静
责任印制：刘 菲

出版发行：清华大学出版社
    网 址：https://www.tup.com.cn, https://www.wqxuetang.com
    地 址：北京清华大学学研大厦 A 座   邮 编：100084
    社 总 机：010–83470000   邮 购：010–62786544
    投稿与读者服务：010–62776969，c-service@tup.tsinghua.edu.cn
    质量反馈：010–62772015，zhiliang@tup.tsinghua.edu.cn
印 装 者：北京联兴盛业印刷股份有限公司
经 **销**：全国新华书店
开 **本**：185mm×260mm **印** **张**：14.75 **字** **数**：294 千字
版 **次**：2025 年 3 月第 1 版 **印** **次**：2025 年 3 月第 1 次印刷
定 **价**：65.00 元

产品编号：101437–01

前　言

　　《中国文化概况》一书是在中国积极推动文化"走出去"的战略大背景下，由编者团队历经多年课程建设与教学实践的积淀编写而成。该教材在编撰过程中，综合考虑了国家的大政方针、中国文化的特点以及学生对中国文化已有的丰富体验，力求较深入地展现中国文化的精髓。

一、编写思路

　　本教材以国家对高校文化教学的要求为纲领。《关于实施中华优秀传统文化传承发展工程的意见》（2017）指出，要围绕立德树人根本任务，遵循学生认知规律和教育教学规律，按照一体化、分学段、有序推进的原则，把中华优秀传统文化全方位融入各级各类的教学领域；"两性一度"的金课标准（2018）指出，课程应具有高阶性、创新性和挑战度；《高等学校课程思政建设指导纲要》（2020）进一步明确，加强中华优秀传统文化教育，教育引导学生传承中华文脉，培养富有中国心、饱含中国情、充满中国味的人才。因此，我们计划并实施了将中国优秀传统文化与英语教学深度融合的教材编写项目。

　　本教材以博大精深、源远流长的中国文化为依托。广义的中国文化涵盖中华民族自诞生以来创造的全部知识和行为总和，既包括人们的日常生活、社会实践，也包括文化中的观念、精神和思维习惯。中华大地上多样的地形、纵横的山脉、交织的河流和差异的气候在历史的长河中滋养、孕育出多种特色文化形态，这些文化不断融合发展，吐故纳新，在时空的流转下，积淀了深厚的文化底蕴和深刻的文化内涵，成为世界上唯一延续至今的古老文明。因此，教材不仅涵盖了孕育并滋养中国文化的历史地理环境，呈现了多种文化元素在历史长河中的发展变迁，还揭示了深刻影响中国人言行的文化思想观念。

　　本教材以文化层次理论为基础。文化层次理论认为文化具有层次性且层次间相互作用，文化的深层不易改变、最能体现文化的特质。因此，教材每章内容均由对表层文化产品的历时介绍，以及对里层文化内核的分析构成。教材借助文化特征，将文化的表层与里层紧密关联，让每章都围绕

特定文化主题，构建起从文化现象（即表层）深入到文化内核（即里层）的内容呈现体系。同时，不同章节之间也通过文化内核与文化特征相互关联，形成有机整体。

二、教材特色

本教材从文化层次理论的视角展开编写，具有以下特色：

1. 注重点面结合，呈现文化脉络

教材以文化主题架构章节，每章选取三个文化点展开文化面的陈述，并以之作为主体课文，历时介绍该章节主题下文化现象的发展与变化，总体呈现中国文化的脉络。同时，各章的拓展阅读材料主要提供对文化点的深入介绍，引导学生进一步了解文化知识，体会文化广泛的意义。这样，通过点面结合的方式帮助学生形成对中国文化的立体认知。

2. 侧重文化层次，凸显文化内核

教材主体课文包括章节主题下的文化产品介绍和文化特征分析两部分。前者侧重特定主题下文化现象的呈现，后者侧重文化内核的呈现。这样，通过文化层次性引导学生探究文化特征及其成因，理解文化因子之间的相互影响，从而培养学生的思维能力。同时，文化特征分析多基于文化观点、思想和情感等文化内涵，它们是"文化育人"的有效资源，也是课程思政的着力点，有利于提升学生的文化认同。

3. 关注文化对比，彰显文化特征

教材依托深植于西方文明土壤、承载着西方文化基因的英语媒介呈现中国文化，在东西方文明对话的场域中帮助学生认识文化差异，拓宽国际视野。在章节设置、文本选取和练习设计中，教材适时地融入了中西文化对比，引导学生以全球视角看待中国文化，理解中国文化的独特之处，进而提升其文化自信。

三、内容安排

本教材依据文化主题进行分类，共设 12 章，依次为中国文化起源、中国概况、中国语言、中国哲学、中国传统教育、中国文学、中国表演艺术、中国建筑、中国节日、中国饮食、中国工艺品和中国传统医学。

每章包括三篇主体课文、两篇拓展阅读课文，并配有相关课后练习。主体课文后附有文化分析和阅读理解。文化分析凝练课文内容所体现的文化特点，探究文化成因，显性呈现中国文化内核；阅读理解部分则是对课文中蕴含的文化知识的检测。每章的课后练习包含文化知识、语言知识、文化思考和文化实践等。

四、教学建议

鉴于学生对中国文化有一定的熟悉度，且有一定的英语听、说、读、写的能力，教师在教学过程中可采用精讲多练的方式，并灵活采用以下教学方法：

1. 任务型教学法

教师可将有关中国文化现象的内容布置给学生进行课前预习，要求学生在课上展示所学，培养学生的自主学习能力。课堂上，教师重点进行文化现象的梳理和文化特点的分析。课后布置讨论题和相关练习，要求学生以小组为单位完成学习任务，提升学生的合作学习能力。

2. 归纳、演绎式教学法

教师可以采用从文化现象到文化分析的归纳式教学法，也可以采用从文化特征到具体实例的演绎式教学法，培养学生的思辨能力。在分析中国文化现象的过程中，教师可注重引导学生深入挖掘、理解中国文化内涵，培养学生的文化自觉。

五、配套资源

本教材有配套视频课程和课后练习参考答案等教学资源，既可辅助教师的教学，也可实现线上线下混合式教学。

六、适用对象

本教材主要面向高校大学生，在编写过程中，我们充分考量了他们的文化背景与认知基础。这些学生在中国文化的熏陶下成长，已经积累起丰富的对中国文化的感性认知，也形成了一定程度的理性认识。基于这一学情，本教材适用于英语专业核心课程教学，也可作为高校人文素养类课程教材，还可供希望深入了解中国文化的读者参考使用。

本教材在编写过程中，参阅了大量相关著作、教材和网站，在此对所有被引用著作的作者、教材的编者、网站的所有者和各类文章的撰写者表示最诚挚的谢意。由于编写时间紧迫，编者水平有限，书中难免有疏漏和不足之处，恳请广大同仁和读者不吝批评指正。

编者

2024 年 10 月

Contents

Chapter One   The Origin of Chinese Civilization 中国文化起源 1

1.1   Yellow River Valley Civilization 2

1.2   Chinese Mythology 5

1.3   Chinese Dragon 9

Chapter Two   The Facts about China 中国概况 21

2.1   History of China 22

2.2   Geography of China 27

2.3   Chinese People 30

Chapter Three   Chinese Language 中国语言 41

3.1   Chinese Language 42

3.2   Chinese Characters 45

3.3   Chinese Dialects 48

Chapter Four   Chinese Philosophy 中国哲学 59

4.1   Conception of the Cosmos 60

4.2   Confucius and Confucianism 63

4.3   Laozi and Taoism 67

Chapter Five   Ancient Chinese Education 中国传统教育 77

5.1   School System in Ancient Chinese Society 78

5.2   The Imperial Examination System 81

5.3   Comparison Between Ancient Chinese and Western Education 84

Chapter Six　Chinese Literature 中国文学.............................93

6.1　Classical Poetry.............................94

6.2　Historical Books.............................97

6.3　Classical Novels.............................101

Chapter Seven　Chinese Performing Arts 中国表演艺术.............................113

7.1　Chinese Opera.............................114

7.2　Chinese *Quyi*.............................117

7.3　Chinese Acrobatics.............................121

Chapter Eight　Chinese Architecture 中国建筑.............................131

8.1　Civilian Housing.............................132

8.2　Classical Chinese Gardens.............................135

8.3　Imperial Palaces.............................139

Chapter Nine　Traditional Chinese Festivals 中国节日.............................151

9.1　The Spring Festival.............................152

9.2　The Qingming Festival.............................155

9.3　The Dragon Boat Festival.............................158

Chapter Ten　Chinese Food and Drinks 中国饮食.............................169

10.1　Chinese Food Culture.............................170

10.2　Chinese Cuisine.............................173

10.3　Chinese Liquor.............................177

Chapter Eleven Chinese Arts and Crafts 中国工艺品.....................187

11.1   Chinese Bronze Ware...188

11.2   Chinese Porcelain 191

11.3   Chinese Paper Cutting 195

Chapter Twelve Traditional Chinese Medicine 中国传统医学 207

12.1   TCM Theory 208

12.2   Chinese Materia Medica 211

12.3   Contrast Between TCM and Western Medicine 214

References..223

Appendix...225

Chapter One

The Origin of Chinese Civilization
中国文化起源

River valley civilization refers to an agricultural nation or civilization that is located on a river and derives its sustenance from the river. The river gives the inhabitants a reliable source of water for drinking and agriculture. The first great civilizations, such as Mesopotamia, ancient India and ancient Egypt, all developed in river valleys. Huanghe (Yellow River, 黄河) civilization, is an ancient Chinese civilization that prospered in the middle and lower basin of the Yellow River. Agriculture was started on the flood plains of the Yellow River, and before long, through flood control and irrigation of the Yellow River, cities were developed and political power was reinforced. Some other rivers in China, such as the Yangtze River (长江) and the Zhujiang River (珠江), also contributed to the development of Chinese civilization. Finally, Chinese culture has persisted continuously in this world as a great civilization.

1.1   Yellow River Valley Civilization

The Yellow River, the principal river in northern China, is the country's second longest river—surpassed only by the Yangtze River. Its drainage basin is the third largest in China, covering approximately 750,000 km^2. The river originates in the southern part of Qinghai Province on the Qinghai-Xizang Plateau and flows through six other provinces and two autonomous regions in its course before emptying into the Bohai Sea, an embayment of the Yellow Sea of the North Pacific Ocean.

The Yellow River basin was the birthplace of ancient Chinese civilization. The basin, nurtured and sustained by the major rivers in northern China, has been the center of China for thousands of years. It is called the Yellow River because its water carries silt, which gives the river its yellow-brown color, and when the river overflows, it leaves a yellow residue behind, further cementing its name. While the river helps create fertile land suitable for farming, during certain times of the year, the Yellow River frequently overflows, and floods damage housing and crops across the North China Plain, an important agricultural region. For thousands of years, the Chinese have been building major public works to control floods and use water from the Yellow River for irrigation, such as hydroelectric dams in modern times. Despite the risk of flooding, the Yellow River basin is home to a huge population, and many of China's oldest cities are situated along its banks.

It is hard to say exactly when villages and tribes began to appear in the Yellow River basin, but most scholars agree that a major consolidation of power took place from around

2070 BC to 1600 BC, marking the establishment of the Xia Dynasty. Da Yu (大禹), a mythical figure who created systems to control floods in the Yellow River basin, is credited as the first emperor of the Xia Dynasty. With the ability to better control the Yellow River and save their crops from floods, Chinese rulers were able to consolidate their rule over China, and subsequently a number of dynasties headquartered in the region. The basin became the cultural, social and academic center of China. Therefore the Yellow River is often called "the cradle of Chinese civilization".

The Yellow River civilization originated in the Neolithic Age, a period characterized by the thriving of numerous regional cultures. Over time, some of these cultures merged, while others gradually declined. Despite these transformations, the Yellow River civilization continued to develop and strengthen. Through the integration and expansion of various cultures, it flourished during the Zhou Dynasty, significantly contributing to the unification of China. In terms of agriculture and technological advancements, the Yellow River civilization achieved remarkable feats, surpassing many of its contemporaries throughout the world.

From the Xia and Shang dynasties to the Tang Dynasty, the Yellow River region remained the center of political, economic, and cultural activities. Many ancient capitals were strategically located along the Yellow River, highlighting its pivotal role. Notable achievements in science and technology, such as the invention of the compass, which revolutionized navigation, and the development of advanced irrigation systems that significantly increased agricultural productivity, underscore the ingenuity of the Yellow River civilization. Handicrafts such as intricate pottery designs, luxurious silk fabrics, and elaborate bronze artifacts are also well-known and have become symbols of Chinese civilization. The written language that originated here has served as a vehicle for cultural transmission and laid the foundation for subsequent literary development. Renowned for these early accomplishments, the Yellow River civilization has laid the cornerstone for Chinese culture, philosophy, and governance, shaping the country's identity and influencing future generations.

The Yellow River valley gave birth to the core elements of Chinese belief, such as the worship of ancestors and Heaven. Ancestor worship was deeply intertwined with the social structure of the time, with each tribe and dynasty organized around a patriarchal clan system. This practice reinforced blood ties, kinship ties, maintained family identity, and influenced power dynamics within the Yellow River civilization. To a large extent, ancestor worship involves rituals that maintain the integrity and continuity of the fundamental unit of Chinese society—the family. Moreover, these ancestral worship practices fostered a deeper sense of identity and intergenerational familial and geographical bonds. Meanwhile, the worship of Heaven cultivated a pervasive Chinese identity and gave rise to the concept of the Mandate of Heaven, which endowed the ruling emperor and dynasty with the divine right to govern as long as they maintained Heaven's favor. This subsequently solidified the sense of a shared cultural and national identity among the people.

The mighty Yellow River is the symbol of the Chinese nation. From the towering Kunlun Mountain to the immense Pacific Ocean, it passes through grasslands and deserts, splitting the Loess Plateau（黄土高原）and moistening the land. It is this melting pot of hundreds of rivers that breeds the brilliant Chinese culture, broadens the minds of the Chinese people, and nurtures the largest nation in the world—the Chinese nation.

(Adapted from Travel China Guide, China Highlights and National Geographic websites.)

◆ Cultural Analysis

The Yellow River, the symbol of the spirit of the Chinese people—braveness, industriousness and assidulity, has facilitated the formation of the following characteristics of Chinese culture.

(1) River Valley Civilization

Ancient Chinese civilization sprouted from the river valleys though there is a long coastline in the east. The Yellow River is the cradle of Chinese civilization, and other river valleys also contributed to the development of Chinese culture in the following historical periods. Thanks to the great rivers, the Chinese created the initial civilization depending on the peaceful rivers during the earliest period of human society.

(2) Inclusiveness of Chinese Civilization

From its inception in the Neolithic Age, the Yellow River civilization has been a fusion of multiple tribal cultures, and throughout its development, it has always been inclusive and eclectic. Meanwhile, China, with its numerous rivers, has witnessed the unique local cultures nurtured by these waterways gradually merge and blend, ultimately shaping the rich and diverse Chinese civilization. Within this vast cultural tapestry, every cultural element is cherished and respected, seamlessly integrating into the intricate fabric of Chinese identity.

◆ Text Comprehension

1. Judge whether the following statements are true (T) or false (F).

1) The river valley civilization refers to an agricultural nation or civilization that is located on a river and derives sustenance from the river.

2) The Yellow River, the principal river in northern China, is the country's second longest river—surpassed only by the Yangtze River.

3) The Yellow River civilization is China's earliest civilization and one of the oldest in the world.

4) From the Xia and Shang dynasties to the Qing Dynasty, the Yellow River area was always the center of politics, economy and culture.

5) The Yellow River valley gave birth to the most basic form of Chinese belief: the worship of ancestors.

2. Answer the following questions.

1) What is the location of the Yellow River in China? How did it contribute to the development of early civilizations?

2) Can you list any achievements of the Yellow River civilization during the Xia and Shang dynasties?

3) Can you illustrate the inclusiveness of the Yellow River Valley culture?

1.2   Chinese Mythology

Chinese mythology is a collection of cultural history, folktales, and religious traditions that have been passed down for centuries in oral or written form. There are several aspects to Chinese mythology, including creation myths and legends, and myths about the founding of Chinese culture and the establishment of Chinese state. Chinese mythology generally concerns moral issues and informs people about their culture and values. Like many other mythologies, some people believe that Chinese mythology, at least in part, reflects a factual historical record.

There has been extensive interaction between Chinese mythology and the major belief systems of Confucianism, Taoism, and Buddhism. Elements of early mythology were adapted into these belief systems, and some of the teachings and beliefs of these systems also became incorporated into Chinese mythology. For example, the spiritual paradise of Taoism was incorporated into mythology as a place where immortals and deities dwelled. Myths glorifying the benevolent rulers of the past, the Three Emperors and Five Sovereigns (三皇五帝), became an integral part of the Confucian political philosophy.

Creation myths in Chinese literature appear relatively late in Chinese culture. Some of the existing ones emerged well after the founding of Confucianism, Taoism, and folk religions. The stories exist in several often conflicting versions, with the creation of the first humans variously attributed to Pangu, Nüwa (女娲), and Yu Huang (玉皇 , the Jade Emperor).

Nüwa, who appeared in literature no earlier than about 350 BC, is said to have created the human race. Her companion was Fuxi (伏羲), the brother and husband of Nüwa. These two beings are sometimes worshipped as the ultimate ancestors of all humankind. They are often depicted as half-snake, half-human creatures. Nüwa was also responsible for repairing the sky after Gonggong (共工) damaged the pillars supporting the heavens.

Pangu, who appeared in literature no earlier than about 200 BC, is considered the first sentient being and creator. In the beginning, there was nothing but a formless chaos. Out of this chaos there was born an egg, which remained for 18,000 years. When the forces of *yin* and *yang* became balanced, Pangu emerged from the egg, and set about the task of creating the world. With a swing of his great axe, he separated the *yin* and *yang*. The heavy *yin* sank to become the Earth, while the light *yang* rose to become the Heaven. Pangu stood between them and pushed up the sky. Eighteen thousand years later, Pangu lay to rest. Each segment of Pangu's colossal form transformed into the countless wonders of nature, including towering mountains, flowing rivers, the blazing sun, the shimmering moon, and more.

Yu Huang appeared in literature well after the establishment of Taoism in China. He is considered to be the first god and the ruler of all gods and goddesses. There are many myths about well-known gods and goddesses who were in charge of different aspects of culture, but all of them were subordinate to Yu Huang.

The early myths of China are scattered throughout various ancient texts, such as the *Shan Hai Jing* (《山海经》, *The Classic of Mountains and Seas*), *Huai Nan Zi* (《淮南子》),

and *Shui Jing Zhu* (《水经注》, *Commentary on the Waterways Classic*).

Shan Hai Jing provides a detailed account of the myths, witchcraft, and religion of ancient China, as well as the geography, seas and mountains, history, medicine, customs, and ethnicities of that era. It is widely regarded as an early encyclopedia of China and has deeply influenced the mythical world portrayed in Qu Yuan's works. The mythological figures, sacred mountains, divine waters, and mystical creatures found in the *Chu Ci* (《楚辞》) can be traced back to the *Shan Hai Jing*.

Huai Nan Zi, a philosophy book compiled during the Western Han Dynasty, preserves abundant materials on mythical legends, including the ancient stories of *Nüwa Mending the Heavens* (《女娲补天》) and *Hou Yi Shooting the Suns* (《后羿射日》). Through this classic work, these splendid mythical stories have been passed down to the present day, becoming well-known to future generations.

Shui Jing Zhu, an ancient Chinese masterpiece of geography written by Li Daoyuan (郦道元) in the late Northern Wei Dynasty, details the flow direction, origins, and landscapes along the banks of various rivers. Additionally, the book records many mythical legends, such as the story of the *Goddess in Wu Mountain* (《巫山神女》) and the tale of *Cun Liu and Lu Ban* (《忖留与鲁班》), among others. These mythical elements have enriched Chinese mythology.

After the Han Dynasty, China witnessed the emergence of independently authored mythological books dedicated solely to the documentation of myths and legends, marking the progression and sophistication of ancient mythology culture. *Hei'an Zhuan* (《黑暗传》, *Epic of Darkness*) is the only collection of legends preserved in epic form by a community of the Han Chinese, the inhabitants of the Shennongjia (神农架) mountain area in Hubei Province. It contains accounts ranging from the birth of Pangu (盘古) in prehistorical myth to the historical era.

Sou Shen Ji (《搜神记》, *Anecdotes about Spirits and Immortals*), written during the Eastern Jin Dynasty, is a pioneering work in ancient Chinese mythology novels. Grounded in a rich array of mythical tales and folklore, it vividly showcases the profound imagination and creativity of the ancient Chinese people. Legends such as those of *Gan Jiang and Mo Ye* (《干将莫邪》) and the story of *Dong Yong* (《董永》) have been widely disseminated and cherished through the ages. During the Ming and Qing dynasties, more mythological fictions appeared, such as *Feng Shen Yan Yi*, a mythological fiction about the founding of the Zhou Dynasty; *Journey to the West* (《西游记》) by Wu Cheng'en, a fiction based on the historical event of Xuanzang's pilgrimage to India, in which the pilgrims encounter a variety of ghosts, monsters, and demons; *Bai She Zhuan* (《白蛇传》), a romantic tale set in Hangzhou involving a snake who attains human form and falls in love with a man.

(Adapted from New World Encyclopedia website.)

◆ Cultural Analysis

Karl Marx took the era of myths as the childhood of human beings, and he proposed that the childhood of Chinese was very short, but as the initial phase of Chinese civilization, it also showed some typical characteristics.

(1) The Fragmentation of Chinese Myths

Myths in ancient China were usually spread in scattered and fragmented forms in various written materials. These sources encompass information pertaining to archaeology, literature, philosophy, geography, history and so on. Many of them preserve only a few myths, while some of them hold a comparative large number of myths. In China, there exists almost no sacred canon recording myths or sacred history like the *Bible* (《圣经》) or the *Koran* (《古兰经》), nor were there any literati who collected myths from oral tradition and compiled them into systematic and integrated mythology like the Greek collections ascribed to Homer (荷马) and Hesiod (赫西俄德).

(2) The Moralization of Chinese Myths

The virtue dominates Chinese myths. All the kings depicted in myths were virtuous and tried to bring peace and harmony to human beings, such as the Yellow Emperor, who united the people and brought order out of chaos, and Yu, who devoted himself to flood control. The ideas and spirit conveyed in myths usually encourage Chinese people to do something helpful to others.

(3) The Historicization of Chinese Myths

Many characters and events in the myths eventually become identified as historical figures and occurrences from the distant past. For example, some great kings in Chinese history have their origins in myths: the Yellow Emperor (黄帝), Da Yu, etc. According to Mao Dun (茅盾), many historical stories in ancient times were originally myths; ancient historians historicized the myths by rationalizing their unreasonable elements.

◆ Text Comprehension

1. Judge whether the following statements are true (T) or false (F).

1) Chinese mythology generally concerns moral issues and informs people about their culture and values.

2) *Shui Jing Zhu* and *Shan Hai Jing* focus on the record of Chinese myths.

3) *Hei'an Zhuan* is the only collection of legends in epic form preserved by a community of the Han Chinese.

4) A unique characteristic of Chinese culture is the relatively early appearance of creation myths in Chinese literature.

5) Some characters in Chinese myths eventually become identified as historical figures and occurrences from the distant past.

2. Answer the following questions.

1) Can you list any legendary kings in Chinese myths and tell some stories about them?

2) Can you name some literary works concerning mythical stories?

3) What connotative meaning can you get from the story of Pan Gu?

1.3 Chinese Dragon

The dragon is a totem of the Chinese nation and a symbol of China. It has the highest status among animals and is deified by and sacred to Chinese people.

People are quite familiar with the image of dragon, but nobody has ever seen a real one. The dragon was born from the imagination of people just like the phoenix (凤凰) and kylin (麒麟), so there is no official and fixed version of the birth of Chinese dragons. According to Wang Fu (王符), a scholar in the Eastern Han Dynasty, a Chinese dragon has the head of a camel, the antlers of a deer, the eyes of a rabbit, the ears of cattle, the neck of a snake, the belly of a clam, the scales of a carp, the claws of a hawk, and the paws of a tiger. The body parts may be different in different sayings, but all of them have their own implied meanings and symbolize strong power.

The dragon is deified as the Dragon King, a supreme deity who reigns over the seas, governing all marine creatures and managing water and weather. In Taoism, there are four Dragon Kings, each with jurisdictions over one of the Four Seas: the East Sea, the South Sea, the West Sea, and the North Sea. As noble deities, the Dragon Kings are welcomed into temples and worshipped by believers. Their majestic and unique powers make them masters of weather and water, enabling them to bring abundant rainfall or decree drought, which significantly affects agriculture. Within temples, dragon motifs and sculptures of the Dragon Kings can be seen everywhere, with some temples even enshrining multiple Dragon Kings.

In terms of the origin of Chinese dragon, there are many explanations. One of the explanations is widely recognized: Chinese dragon is created through totems. The origin is clearly stated in the *Records of the Grand Historian* (《史记》): The Chinese dragon is an integrated creature composed of several animals that served as totems for tribes involved in tribal wars, in which the Yellow Emperor defeated other tribes and united the country. As such, Chinese dragon became a totem of the whole nation, and headed forward with the nation into a new chapter of unification. The Yellow Emperor is considered to be the emblem of the dragon, and the Chinese people regard themselves as descendants of this nation and the dragon. In the thereafter several thousand years, dragon is a symbol of China, and an intangible bond uniting Chinese people. To Chinese, dragon brings them luck, well-being and all good things.

The legendary story of the Yellow Emperor and dragon influenced other emperors to follow his example. Therefore, emperors in ancient China considered themselves as the incarnation of dragon, and everything used by the emperors was ornamented with dragon motifs to show their status as the highest ruler, and their strong power and majesty. Chinese dragon's deep relationship with emperors can be seen from emperors' birth to death: on the day of an emperor's birth, strange phenomena related to dragons, like strange weather, would take place.

Several items used by emperors are believed to have special functions and significance. First is the clothes. Clothes embroidered with five-clawed dragons symbolize imperial authority, which should be worn by emperors only, called the Dragon Robes. Anyone other than the emperor who wears this special robe will be deemed a traitor to the nation. Specific rules govern the production of garments with dragon motifs, which are worn by princes or other members of the royal family. Second are the seals, which are usually carved from jade. The Heirloom Seal of the Realm (传国玺), first carved during the

Qin Dynasty, was exclusively possessed by emperors and served as a symbol of imperial power. Historically, it was passed down through generations of emperors. And other kinds of seals with dragon ornaments were also used by emperors and held official validity and authority.

Dragon is not only worshipped by the royal, but also by ordinary people. People's love and worship for dragons can be seen everywhere, from a person's name to a person's possessions. Ordinary people may have a name related with dragons, like Jackie Chan's Chinese name Cheng Long（成龙）means "to become a dragon", and they may name a place or a thing after dragons, like the Heilongjiang Province（黑龙江省）. People may have a piece of furniture, wares, and other things ornamented with dragons, and may worship the Dragon King in a temple. They may go somewhere by dragon boat, and may perform dragon dances during festivals.

(Adapted from Top China Travel website.)

◆ Cultural Analysis

The Chinese dragon is benevolent, powerful and brings good fortune. It has played an important role in the history, politics and culture of the Chinese nation and the Chinese language.

(1) The Symbol of Chinese People

The origin of the Chinese dragon is connected with China's tribal history. It is said that when the Yellow Emperor defeated another tribe, he incorporated that tribe's animal totem into his own coat of arms—the snake. The body of the snake became mixed with the limbs and features of other animals as tribes were annexed, creating a dragon. The Yellow Emperor at last united all the tribes of ancient China, so the dragon symbolizes a unified China and till today all Chinese call themselves the descendants of the dragon.

(2) The Symbol of Imperial Power and Authority

According to legend, the dragon can walk on land, swim under water, and soar through the sky. It has incredible power. For thousands of years, Chinese emperors revered it as the symbol of power and dignity. While all Chinese people are said to be descendants of the dragon, the emperor has long been considered the human incarnation of the dragon. Historically, the Chinese emperor was the only person with the right to wear robes with dragon patterns.

(3) The Symbol of Good Luck

The Chinese dragon represents prosperity and good luck, and is also a rain deity that fosters harmony, which is different from the connotation of the European dragon— in European cultures, the dragon is a fire-breathing creature with aggressive connotations. Usually they are mean-spirited, greedy beings who hoard treasure.

◆ Text Comprehension

1. Judge whether the following statements are true (T) or false (F).

1) People are quite familiar with the image of the dragon though it was born from the imagination of people.

2) The body parts of the Chinese dragon may vary in different sayings, but all of them have their own implied meanings and symbolize strong power.

3) In Buddhism, there are four Dragon Kings who have respective jurisdictions over the East Sea, the South Sea, the West Sea and the North Sea.

4) Dragon is a totem of the Chinese nation, a symbol of China and all Chinese are proud to call themselves "the offspring of the dragon".

5) In feudal society, clothes embroidered with five-clawed dragons to show imperial authority could only be worn by the royal families.

2. Answer the following questions.

1) What is the appearance of Chinese dragon and what does dragon mean to Chinese?

2) How is the dragon connected with imperial power in China?

3) Can you list some activities to illustrate Chinese people's love for dragons?

◆ Exercises

1. Match each of the mythological fictions with its description.

Mythological Fictions	Descriptions
1) *Shui Jing Zhu*	a) The collection of legends in epic form preserved by the inhabitants of the Shennongjia mountain area in Hubei Province
2) *Shan Hai Jing*	b) A fiction based on the historical event of Xuanzang's pilgrimage to India, in which the pilgrims encounter a variety of ghosts, monsters, and demons
3) *Feng Shen Yan Yi*	c) Characterized by rich allusions to ancient historical mythology dating back to the dawn of Chinese civilization
4) *Hei'an Zhuan*	d) An early encyclopedia of China describing the myths, witchcraft, and religion of ancient China
5) *Li Sao*	e) A romantic tale set in Hangzhou with a snake who attains human form and falls in love with a man
6) *Journey to the West*	f) Commentaries on the briefer work *Waterways Classic* and famous for its extensive record of geography, history, and associated legends
7) *Bai She Zhuan*	g) A mythological fiction about the founding of the Zhou Dynasty

2. Choose the best answers to each of the following questions. You may choose MORE THAN ONE answer.

1) The Yellow River is nicknamed as _____.

   A. The Cradle of Chinese Civilization

   B. The Great River

   C. China's Sorrow

   D. The Long River

2) Chinese mythology has extensive interaction with major belief systems such as _____.

   A. Confucianism

   B. Legalism

   C. Mohism

   D. Taoism

3) Which of the following statements is true about the image of Chinese dragon?

A. People have seen a real dragon in history.

B. Chinese dragons have an official and fixed appearance at their birth.

C. The body parts of Chinese dragons symbolize strong power.

D. According to Wang Fu, Chinese dragon has ears of an elephant.

4) Which of the following statements is true about Chinese dragon's deep relationship with emperors?

A. Chinese emperors, princes and other members of royal family have the right to wear Dragon Robes.

B. Ancient Chinese emperors consider themselves as the incarnation of dragon.

C. On the day of an emperor's death, strange phenomena related to dragon would take place.

D. Dragon motifs can show the emperor's status as the highest ruler, his strong power and majesty.

3. Translate the following sentences.

1) 黄河文明是在黄河中下游地区繁荣起来的古老的中华文明。

2) 中国古代文明属于大河文明，具有典型的农业文明特征。

3) 中国神话故事里的帝王都是善良的，他们努力给人类带来和平与和谐。

4) 龙王是海洋中的最高统治者，控制着所有海洋生物、水和天气。

5) 龙象征着统一的中国，直到今天，中国人仍自称为龙的传人。

4. Discuss the following questions.

1) Can you list the benefits a river can bring to the inhabitants? What is the role of the Yellow River in Chinese culture?

2) What are the functions of the myths in a culture?

3) What are the differences between Chinese dragon and Western dragon?

5. Work in groups. Do research on the river civilizations and fill in the table below. Then report your findings to the class.

River Civilization	Time/Period	Rivers/Places	Main Achievements
Ancient Chinese civilization			
Mesopotamian civilization			
Harappan civilization			
Ancient Egyptian civilization			

◆ Extended Readings

Chu Culture 楚文化

According to legends recounted in Sima Qian's *Records of the Grand Historian*, the ruling family of Chu descended from the Yellow Emperor and his grandson and successor Zhuanxu (颛顼). Zhuanxu's great-grandson Wuhui (吴回) was put in charge of fire by the Emperor Ku (喾) and was given the title of Zhurong (祝融). One of his descendants, Xiong Yi (熊绎), was enfeoffed by King Cheng (周成王) with the fiefdom of Chu. Then the first capital of Chu was established in Danyang (丹阳).

In the mid-8th century BC, Chu rose around the present Hubei Province, in the fertile valley of the Yangtze River in southern China. Sometime between 695 and 689 BC, the capital of Chu moved southeast from Danyang to Ying (郢). Ying was one of the largest cities in the world then with an area of 15.75 km² and walls 16 km long. It was a large-scale ancient city with magnificent palaces, large handicraft workshops, dense residences, wide city gates and a good drainage system.

According to archaeological findings, Chu's culture was initially quite similar to that of other Zhou states of the Yellow River basin. However, subsequently, Chu absorbed indigenous elements from the conquered Baiyue lands to its south and east, integrating these unique features into its own cultural fabric. As a result, Chu evolved into a hybrid culture that was distinct from those of the northern plains. Therefore, Chu fostered a brilliant culture that ultimately surpassed all other regional cultures in terms of achievements, leaving an enduring legacy on the historical and cultural landscape of China. Among these legacies is the unique and famous epic poem Li Sao written by Qu Yuan, a nobleman of Chu, which initiated a tradition of romanticism in Chinese literature. Ultimately, with the unification and development of Chinese society, the cultural heritage of Chu became an integral part of the broader Chinese culture.

Despite the fact that early Chu burial offerings consisted primarily of bronze vessels in the Zhou style, the bronze wares of the Chu State also have their own characteristics. For example, the bronze *jin* (铜禁 , altar table) unearthed from the Chu tomb in Xichuan (淅川), Henan Province, is complex in shape. Dated to the mid-6th century BC, it was one of the early confirmed example of lost-wax cast artifacts discovered in China. Later Chu burials, especially during the Warring States Period, featured distinct burial objects, such as colorful lacquerware, iron implements, and silk fabrics, accompanied by a reduction in bronze vessel offerings.

Common Chu motifs are vivid depictions of wildlife, mystical animals, and natural imagery, such as snakes, dragons, phoenixes, tigers, free-flowing clouds, and serpent-like beings. Usually the phoenix is considered as the totem of Chu people. Some archaeologists have speculated that Chu may have had cultural connections with the previous Shang Dynasty, since many motifs used by Chu appeared earlier at the Shang sites, such as serpent-tailed gods. Later Chu culture was known for its affinity for witchcraft. With the development of Chu culture, there was a shift in the witchcraft doctrine. Some rational aspects were integrated into Taoism, while some imaginative elements were recorded in Li Sao. The basic belief of the Chu people was the "Worship of the sun and fire", which was based on their worship of nature and ancestors. The Yan Emperor (炎帝), the God of the sun, was venerated by the Chu people, and Zhurong, the God of fire, was revered as their ancestor. Therefore, they used red color in garments, architecture, wares, etc. They liked the east because the sun rises in the east, and they buried the dead in tombs facing east.

Chu had achieved a remarkable level of expertise in various fields, including bronze smelting, colorful silk weaving, embroidery, and lacquer ware manufacturing. Great accomplishments were also made in the artistic realm, particularly in music, dance, painting, and sculpture. Because of rich mine resources, the melting and casting techniques were finely developed. The bronze wares, gold wares and iron tools of Chu represented the highest standards at that time. The musical bells and chimes were dug out in 1978 from the Tomb of Marquis Yi of State Zeng (曾侯乙墓), which represented the highest level of bronze casting.

(Adapted from Wikipedia and Britannica websites.)

The Xia Dynasty 夏朝

The Xia Dynasty was the first government to emerge in ancient China and the first to adopt the policy of dynastic succession. Consequently, the Xia was the first dynasty of China.

The Xia Dynasty was overthrown by the Shang Dynasty, a historically more certain governmental entity, which was subsequently overthrown by the Zhou Dynasty. The argument that regards the Xia Dynasty as mythological holds that the Zhou (and later dynasties) wanted to make clear that the previous dynasties lost their right to rule because of immoral conduct, and thus created a proto-dynasty—the Xia—as a prehistoric model.

According to historians like Sima Qian (145–86 BC), there was once a great ruler named Huangdi better known as the Yellow Emperor who emerged from prehistoric tribal system to rule the region of Shandong. The Yellow Emperor is credited with laying the foundations of Chinese culture and establishing a government system that lasted for centuries. He is attributed with the invention of musical instruments, the development of silk production, the institution of laws and customs, and significant advancements in the fields of medicine and agriculture. After his death, he was buried in the mausoleum in what is now Huangling County（黄陵县）, Shaanxi Province, which is now a popular tourist attraction.

Huangdi was succeeded by his grandson Zhuanxu, one of the famous Five Emperors, who founded the Xia tribe. After defeating their rivals, the Xia established the first dynasty in China under the leadership of the Emperor Yao（尧）. Yao ordered the construction of great palaces, and small villages of huts grew into urban centers. He is considered a great philosopher king who ruled his people wisely and worked for their best interests following the precepts of Huangdi.

During his reign, Yao had a serious problem in controlling the flooding of the Yellow River which disrupted agriculture as well as caused his people to drown or be displaced. He appointed a man named Gun（鲧）to take care of this situation. Gun tried for nine years to stop the flooding but every year it grew stronger and more lands were flooded and more people were killed. Finally, Gun constructed a series of dykes which he hoped would hold back the water, but the dykes collapsed, causing more destruction and deaths. By this time Yao had relinquished rule to his successor Shun（舜）, who was not pleased at Gun's failure to control waters. According to some versions of the tale, Gun then killed himself, while according to others he was imprisoned by Shun. After him, Emperor Shun appointed Gun's son Yu（禹）to complete the work and stop the flooding.

Yu learned from his father's mistakes: Gun tried to do too much by himself, underestimated his need for help, and overestimated his abilities. He also acted without respect for the forces of nature and worked against the water instead of working with it. Yu sought help from the surrounding tribes and had them construct canals to channel the water to the sea.

Yu's project lasted 13 years, during which he was so dedicated to his task that he never returned his home once, even though he passed by it three times. Yu's wife and young son would call out to him as he passed by and his colleagues would advise him to go home and rest, but Yu would not abandon his task until it was completed. His single-mindedness and dedication inspired those around him, who looked up to him as a role model and worked harder until the river was brought under control and there were no more floods.

Once the water problem had been solved, Shun was very proud of Yu and placed him in command of his army. Yu led his men against the Sanmiao (三苗), a tribe hostile to the Xia, who were constantly raiding its borders. He defeated the Sanmiao and drove them out of the land, and as a reward for his victory, Shun declared him heir to the throne.

Yu's reign is considered to be the beginning of the Xia Dynasty, and he is known as Yu the Great not only for his victories over the floods and the Sanmiao but also because he established a stable central government and divided the country into nine provinces, making such a huge area easier to govern.

Yu ruled for 45 years, and on his deathbed, he named his son Qi (启) as his successor. Qi had been a young boy during the time of the great flood, and many people loved the story of how his father refused to return home until the flood stopped and how well young Qi accepted his father's absence. Yu intended to name his minister as successor, and did not want his son to have the burden of ruling, but so many people favored Qi that Yu had no choice. In naming Qi as his successor, Yu initiated the policy of dynastic succession.

Qi's son, Tai Kang (太康), was a poor ruler but many of his successors were highly skilled and numerous inventions and innovations were attributed to the later years of the Xia Dynasty, such as the development of armor in warfare and rules of chivalry in battle. The fourth ruler after Qi was the great hero Shao Kang (少康), who revitalized the country and was well known through many legends about him. The Xia Dynasty began to decline under the rule of Kong Jia (孔甲), who preferred drinking strong liquor to his responsibilities. He was succeeded by Gao (皋) who was succeeded by Fa (发), and neither of them did much to improve the lives of anyone but themselves. The last emperor was Jie (桀), who was known as a tyrant and lost the mandate of heaven to rule. He was overthrown by Tang (汤) who established the Shang Dynasty.

Most of the above had been considered mythology until archaeological evidences began to emerge between 1920s and mid 1960s to confirm the recording of historians. Even now, the academic consensus is that the history of the Xia Dynasty is largely mythological, even if such a dynasty did actually exist. The skepticism grew because there were no early accounts of the Xia Dynasty and no physical evidence argued for its existence. It is believed that historians, especially the famous Sima Qian, created the Xia Dynasty as a model precedent to explain and justify dynastic changes in China.

(Adapted from World History website.)

Chapter Two

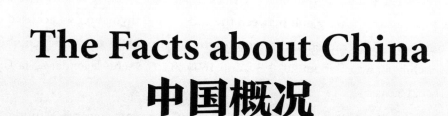

The Facts about China
中国概况

China is located in eastern Asia on the western shore of the Pacific Ocean. It spreads over a vastly diverse geographical area of about 9.6 million square kilometers, and the total sea area is about 4.73 million square kilometers. It is home to approximately 1.4 billion people who are from different ethnic groups. Most of China has a continental climate, though it has an ocean coast. Its latitudes range from tropical to Siberian, meaning that temperatures and weather differ strikingly across the country. With written records dating back 4,000 years, it is recognized as one of the ancient civilizations of the world. Moreover, it is the only ancient civilization that has continued to this very day.

2.1　History of China

Chinese history embodies a prolonged, multifaceted, and resplendent journey of civilization development, spanning across the ages from ancient times to the present day. By 2000 BC, the Chinese had learned to make pottery, lacquerware, baskets and bronze ware and made ritual objects from jade such as knives, axes, and rings. Almost at the same time there was also a growing gulf between the classes, and divination was carried out by heating bones till they cracked and then interpreting the cracks to predict good or bad luck. Meanwhile, between about 2070 BC and 1600 BC, the semi-legendary Xia Dynasty ruled parts of China.

During the Shang Dynasty, the veneration of ancestors became a fundamental practice. Silk production is believed to have originated during this period. Bronze ware gained broader applications, including use in ritual vessels, weapons, tools, and decorative items. However, essential tools for daily life and agriculture, such as sickles, plows, and spades, were predominantly crafted from wood and stone. The inhabitants of the Shang Dynasty constructed the earliest cities, palaces, and temples, which serve as a testament to their remarkable architectural prowess and advanced civilization. Divination was practiced using turtle shells and animal bones, which were widely used to seek guidance from ancestors and gods on war, agriculture, and governance.

During the Zhou Dynasty, particularly in the later periods such as the Spring and Autumn and Warring States periods, the increasing prevalence of iron weapons marked a significant advancement in military technology. This era also witnessed the ingenuity of the Chinese people in crafting kites, and tea was first documented in the annals of the Zhou. The umbrella, a marvel of engineering, provided graceful protection from both the scorching sun and relentless rain. During this period, divination practices continued. The Chinese concept of Heaven emerged, and in its wisdom, Heaven granted the emperor a divine right to rule. The Spring and Autumn Period and the subsequent Warring States Period fostered an unparalleled era of cultural flourishing, known as the Contention of a Hundred Schools of Thought.

Qin Shi Huang (秦始皇), the first emperor, united China in 221 BC. He introduced standard writing, currency, weights and measures, and even insisted that axles of vehicles should be of a standard width. The Qin emperors continued their legalist policies and banned private ownership of weapons. They ordered many aristocratic families to move to the capital, Xianyang (咸阳), and divided the whole land into 36 areas called prefectures (郡), each of which was made up of counties.

In the Han Dynasty, the Chinese created brilliant civilization. The first Han emperor was more humane than the Qin emperors and he abolished many of their savage punishments. He retained some of the legalist policies of his predecessors, but he also adopted some Confucian policies. His successors increasingly came to favor Confucianism, thereby establishing the cultural and philosophical foundations that would shape China for centuries to come. In this period, agriculture continued to be improved partly due to an increasing number of irrigation schemes, the increasing use of buffaloes to pull plows, and the introduction of crop rotation into China. These advancements not only increased crop yields but also promoted economic prosperity. Silk was widely exported to the West, passing through many hands before reaching as far as the Roman Empire, where it was highly valued as a prestigious commodity. In return, merchants introduced gems, glassware, and grapevines into China, facilitating extensive cultural and economic exchanges between the East and the West.

After the fall of the Han Dynasty, China was split into the Three Kingdoms, Wei (魏), Shu (蜀) and Wu (吴). Following the Three Kingdoms Period were consecutively the Jin Dynasty, the Sixteen Kingdoms Period and the Northern and Southern Dynasties (两晋 , 十六国 , 南北朝). It was an age of civil wars and disunity for China. During this period of division, Buddhism flourished in China, leading to the construction of many temples and monasteries. Taoism also underwent development during this period.

In 581 AD, the short-lived Sui Dynasty emerged, marking a new era in Chinese history. The government initiated ambitious public works projects, including the reconstruction of cities to enhance their grandeur and the excavation of China's Grand Canal (京杭大运 河), an engineering marvel of its time. Stretching from north to south, the Grand Canal was constructed not only to facilitate trade and transportation but also to strengthen cultural and economic ties across China's diverse regions.

In 618 AD, Li Yuan (李渊) founded the Tang Dynasty, and later Li Shimin (李世民), the son of Li Yuan, adopted a series of policies known as the "Zhenguan Reign Reforms (贞观之治)", which brought the feudal society to the height of prosperity. Agriculture, handicrafts and commerce flourished; land and water transportation was fairly well developed, and economic and cultural relations with Japan, Korea, India, Persia, Arabia and other countries were extensive. The capital Chang'an housed Buddhists, Christians, and Muslims. By the 9th century, Buddhism had a great influence on China and the *Diamond Sutra* (《金刚经》) was the earliest known book printed using woodblock printing, a technique invented in the Tang Dynasty. Additionally, the Tang Dynasty witnessed a golden age of poetry, during which numerous talented poets emerged and created masterpieces that have been celebrated and cherished for centuries.

In the Song Dynasty, China's economy boomed. The application of new planting techniques promoted the development of agriculture; trade and commerce prospered and towns and cities expanded significantly. Industries like iron making, ceramics making, silk spinning, lacquerware making, and papermaking flourished. The compass had been utilized for navigating ships since the 12th century, whereas for several centuries prior to that, it was employed for divination purposes. Buddhism declined in popularity, while Confucianism underwent a revival. Scholars wrote commentaries on Confucian classics, and a new philosophy known as Neo-Confucianism emerged, which dominated China for centuries. The number of schools increased greatly in the Song Dynasty and China came to be ruled by elite scholar-officials.

In 1264, Kublai Khan (忽必烈), the grandson of Genghis Khan (成吉思汗), made Beijing his winter capital (the summer capital was in Mongolia). Kublai Khan invaded southern China in 1268 and eventually conquered it. However, Kublai khan realized it would be more beneficial to rule China and collect taxes than to simply plunder it. Thus, after gaining control over China, he recruited Chinese officials to assist him in governing.

The first Ming emperor, Zhu Yuanzhang (朱元璋), conquered Beijing in 1368 and established Nanjing as the capital city. Subsequently, emperor Zhu Di (朱棣) relocated the capital back to Beijing and commissioned the construction of the Forbidden City between 1406 and 1421. Within its walls was the imperial city, which was exclusively reserved for officials, while the outer areas were inhabited by ordinary people. Under the reign of the Ming emperors, China once again became prosperous and powerful, with industry and trade flourishing. A vast quantity of cotton was spun and a huge amount of porcelain was produced. In the early 15th century, the emperor dispatched ships on seven expeditions, sailing as far as India, Arabia, and the east coast of Africa. However, the later Ming emperors became increasingly inward-looking and tried to isolate China from the outside world.

In the late Ming Dynasty, the Manchus in the northeast China grew in strength. Over the course of three successive generations, they invaded the Central Plains region and finally founded the Qing Dynasty, the last imperial dynasty of China. The two most famous emperors of the Qing Dynasty were Emperor Kangxi (康熙皇帝) and Emperor Qianlong (乾隆皇帝), whose reign periods were known as the "Age of Prosperity". During the Qing Dynasty, some novels of high artistic value were created, among which Cao Xueqin's *Dream of Red Mansions* is the best known one. It describes the decline of a prosperous feudal aristocratic family.

Towards the end of Qing Dynasty, the historically called "Opium War" broke out, marking the beginning of China's transition into a semi-colonial and semi-feudal society. In the late 19th century, the Chinese government made some attempts to introduce and implement European technology and institutions; however, these efforts achieved only limited success. Additionally, several peasant rebellions erupted, yet none of them ultimately succeeded.

The Revolution of 1911, led by Sun Yat-sen, abolished the feudal monarchy, and established the Republic of China. With the introduction of Marxism-Leninism into China and the influence of the October Revolution in Russia, the May Fourth Movement broke out in 1919; and in 1921, the Communist Party of China (CPC) was founded. After the War of Resistance against Japanese Aggression and the War of Liberation, the Communist Party of China established the People's Republic of China (PRC) in 1949.

(Adapted from Local Histories website.)

◆ Cultural Analysis

With a recorded history spanning nearly 4,000 years, China's rich cultural heritage has been shaped by its status as one of the world's most ancient civilizations.

(1) Cycles of Dynasties

In the slave society, the changes in politics were reflected in the rise and fall of the

Xia, Shang and Zhou dynasties. The 2,000 years of feudal society were mainly comprised of dynasties which usually experienced establishment, prosperity, decline and collapse. Each developed itself on the cultural achievements of the previous ones.

(2) Continuity of Culture

In the history of China, it is true that there were periods of division, but these divisions were transient. There seem to be cycles of division and unity, with unity lasting longer than division. Over time, Chinese culture has continuously interacted and integrated with other cultures, yet its core cultural genes has remained unchanged.

◆ Text Comprehension

1. Judge whether the following statements are true (T) or false (F).

1) By 2000 BC, there was a growing gulf between the classes and divination was no longer practiced in China.

2) During the Zhou Dynasty, the Chinese invented the umbrella and the kite, and tea was first mentioned.

3) After Qin Shi Huang unified China in 221 AD, he introduced standard writing, currency, weights and measures and the standard width of axles.

4) The number of schools increased greatly in the Tang Dynasty, and China came to be ruled by elite scholar-officials.

5) At the end of the Qing Dynasty, the historically called "Opium War" broke out, which ushered China to the semi-colonial and semi-feudal society.

2. Answer the following questions.

1) What progress did China make in prehistoric periods?

2) When did China step into the civilization era?

3) What historical activities promoted the international communication in the history of China?

2.2　Geography of China

China's land stretches for about 5,200 km from east to west and 5,500 km from north to south. Its land frontier is about 22,000 km in length, and its coastline extends for some 18,000 km, bordered by the Bohai Sea, the Yellow Sea and the East China Sea to the east, and the South China Sea to the southeast. The country is bordered by Mongolia to the north; Russia and North Korea to the northeast; Vietnam, Laos, Myanmar (Burma), India, Bhutan, and Nepal to the south; Pakistan to the southwest; and Afghanistan, Tajikistan, Kyrgyzstan, and Kazakhstan to the west. In addition to the 14 countries it borders directly, China also faces South Korea and Japan across the Yellow Sea, and the Philippines across the South China Sea.

Broadly speaking, the topography of China is high in the west and low in the east; consequently, major rivers generally flow eastward. The landforms can be divided into three steps, or levels. The first step is represented by the Qinghai-Xizang Plateau (青藏高原), which is located in both the Xizang Autonomous Region and the Qinghai Province, with an average altitude of well over 4,000 metres, making it the loftiest highland area in the world. The second step lies to the north of the Kunlun Mountains (昆仑山) and Qilian Mountains (祁连山) and (farther south) to the east of the Qionglai Mountains (邛崃山脉) and Daliang Mountains (大凉山脉). There, the mountains descend sharply a height of between 1,800 and 900 metres, after which basins intermingle with plateaus. This step includes the Inner Mongolian Plateau (内蒙古高原), the Tarim Basin (塔里木盆地), the Loess Plateau (黄土高原), the Sichuan Basin (四川盆地), and the Yunnan-Guizhou (Yungui) Plateau (云贵高原). The third step extends from the east of the Greater Khingan Mountains (大兴安岭), Taihang Mountains (太行山脉), and Wushan Mountains (巫山) and from the eastern perimeter of the Yunnan-Guizhou Plateau to the Sea. Almost all of this area is made up of hills and plains below 450 metres.

The most remarkable feature of China's landscape is its vast mountain range; the mountains, indeed, have exerted a tremendous influence on the country's political, economic, and cultural development. According to a rough estimate, approximately one-third of China's total area is covered by mountains. China is home to the world's tallest mountain and the world's highest and largest plateau, as well as extensive coastal plains. The five major landforms—mountain, plateau, hill, plain, and basin—are all well represented in China. The country's diverse natural environment and abundant natural resources are closely linked to the varied nature of its relief (地形).

China's relief has determined its development in many aspects, including the early development of the Han people. The civilization of Han Chinese originated in the southern part of the Loess Plateau, and extended outward until it encountered the combined barriers of relief and climate. The long and narrow corridor, commonly known as the Hexi Corridor, exemplifies this fact. To the south of the corridor is the Qinghai-Xizang Plateau, which was too high and cold for the Han Chinese to gain a foothold. To the north of the corridor stretches the Gobi Desert, which also formed a barrier. Consequently, Chinese civilization was forced to spread along the corridor, where the melting snow and ice of the Qilian Mountains provided water for oasis farming. The westward extremities of the corridor became the ancient meeting place between East and West. Thus, for a long time the ancient political centre of China was located along the middle and lower reaches of the Yellow River.

China's terrain has profoundly influenced its agricultural development. The drainage basins of China's rivers differ in terms of scope and topography, providing different opportunities for agricultural development. Rice, wheat, corn, barley and millet are the principal grain crops, each representing a particular adaptation to specific environmental conditions. Rice cultivation is particularly prevalent in the fertile areas of southern and central China where a mild climate favors two and sometimes three crops per year. Rice is frequently rotated with other crops, such as winter wheat, sweet potatoes, corn, and vegetables of various types.

Throughout the rugged areas of northern and southern China, farmers over the centuries have sculpted the hilly land into step-like landscapes of terraces. Sometimes terraces are relatively natural features that require only minor modifications to produce flat areas for planting, while in other cases extraordinary efforts are required to move earth and rocks, stabilize retaining walls, and build sluices to control water flow. Drainage control and water storage are as important as the flat land itself. Besides the irrigation systems fundamental to terraced rice production, small- and large-scale water conservancy projects continue to be an important means of increasing crop production as well as reducing flood and drought hazards.

(Adapted from Britannica and Asia for Educators websites.)

◆ Cultural Analysis

The varied landforms and diverse climates inevitably have a great effect on the Chinese culture in the following ways.

(1) Different Lifestyles

The eastern part of China is flat and moist, with abundant arable farmland, while the northeastern part and the area north of the Great Wall are dry all year round, and mainly fit for animal husbandry. Different temperatures and humidity lead to the fact that in the north of Qinling Mountains-Huaihe River line, wheat and corn are the staple grains while in the south of it, rice takes its place. The regional diversity is the natural basis of the co-existing multi-cultures in China.

(2) A United Nation

China is a country with many towering mountains in the west and southwest borders, deserts and Gobi in the far north, and boundless waters in its east and southeast. In another way, China, with the central plain region serving as the birthplace of its civilization and surrounded by land on three sides, has long been isolated, which has given birth to a less open but very united nation most of the time. After a long period of continuous development, a strong and unified culture has been formed.

(3) Agricultural Civilization

The geographic environment provides the favorable conditions for agriculture. In ancient China, farming was conducted for thousands of years with each household as a productive unit. The major productive mode was the natural family economy with men cultivating the land and women weaving at home. Therefore, it was a type of self-sufficient natural economy with limited reliance on the market economy. The Chinese culture is of strong agricultural nature, which has created a people with love of nature, their home and world peace.

◆ Text Comprehension

1. Judge whether the following statements are true (T) or false (F).

1) China has both marine and land boundary line.

2) The eastern plains and southern coasts of China consist of fertile lowlands and foothills.

3) The eastward extremities of Hexi Corridor was the ancient meeting place between East and West.

4) The drainage basins of China's rivers are helpful for agricultural development.

5) Chinese over the centuries have sculpted the hilly land into step-like landscapes of terraces throughout the rugged areas of northern and southern China.

2. Answer the following questions.

1) What are the characteristics of topography in China?

2) Which geographic characteristics have promoted the development of agriculture in China?

3) What are the characteristics of the rivers in China?

2.3 Chinese People

The People's Republic of China is a united multi-ethnic state founded jointly by the people of all its ethnic groups. So far, there are 56 ethnic groups identified and confirmed. As the majority of the population belongs to the Han ethnic group, China's other 55 ethnic groups are customarily referred to as the ethnic minorities.

China has been a united multi-ethnic country since ancient times. In 221 BC, the first united, multi-ethnic, centralized state—the Qin Dynasty—was founded in China. Today's Guangxi Zhuang Autonomous Region and Yunnan Province, where ethnic minorities are concentrated, were prefectures and counties under the jurisdiction of the united Qin regime. During the Han Dynasty, the centralized feudal state became even more powerful by inheriting the Qin system. The Han set up Frontier Command Headquarters in the Western Regions (西域都护府 , a general term for today's territory west of Dunhuang in Gansu Province since the Han Dynasty) and added 17 prefectures governing the people of all ethnic groups there. In this way, a state with a vast territory embracing the ancestors of the various ethnic groups living in today's Xinjiang emerged. In the course of frequent communication between the Han and the surrounding minority nationalities, the people of the Chinese nation were called the Han by other ethnic groups, forming the most populous ethnic group in the world—the Han. China, as a united multi-ethnic country, was created by the Qin Dynasty and consolidated and developed by the Han Dynasty.

The central governments following the Han Dynasty developed and consolidated the united multi-ethnic entity. The central governments of the successive dynasties were established not only by the Han people but also by ethnic minorities. In the 13th century, the Yuan Dynasty practiced a system of xingsheng (行省) across the country and appointed aboriginal officials (土司) in the prefectures and subprefectures of the southern regions where ethnic minorities lived in concentrated communities. It established the Pacification Commissioner's Commandery (宣慰使司都元帅府) in charge of military and administrative affairs in Xizang, whereby Xizang has became thenceforth an inalienable part of Chinese territory; the Penghu Police Office (澎湖巡检司) for the administration of the Penghu Islands and Taiwan was also established. Ethnically, the Yuan Dynasty included most of modern China's ethnic groups. The Qing Dynasty set up the Ili Generalship (伊犁将军府) and Xinjiang Province in the Western Regions, appointed resident officials in Xizang and established the historical convention of conferring honorific titles on the two Living Buddhas Dalai (达赖) and Panchen (班禅) lamas by the central government. In addition, the Qing government carried out a series of policies, including a system of local administrators in minority areas appointed by the central government, in southwestern China.

China's ethnic groups live together over vast areas, while some live in individual concentrated communities in small areas. This distribution pattern has taken shape throughout China's long history of development as ethnic groups migrated and mingled. The national minorities, though small in population, are scattered over vast areas. Ethnic minorities live in every province, autonomous region and municipality directly under the central government, and in most county-level units, usually two or more ethnic groups live together.

During the long process of unification, economic and cultural exchanges have brought the people of all ethnic groups in China closely together, giving shape to a relationship of interdependence, mutual promotion and mutual development among them, and contributing to the creation and development of the Chinese civilization. Due to their interdependent political, economic and cultural connections, all ethnic groups in China have shared common destiny and interests in their long historical development, creating a strong force of affinity and cohesion.

(Adapted from the Ministry of Foreign Affairs of the People's Republic of China website.)

◆ Cultural Analysis

China has been a united multi-ethnic country throughout its long history. Over thousands of years, many ethnic groups have taken an active part in the stage of Chinese history.

(1) National Integration

For a long time, the different ethnic groups "living together in one area while still living in individual compact communities in special areas" have provided a practical basis for the political, economic and cultural exchanges between the Han and the various ethnic minorities.

(2) National Cohesion

China has always been a country of many ethnic groups. No matter which ethnic group was dominating, whether it was Hans, Mongols, or Manchus, all ethnic groups could always live under the same roof and under the same emperor. All these ethnic groups have their own cultural legacies, but they share common legacy as well, and together constitute the Chinese nation.

◆ Text Comprehension

1. Judge whether the following statements are true (T) or false (F).

1) China has been a united multi-ethnic country throughout its long history and there are 55 ethnic minorities in China.

2) Two or more ethnic groups live together in most province-level units in China.

3) The central governments of all dynasties developed and consolidated the united multi-ethnic entity.

4) The Ming government set up the Ili Generalship and Xinjiang Province in the Western Regions, and appointed resident officials in Xizang.

5) The people of all ethnic groups in China closely together have given shape to a relationship of interdependence, mutual promotion and mutual development among them.

2. Answer the following questions.

1) What is the distribution pattern of ethnic minorities in China?

2) How did the central government in Chinese history develop the united multi-ethnic entity?

3) How is the ethnic relationship in China?

◆ Exercises

1. Choose the corresponding achievements and school of philosophy for each dynasty and fill in the table.

1) Paper-making and compass	a) Confucianism
2) The abolishment of many savage punishments	b) Neo-Confucianism
3) Standard writing, currency, weights and measures	c) Legalism
4) Gunpowder and printing	d) Buddhism

	Achievements	School of Philosophy
Qin Dynasty		
Han Dynasty		
Tang Dynasty		
Song Dynasty		

2. Choose the best answer to each of the following questions.

1) Agriculture improved during the Han Dynasty for all of the following reasons EXCEPT _____.

A. the increasing use of buffaloes to pull plows

B. crop rotation

C. the application of new planting techniques

D. an increasing number of irrigation schemes

2) Which of the following is true during the Ming Dynasty?

   A. The Great Wall was built.

   B. The Forbidden City was built.

   C. The emperors were outward-looking.

   D. The emperor sent ships to America.

3) Which of the following is true about the relief of China?

   A. Major rivers flow southward.

   B. Basins intermingle with plateaus in the first step.

   C. The second step is the lofty highland area.

   D. The third step is made up of hills and plains.

4) Which of the following is true about grain crops in China?

   A. Wheat and corn are the staple grains in the south.

   B. Rice can grow two or three crops per year all over China.

   C. The growing of rice is frequently rotated with other crops.

   D. Grain accounts for 50% of all agricultural crops in China.

5) China's agricultural civilization has the following characteristics EXCEPT
   _____.

   A. men cultivating the land and women weaving at home

   B. a type of self-sufficient natural economy

   C. a people with love of nature, their home and world peace

   D. reliance on the market economy

3. Translate the following sentences.

1) 中国自古以来就是一个统一的多民族国家。

2) 在长期的统一进程中，经济和文化交流使中国各族人民紧密团结在一起。

3) 大运河和长城等重大工程是数百年来人类对中国自然景观的改造。

4) 中国的地势西高东低，主要河流的流向通常是自西向东。

5) 四川盆地是中国西南部一个与世隔绝的地区，受高山保护，农产品自给自足。

4. Discuss the following questions.

1) How did the four great inventions in ancient China promote the development of world civilization?

2) What characteristics can be manifested in the Chinese history?

3) How have the geographic characteristics influenced the development of Chinese civilization?

5. Work in groups. Do research on China's three steps and fill in the table below. Then report your findings to the class.

Three Steps	Major Landforms	Major Crops	Major Ethnic Groups
The first step			
The second step			
The third step			

◆ Extended Readings

Silk Road 丝绸之路

The Silk Road was a network of ancient trade routes, formally established in the Han Dynasty of China in 130 BC, which linked the regions of the ancient world in commerce between 130 BC and 1453 AD. The Silk Road was not a single route stretching from east to west; thus, historians prefer the name "Silk Routes", though "Silk Road" is commonly used. The European explorer Marco Polo (1254–1324) traveled these routes and provided detailed descriptions of them in his famous work, but he did not name them. Both terms for this network of routes—Silk Road and Silk Routes—were coined by the German geographer and traveler, Ferdinand von Richthofen (费迪南·冯·李希霍芬) in 1877, who designated them "Seidenstrasse" (silk road) or "Seidenstrassen" (silk routes).

The network was used regularly from 130 BC when the Han Dynasty officially opened trade with the West, to 1453 AD, when the Ottoman Empire (奥斯曼帝国) boycotted trade with the West and closed the routes. By this time, Europeans had become used to the goods from the East, and when the Silk Road closed, merchants needed to find new trade routes to meet the demand for these goods. The closure of the Silk Road initiated the Age of Discovery which would be defined by European explorers taking to the sea and charting new water routes to replace overland trade. The Silk Road—from its opening to its closure—had so great an impact on the development of world civilization that it is difficult to imagine the modern world without it.

The history of the Silk Road predates the Han Dynasty in practice, however, as the Persian Royal Road, which would come to serve as one of the main arteries of the Silk Road, was established during the Achaemenid Empire (阿契美尼德王朝，波斯帝国第一王朝, 550–330 BC). The Persian Royal Road ran from Susa, in north Persia (modern day Iran) to the Mediterranean Sea in Asia Minor (小亚细亚, modern-day The Republic of Türkiye) and featured postal stations along the route with fresh horses for envoys to quickly deliver messages throughout the empire. The Persians maintained the Royal Road carefully and, in time, expanded it through smaller side roads. These paths eventually crossed down into the Indian subcontinent, across Mesopotamia (美索不达米亚), and over into Egypt.

In 138 BC, Zhang Qian (张骞) was sent on a diplomatic mission to the West to negotiate with the Dayuezhi (大月氏) people for their help in combating the Xiongnu

（匈奴）. At that time, the Han Dynasty of China was frequently harassed by the nomadic Xiongnu tribes along its northern and western borders. Zhang Qian's journey not only facilitated further interactions between China and the West, but also led to the establishment of a systematic and efficient horse-breeding program across the country, aimed at equipping the cavalry. With the introduction of superior horses from Dayuan （大宛）, the Han Dynasty eventually defeated the Xiongnu. Encouraged by this success, Emperor Wu （汉武帝） evaluated the potential benefits that could be gained through trade with the West, which ultimately led to the official establishment of the Silk Road in 130 BC.

While many different kinds of merchandise traveled along the network of trade of the Silk Road, the name comes from the popularity of Chinese silk with the West, especially with Rome. The Silk Road routes stretched from China through India, Asia Minor, up throughout Mesopotamia, to Egypt, the African continent, Greece, Rome and Britain.

The northern Mesopotamian region (present-day Iran) became China's closest partner in trade, as part of the Parthian Empire （帕提亚帝国）, initiating important cultural exchanges. Paper and gunpowder invented by the Chinese had a much greater impact on culture than silk. The rich spices of the East, also, contributed more than the fashion which grew up from the silk industry. Even so, by the time of the Roman Emperor Augustus (27 BC–14 AD), trade between China and the West was firmly established and silk was the most sought-after commodity in Egypt, Greece, and especially, in Rome.

The Romans thought silk a vegetable product combed from trees and valued it by the weight of gold. Much of this silk came to the island of Kos （科斯岛）, where it was woven into dresses for the ladies of Rome and other cities. In Rome, silk had remained popular, though increasingly expensive, until the fall of the Roman Empire in 476 AD. The eastern half of Rome survived, which came to be known as the Byzantine Empire （拜占庭帝国） and carried on the Romans' infatuation with silk. Around 60 AD the West had become aware that silk was not grown on the trees in China but was actually spun by silkworms. The Chinese had very purposefully kept the origin of silk a secret, and once the secret was out, they carefully guarded their silkworms and their process of harvesting the silk.

The Byzantine Emperor Justinian （查士丁尼一世, 482–565 AD), tired of paying the exorbitant prices the Chinese demanded for silk, sent two emissaries, disguised as monks, to China to steal silkworms and smuggle them back to the West. The plan was successful and initiated the Byzantine silk industry. When the Byzantine Empire fell to the Turks in

1453, the Ottoman Empire closed the ancient routes of the Silk Road and cut all ties with the West.

The greatest value of the Silk Road was the exchange of culture. Art, religion, philosophy, technology, language, science, architecture, and every other element of civilization were exchanged along these routes, carried with the commercial goods the merchants traded from country to country. The closing of the Silk Road forced merchants to take to the sea for trade, thus initiating the Age of Discovery which led to worldwide interaction and the beginnings of a global community. In its time, the Silk Road served to broaden people's understanding of the world they lived in.

(Adapted from World History website.)

Mount Tai 泰山

Mount Tai is a mountain of historical and cultural significance, located in the north of the city of Tai'an（泰安市）. It is the highest point in China's Shandong Province. The tallest peak is the Jade Emperor Peak（玉皇顶）, which is commonly reported to be 1,545 metres tall.

Mount Tai was originally known as Daizong or Daishan. Since the Qin Dynasty it has also been known as Eastern Mountain（东岳）, one of the Five Great Mountains（五岳）of China, and has usually ranked as the first among them for it is associated with sunrise, birth, and renewal; the other four are: Mount Heng（衡山）in Hunan Province (Southern Mountain), Mount Hua（华山）in Shaanxi Province (Western Mountain), Mount Heng（恒山）in Shanxi Province (Northern Mountain), and Mount Song（嵩山）in Henan Province (Central Mountain). Mount Tai has been a place of worship for at least 3,000 years and served as one of the most important ceremonial centers of China during this period. Because of its sacred importance and dramatic landscape, it was made a UNESCO（联合国教科文组织）World Heritage Site in 1987. It meets 7 of the 10 evaluation standards of World Heritage, and is listed as a World Heritage Site, along with the Tasmanian Wilderness World Heritage Area（塔斯马尼亚荒原世界遗产区）in Australia.

Mount Tai is located in the west of Shandong Province, which used to be a huge subsiding belt or sea canal. The orogeny made the rock layers in the subsidence zone folded and uplifted into ancient land, forming a huge mountain system, which has experienced 2 billion years of weathering and denudation, and the terrain has gradually become flat. About 600 million years ago, Mount Tai sank into the sea again. After more than 100 million years, the entire area rose to land again, and the ancient Mount Tai uplifted into a relatively low barren hill. In the late Mesozoic period（中生代时期）about 100 million years ago, due to the extrusion and subduction of the Pacific Plate to the Eurasian Plate, the stratum of Mount Tai experienced extensive folds and fractures under the influence of the Yanshanian（燕山期，地质学名词）. During the crustal movement above, Mount Tai was rapidly uplifted. In the mid-Cenozoic period（新生代中期）about 30 million years ago, the outline of today's Mount Tai was basically formed.

Due to its height, Mount Tai also has a vertical climate variability. The lower part of the mountain is a warm temperate zone and the top of the mountain is a medium temperate zone. The mountain top is cloudy and foggy, with an average annual precipitation of 1,132 mm, while at the mountain foot is only 750 mm. Its vegetation coverage rate reaches 80%. On the foothills, deciduous forests, broad-leaved coniferous mixed forests, coniferous forest, alpine shrubs and grass can be seen in sequence. The vertical boundaries of the forest belts are distinct and the vegetation landscapes are different.

Traces of human presence at Mount Tai date back to the Paleolithic period（旧石器时代）. Evidence of human settlement in the area can be proven from the Neolithic period（新石器时代）onwards. During this time, two cultures had emerged near the mountain, the Dawenkou culture（大汶口文化）to the south and the Longshan culture（龙山文化）to the north.

The religious worship of Mount Tai dates back 3,000 years, from the time of the Shang Dynasty to the Qing Dynasty. Over time, this worship evolved into the Feng（封）and Shan（禅）sacrifices. The sacrifices were official imperial rites and Mount Tai became one of the principal places where the emperor would carry out the sacrifices to pay homage to heaven (on the summit of the mountain) and earth (at the foot of the mountain) in the Feng and Shan sacrifices respectively. The two sacrifices are often referred to together as the Fengshan sacrifices（封禅）. The carving of inscriptions as part of the sacrifices marks the attainment of the "great peace".

Mount Tai was not only the site of imposing state ceremonies. It was also home to powerful spirits, for whom rituals were performed in spring for a good harvest and in autumn to give thanks for the harvest. Since Mount Tai was the chief ceremonial centre in eastern China, rites were also performed to seek protection from floods and earthquakes.

Mount Tai became associated with a wide range of beliefs that were connected with Taoism, a philosophy integral to Chinese life and thought for more than 2,000 years. It was considered to be the centre of the *yang* (male) principle, the source of life, and from the Eastern Han Dynasty onward it was believed that the spirits of Mount Tai determined all human destiny and that after death the souls of people returned to Mount Tai for judgment. The name of the most important spirit, originally Taishan Fujun (泰山府君), was changed to Dongyue Dadi (东岳大帝) with the emergence of organized Taoism.

In 2003, Mount Tai attracted around six million visitors. A renovation project was completed in late October 2005, which aimed at restoring cultural relics and renovating damaged buildings of cultural significance. Widely known for its special ceremonies and sacrifices, Mount Tai has seen visits by many poets and literary scholars who have traveled there to gain inspiration.

(Adapted from Britannica and Wikipedia websites.)

Chapter Three

Chinese Language
中国语言

Chinese language, also called Sinitic language, is the principal language group of eastern Asia, belonging to the Sino-Tibetan language family, and is spoken by the largest number of people in the world. Chinese characters (汉字) are one of the earliest writing systems in the world, dating back several thousand years. There are many varieties of Chinese which are called dialects and usually classified as groups by scholars. The modern standard Chinese is one of the six official languages used in the United Nations. The vast majority of the Chinese-speaking population is in China, but a substantial number are also found throughout Southeast Asia, especially in Singapore, Indonesia, Malaysia, and Thailand.

3.1 Chinese Language

Chinese employs a logographic (字符的) writing system, while English uses an alphabetic writing system. An alphabetic writing system is one which uses individual letters—each of which roughly corresponds to particular phonemes—to spell out how words sound. A logographic system is made up of visual symbols which represent words but not sounds. This means that the pronunciation of a Chinese character is not implied by the way the character is written. While there may be elements within individual Chinese characters that hint at pronunciation, in most cases the pronunciation of a character cannot be learned by looking at the logogram (字符) itself.

Chinese characters, in general, are composed of a dozen basic strokes, which have similar functions to letters of most European languages, though they do not combine into syllables. There are some basic strokes, such as dot, horizontal stroke, vertical stroke, right-upward stroke, left-downward stroke and right-downward stroke, hook stroke, turning stroke. These strokes can be arranged in linear, irregular, close and loose ways, which differ from letters in European languages arranged from left to right.

Most Chinese speakers had no uniform phonetic transcription system until the mid-20th century, although enunciation patterns were recorded in early rhyme books and dictionaries. *Hanyu pinyin* (汉语拼音), often abbreviated to *pinyin*, is the official Romanization system for standard Mandarin Chinese in China. The earliest attempts at romanizing the Chinese language were made by Jesuit missionaries, who began arriving in China at the end of the 16th century, during the late Ming Dynasty. After the Opium War, the missionaries created Romanization system for many varieties of Chinese spoken in coastal provinces of the southeast, where people predominantly spoke local dialects and were largely illiterate. After the founding of the People's Republic of China, a phonetic script, *pinyin*, was introduced as the official phonetic transcription system for Chinese.

The grammar of Standard Chinese or Mandarin shares many features with other varieties of Chinese. The language almost entirely lacks inflection so that words typically have only one grammatical form. The basic word order of Chinese is subject–verb–object (SVO), the same as English. Additionally, Chinese is chiefly a head-final language, meaning that modifiers precede the words that they modify. In a noun phrase, for example, the head noun comes last, and all modifiers, including relative clauses, come in front of it. This phenomenon is more typically found in subject–object–verb languages, such as Turkish and Japanese. There was no grammar book until *The Elements of Chinese Grammar* was published in 1814, which was written by a missionary named Joshua Marshman. In 1898, the first Chinese-authored grammar book *Ma Shi Wen Tong* (《马氏文通》), written by Ma Jianzhong (马建忠), was published.

Categories such as number (singular or plural) and verb tense are frequently not expressed by any grammatical means in Chinese, but there are several particles that serve to express verbal aspect and, to some extent, mood. In Chinese, the meaning conveyed by a sentence is determined not by grammatical structures, but rather by the words themselves, their inherent relationships, and the context in which they are used.

Modern Standard Chinese, a form of Mandarin, takes its phonology from the Beijing dialect, adopts vocabulary from the Mandarin group, and bases its grammar on literature in the modern written vernacular, which is one of the official languages of China. Since the May Fourth Movement of 1919, classical Chinese (文言文) was rejected as the standard written language. After the establishment of the People's Republic of China, some government regulations were successfully implemented, and the tremendous task of ensuring that Modern Standard Chinese understood throughout China was effectively undertaken. Millions of Chinese, whose mother tongues were divergent Mandarin or non-Mandarin languages or non-Chinese languages, have learned to speak and understand the national Language, or Putonghua.

(Adapted from Wikipedia and Britannica websites.)

◆ Cultural Analysis

Chinese is one of the oldest languages that evolved from graphics. It is spoken by the Han ethnic group and many other ethnic groups in China. It is not only a carrier of Chinese culture, but also a kind of culture in its own right.

(1) Parataxis-based Language

Chinese is a language focusing more on parataxis, which means that the sentences are organized on the semantic connection, instead of the conjunctive words. In Chinese, semantic and pragmatic elements are more prominent than syntactic ones, in contrast to Western languages. Sentences formed in this way can carry the maximum amount of information and express multiple meanings, enhancing the expressiveness of the Chinese language. This may be one of the reasons why the Chinese language has flourished and evolved so vibrantly over thousands of years, even without the aid of formal grammar books.

(2) Block-shaped Character

Chinese characters are square and each occupies a similar-sized square space on the paper though the number of each one's strokes may be different. Compared with the linear alphabet language, it can reflect the inward seeking characteristic of its users. During the writing process, the writer should adjust to make the characters well balanced and fit together.

◆ Text Comprehension

1. Judge whether the following statements are true (T) or false (F).

1) The Chinese writing system is alphabetic.

2) The strokes should not be arranged in an irregular or loose way when writing Chinese characters.

3) Romanization was introduced to Chinese by missionaries at the end of the Qing Dynasty.

4) There is no grammatical tense in Chinese.

5) Since the May Fourth Movement of 1919, classical Chinese was rejected as the standard written language.

2. Answer the following questions.

1) What are the different characteristics of Chinese and English writing systems?

2) How has the phonetic transcription system of Chinese developed?

3) What are the characteristics of Chinese grammar compared with English?

3.2　Chinese Characters

Chinese characters are one of the oldest forms of writing in the world, carrying more than 5,000 years of Chinese culture and civilization. Chinese characters developed from early pictograms (象形符号). Today, we can still see traces of these pictograms in the form and structure of some characters, allowing us to easily guess their meaning. The general ideographic (表意的) nature of Chinese writing system sets it apart from alphabetic writing system.

According to legend, Chinese characters were invented by Cangjie (仓颉), a bureaucrat under the legendary Yellow Emperor. Inspired by his study of the animals of the world, the landscapes of the earth and the stars in the sky, Cangjie is said to have invented symbols called *zì* (字) —the first Chinese characters. The legend relates that on the day the characters were created, grain rained down from the sky and that night people heard ghosts wailing and demons crying because the human beings could no longer be cheated.

The earliest confirmed evidence of the Chinese scripts discovered so far is inscriptions carved on bronze vessels and oracle bones from the late Shang Dynasty. In 1899, pieces of these bones were being sold as "dragon bones (龙骨)" for medicinal purposes, when scholars identified the symbols on them as Chinese characters. Oracle bone inscriptions are records of divination performed in communication with royal ancestral spirits.

In the Qin Dynasty, the first government standardization of the characters took place. A very beautiful style known as small seal script (小篆) was introduced by the statesman Li Si (李斯). Since the seal script (篆书) was very time-consuming, people of the Qin Dynasty further improved the characters and created a new style, clerical script (隶书). In the Han Dynasty, the clerical script became the main typeface. Clerical script changed the curved and round strokes of the seal script into linear and flat square shapes, breaking away from the pictographic elements of ancient Chinese characters.

Regular script (楷书) came into being in the late Han Dynasty and was based on clerical script. After regular script appeared, the block-shaped Chinese characters were finalized and have been in use ever since. *Kai* (楷), the Chinese equivalent of regular script, means good examples for standard writing. It is simpler in form, has fewer strokes, and features straight lines. During the Tang Dynasty, regular script prevailed due to its rigorous rules and diverse styles. Cursive script (草书) is a kind of traditional Chinese script created for convenience of writing. It improves writing speed, but is difficult to read and understand for those who are not familiar with it. Cursive script broke the regularity of clerical script and gradually became a pure form of calligraphic art with aesthetic value. During the Jin Dynasties, especially the Eastern Jin Dynasty, cursive script flourished due to its unique artistic charm and practicality. Running script (行书) is somewhere between regular script and cursive script, allowing simpler and faster writing.

By the 20th century, traditional Chinese characters were thought to be too cumbersome and an impediment to progress. After the founding of the People's Republic of China, for the sake of the popularization of education, the Chinese government simplified the Chinese characters on a large scale. There were more than 2,000 complex Chinese characters that were simplified to today's appearance. The simplified writing system differs in two ways from the traditional writing system: the reduction of the number of strokes per character and the reduction of the number of characters in common use. Nowadays, the simplified Chinese is one of the working languages used by the United Nations.

With regard to the formation of Chinese characters, Xu Shen (许慎), a distinguished scholar in the Eastern Han Dynasty, classified Chinese characters into six categories. However, two of them are often omitted, and Chinese characters may fall into four main categories in view of their origin.

Pictograms (象形字 , hieroglyphs) refer to the characters that draw the profile of the involved subject, such as 月 (moon) which looks like a crescent moon. Over a long history, pictograms have evolved from irregular drawing into a definite form, mostly by reducing certain strokes to simplify writing. Ideographs (指事字) usually describe abstract concepts. They are combinations of indicators, or adding indicators to pictographs. For example, 刃 (blade), which is made up by adding a point on the cutting edge of a knife (刀), pointing out the position of the blade. Logical aggregates (会意字 , associative compounds) are combinations of two or more symbols to represent new characters with new meanings. For instance, the character 明 (bright) is composed by 日

(sun) and 月 (moon). Definitely, it will be bright when the sun and the moon appear in the same place. Pictophonetic compounds (形声字) are also called semantic-phonetic compounds, just as the name implies, they combine a semantic element with a phonetic element, taking the meaning from one element and the sound from the other. Semantic element indicates the word's meaning and characteristic, while phonetic element indicates the pronunciation of the word. For example, 湖 (lake) is composed of three dots which represent water, and 胡 which indicates the pronunciation.

(Adapted from Britannica website.)

• Cultural Analysis

Chinese characters, a combination of both meaning and pronunciation, are one of the most ancient writing scripts, which developed from early pictograms, and their development has gone through a number of stages.

(1) A Constant State of Simplification

Throughout their many stages of development, Chinese characters have been in a constant state of simplification, which is usually characterized by a less complex combination of strokes or a reduction in the number of strokes.

(2) The Carrier of Chinese Culture

Based on pictographs, Chinese characters combine shapes with sounds and connotations to form unique, block-shaped characters that carry meaning. This characteristic can help us read the signs left by the people thousands of years ago, which can help us communicate with the ancient culture and then inherit and develop it. For example, the character 财 (money) can tell us that the shell had been used as money in the history of China, because 贝 (shell) is the semantic element of the character.

• Text Comprehension

1. Judge whether the following statements are true (T) or false (F).

1) According to legend, Cangjie was inspired by his study of nature and invented Chinese characters.

2) The oracle bones were one of the traditional Chinese medicine in Chinese history.

3) After regular script appeared, the block-shaped Chinese characters were finalized and they have been used ever since.

4) The clerical script gradually became a pure form of calligraphic art with aesthetic value.

5) A pictophonetic compound usually combines a semantic element with a phonetic element, taking the meaning from one element and the sound from the other.

2. Answer the following questions.

1) What happened according to the legendary story on the day when the Chinese characters were created? Why?

2) What was the original function of oracle bone inscriptions?

3) What measurements have been taken by the government to address the issues of the Chinese writing system after the founding of PRC?

3.3   Chinese Dialects

At the end of the 2nd millennium BC, a form of Chinese was spoken in an inhabited area around the lower Wei River and middle Yellow River. From there, it expanded eastwards across the North China Plain to Shandong Province, and then southwards into the valley of the Yangtze River and into the hills of southern China. As the language spread, it replaced formerly dominant languages in those areas, and regional differences grew. Simultaneously, especially in periods of political unity, there was a tendency to promote a central standard to facilitate communication between people from different regions. Though there was wide variation in pronunciation among regions in Chinese history, the governments set out to define a standard pronunciation for reading the classics. The North China Plain provided few barriers to migration, leading to relative linguistic homogeneity over a wide area in northern China. In contrast, the mountains and rivers of southern China have spawned the other six major groups of Chinese languages with great internal diversity, particularly in Fujian Province.

The classification of Chinese dialects in the late 19th century and early 20th century was based on impressionistic criteria. Different dialects are often distributed along rivers, which were historically the main routes of migration and communication in southern China. The first scientific classification, based primarily on the evolution of Middle Chinese voiced initials（声母）, was proposed by Wang Li（王力）in 1936 and Li Fanggui（李方桂）in 1937, and has since been slightly modified by other linguists. The conventionally accepted seven dialect groups are Mandarin, Wu（吴）, Min（闽）, Xiang（湘）, Gan（赣）, Hakka（客家）and Yue（粤）dialects.

Mandarin is spoken in northern and southwestern China and is currently spoken by the largest number of people. Mandarin, also called Guanhua, has existed for a long time. In the Yuan, Ming and Qing dynasties, Beijing was the political, economic and cultural center. Officials in Beijing spoke the Northern Dialect which was based on the local dialect of Beijing. Naturally, travelling merchants had to learn it as well so that they could negotiate and do business with those who lived in the capital city. Moreover, when government officials were designated to work in other provinces across the country, they could only speak the Northern Dialect as they probably could not speak the local dialects of the provinces in which they were working. As a result, for administrative purposes, when locals were dealing with the government officials, the official language would be used, and people could not join the civil service unless they were able to speak the language. Hence, the dialects used in the north of China came to sound similar.

Wu is spoken in Jiangsu Province, Zhejiang Province and Shanghai. Wu includes Shanghainese, which is sometimes taken as the representative of all Wu Dialect. Wu's subgroups are extremely diverse, especially in the mountainous regions of Zhejiang Province and eastern Anhui Province. Wu possibly comprises hundreds of distinct spoken forms, which are not mutually intelligible.

Gan is spoken in Jiangxi Province. In the past, it was thought to be closely related to Hakka Dialect because Middle Chinese voiced initials became voiceless aspirated initials in Hakka, and hence it was called by the umbrella term（涵盖性术语）as Hakka-Gan Dialect.

Xiang is spoken in Hunan Province. Xiang is usually divided into the old dialect and the new dialect, and the new dialect is significantly influenced by Mandarin. The Xiang dialect has retained many ancient Chinese vocabulary and phonetic features. Its formation can be traced back to the Chu dialect of the pre-Qin period.

Min is spoken in Fujian Province, Taiwan region, and parts of Southeast Asia (particularly Malaysia, the Philippines, and Singapore). Min is the only branch of Chinese that cannot be directly derived from Middle Chinese. It is also the most diverse, with many varieties used in neighboring countries. In the mountains of western Fujian Province, even in adjacent villages, the dialects are mutually unintelligible.

Hakka is spoken by the Hakka people, a subgroup of the Han Chinese, in several provinces across southern China, in Taiwan region, and in parts of Southeast Asia such as Malaysia and Singapore. The term "Hakka" itself translates as "guest families", and Hakka people consider themselves descendants of the Song Dynasty and later refugees from northern China. Hakka has kept many features of northern Middle Chinese that have been lost in northern China.

Cantonese is spoken in Guangdong and Guangxi provinces, Hong Kong, Macao, parts of Southeast Asia, and among overseas Chinese people with an ancestry tracing back to the Guangdong region. But not all varieties of Cantonese are mutually intelligible.

Chinese varieties differ most in their phonology, and less in vocabulary and syntax. Local varieties from different areas of China are often mutually unintelligible, and these varieties form the Sinitic branch of the Sino-Tibetan language family. Because speakers share a standard written form, and have a common cultural heritage due to a long period of political unity, the varieties are popularly perceived among native speakers as variants of Chinese language.

Until the mid-20th century, most Chinese people spoke only their local language. In the early years of the Republic of China, classical Chinese was replaced as the standard written language by vernacular Chinese, which was based on northern dialects. In the 1930s, a standard national language was adopted, with its pronunciation based on the Beijing dialect, but with vocabulary also drawn from other Mandarin varieties. It is the official spoken language of the People's Republic of China and one of the official languages of Singapore. Standard Mandarin now dominates public life in China, and is much more widely studied than any other variety of Chinese language.

(Adapted from Wikipedia website.)

◆ Cultural Analysis

Dialects, generally referred to as local languages, are branches of the Chinese language in different regions and are only used in certain areas. The major dialect groups of Chinese are mutually unintelligible and each of them has numerous dialects.

(1) Unintelligibility in Oral Communication

Chinese dialects are very complicated. Various dialects differ in pronunciation, vocabulary and grammar. And the difference in pronunciation is the most obvious. There is a saying in coastal areas of southeastern China, which goes "People who live 10 li away from each other speak in different pronunciations (十里不同音)". If all people in different areas speak in their local dialects, it will lead to trouble in communication.

(2) More Dialects in the Southeast and Fewer in the North

Generally speaking, there are many more dialect groups in the southeastern area than in the northern part of China. Actually, there are a lot of factors which cause the formation of dialects, such as small-scale peasant economy, the division within society, the isolation caused by mountains and rivers, population migration, etc. The northern part of China was the political center for a long time, while the southern part was full of lakes and swamps, mountains and rivers, and lush vegetation, which hindered easy communication among different dialect speakers. So there is a relatively unified dialect group in the north but many dialect groups in the south.

(3) The Significance of Dialects to Chinese Language Research

There are seven major dialect groups in the Chinese language and each dialect group consists of a large number of dialects. The boundaries between one so-called dialect and another are not always easy to define. Because each dialect group preserves distinct features of Middle Chinese, they have proven invaluable as research tools for the phonological reconstruction of Middle Chinese and even, to some extent, its ancestor, Old Chinese.

◆ Text Comprehension

1. Judge whether the following statements are true (T) or false (F).

1) The variation of Chinese is particularly strong in the more mountainous southeast of China.

2) In the Yuan Dynasty, the officials usually could speak Mandarin.

3) Gan Dialect has kept many features of northern Middle Chinese that have been lost in northern China.

4) The varieties of Chinese can only be classified into several groups: Mandarin, Wu, Min, Xiang, Gan, Hakka and Yue.

5) Chinese varieties differ most in their phonology, and less in vocabulary and syntax.

2. Answer the following questions.

1) What is "dialect" and what is "Mandarin"?

2) What caused the relative linguistic homogeneity across a wide area in northern China?

3) Why are there so many dialect groups in southeastern China?

◆ Exercises

1. Choose the best answer to each of the following questions.

1) Large Chinese-speaking populations can be found in all of the following regions EXCEPT _____.

A. Singapore

B. Thailand

C. North Korea

D. Indonesia

2) Which of the following is true about strokes of Chinese characters?

A. Strokes are arranged from left to right.

B. Strokes can be combined into syllables.

C. Strokes should be adjusted to make the character well balanced.

D. Strokes cannot be arranged in a loose way.

3) Which of the following is true about the grammar of Standard Chinese?

A. Chinese words typically have several grammatical forms.

B. Chinese is chiefly a head-final language.

C. Verb tense is expressed by grammatical means.

D. Chinese does not involve two or more verbs or verb phrases in sequence.

4) Which of the following description is inaccurate about Chinese script?

A. Block-shaped

B. Pictographic

C. Ideographic

D. Alphabetic

5) Chinese varieties differ in all of the following EXCEPT _____.

A. Phonology

B. Syntax

C. Written form

D. Vocabulary

2. Match the following types of Chinese scripts with their corresponding features.

Types	Features
1) Seal script	a) Breaking away from the pictographic element of ancient Chinese characters
2) Clerical script	b) Characterized by the curved and round strokes
3) Regular script	c) A pure form of calligraphic art with aesthetic value
4) Cursive script	d) Finalizing the block-shaped Chinese characters

3. Translate the following sentences.

1) 汉语属于汉藏语系，是世界上使用人口最多的语言。

2) 现代标准汉语是联合国六种官方语言之一，其音韵来源于北京方言。

3) 书法是中国传统的汉字书写艺术，经过千百年的创作和发展，已成为一门风格独特的艺术。

4) 汉字历史悠久，它起源于记事图画。目前发现的最古老的汉字是距今 3000 多年前的甲骨文，它们已是很成熟的文字。

5) 因为讲普通话有利于各民族、各地区人民之间的文化交流和信息传递，所以中国政府十分重视推广普通话的工作，鼓励大家都说普通话。

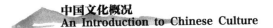

4. Discuss the following questions.

1) What is a parataxis-based language? What are the characteristics of parataxis-based language?

2) Why did vernacular Chinese replace classical Chinese as the standard written language in the early years of the Republic of China?

3) Why could Chinese people communicate effectively despite the existence of so many dialects in China?

5. Work in groups. Do research on the differences between Chinese and English based on your own experience of learning English and fill in the table below. Then report your findings to the class.

Differences	Chinese	English

◆ Extended Readings

Oracle Bone Script 甲骨文

Oracle bones (also known as dragon bones) are the shoulder blades of oxen or plastrons of turtles (the flat, underside of the turtle's shell), which were used in the Shang Dynasty of China for divination. The symbols carved on the bones eventually became words and a recognizable Chinese script developed from this practice.

A fortune-teller would carve (and later paint) symbols onto the ox bones or the turtle shells, heating them with a hot poker or fire until cracks appeared. Then, they would interpret the direction of the cracks in conjunction with the carved symbols to predict the future. Most of the oracle bones discovered come from the Shang Dynasty but some are from the early Zhou Dynasty. The practice of telling the future through oracle bones is known as scapulimancy (telling the future through the scapula, the shoulder bone, of an animal), plastromancy (using a turtle's plastron) or pyromancy (using fire). These methods all declined when the book known as *The Book of Changes* (《易经》, a fortune-telling manual which uses hexagrams and narrow sticks) gained wider acceptance in the Zhou Dynasty.

Oracle bones continued to be used in later dynasties, but not as frequently as in the Shang Dynasty. These bones are important primary sources for understanding the history of the Shang Dynasty and the origin of Chinese characters. Historian Harold M. Tanner writes, "oracle bones are the earliest written records of Chinese civilization. The inscriptions provide us with a limited view of some of the concerns and events that were relevant to the Shang elite. The earliest of these records can be traced back to to the reign of King Wu Ding (武丁) in the late Shang." Even though everyone was curious about the future, the majority of the inscriptions were questions posed by the wealthier classes in China. This is probably because they could afford to consult oracle bone diviners more often than the poor.

The desire to know the future has been constant in human history and the people of China in the Shang Dynasty were not different from people today in this respect. Fortune-telling in the Shang Dynasty was considered an important resource in making decisions, and these psychics were consulted by everyone from the farmer to the king. These fortune-tellers were thought to be in touch with the spirit world of the ancestors who lived with the gods and knew the future. These spirits would communicate with the psychics through the oracle bones. Each fortune-teller had his or her area of expertise (love, money, work, etc.) but could answer questions on any topic.

Fortune-tellers either got the bones and shells themselves (and prepared them) or bought them from a merchant who scraped and cleaned them. The bones or shells were then kept in the fortune-tellers' shop. If someone wanted to know whether they should take their cattle to market, or go to visit a friend on a certain date, they would visit a fortune-teller who could predict how well their plans would work out.

The Shang Dynasty was replaced by the Zhou Dynasty, which still used oracle bones but mainly relied on *The Book of Changes* and other methods of telling the future. The capital of the Shang Dynasty, which is now Anyang (安阳), was renovated during the Zhou Dynasty, and the areas of the bone workshops and places of divination were neglected.

In 1899, the Chancellor of the Imperial Academy, Wang Yirong (王懿荣), became sick with malaria. He asked his doctor for medicine and was sent to an apothecary (药商) for the best-known remedy: dragon bones. This medicine was supposed to be made from the ancient bones of dragons and had mystical properties for healing. Taking a dose of dragon bones in the Shang Dynasty was like taking aspirin or a prescription drug today, and the apothecaries, doctors, and suppliers all made money from the dragon bones, which were always given to patients in their ground up, powdered form. When Wang Yirong got his dragon bones, however, they were not ground up. On the night of this incident, he had a friend visiting named Liu E (刘鹗) who examined the dragon bones with him. They were both interested in palaeography (古文字学) and noticed that these bones seemed to be covered with ancient Chinese characters.

Wang Yirong and Liu E went to the apothecary to find out where he got these bones, but the man would not tell them. He agreed to sell them all the unground bones he had in his shop. After Wang and Liu told other people about their discovery, scholars quickly became interested in finding out where these bones were coming from. But the apothecaries and dragon bone dealers kept it a secret and thus made a lot of money from the medicine.

(Adapted from World History website.)

Chinese Phonetic Transcription 汉语注音系统

Chinese uses pictograms and its characters do not represent phonemes directly. Many different ways have been devised to represent the sounds of spoken Chinese. Most use a version of the Latin or Roman alphabet, known as "Romanization" or "Latinization".

The Indian Sanskrit grammarians who came to China two thousand years ago to work on the translation of Buddhist scriptures into Chinese and the transcription of Buddhist terms into Chinese, discovered the "initial sound", "final sound", and "suprasegmental（超音段的）tone" structure of spoken Chinese syllables. This understanding is reflected in the precise *Fanqie*（反切）system, and it is the core principle of all modern systems. While the *Fanqie* system was ideal for indicating the conventional pronunciation of single, isolated characters in written classical Chinese literature, it was unworkable for the pronunciation of essentially polysyllabic Chinese characters.

Romanization of Chinese is the transliteration of Chinese with the Latin alphabet. There have been many systems using Roman letters to represent Chinese characters throughout history. The first people to attempt the Romanization of Chinese were Jesuit missionaries, mainly from Spain and Portugal, who began to arrive in China during the early 16th century, towards the end of the Ming Dynasty. The first Romanization systems were created by Matteo Ricci（利玛窦）, in 1605, and Nicolas Trigault（金尼阁）, in 1625, who used them only as an aid to studying Mandarin.

When Protestant missionaries were permitted to work in China after the Opium War of 1840–1842, at first they had to confine their activities to the southeastern coastal provinces, where people didn't speak Mandarin and were mainly illiterate. The missionaries created Romanization systems for many varieties of Chinese spoken in those areas, taught their converts to read, and published millions of copies of religious works and other materials. The Wade-Giles system（威妥玛拼音）was popular and used in English-language publications outside China until 1979, which was produced by Thomas Wade in 1859, and further improved by Herbert Giles in a Chinese-English Dictionary in 1892.

At the end of the 19th century and the beginning of the 20th century, there was general discontent with the policies of the Qing Dynasty, which led to calls for reform in many areas, including language reform. Many phonetic scripts were devised by Chinese patriots who saw them as a way of making China "wealthy and strong" again. There was also much debate about whether the transcription systems should be used in conjunction with Chinese characters to show their pronunciation, or whether they should replace the Chinese characters altogether. Another issue was about which varieties of Chinese should be represented by the transcription systems: some favoured Mandarin only, and others argued that separate systems need to be devised for other varieties of Chinese.

Eventually, it was decided that a northern dialect spoken by educated people in northern China should be used as the basis for a new form of written Chinese. It also became the standard spoken language for the whole country. The *pinyin* system includes four diacritics denoting tones. *Pinyin* without tone marks is used to spell Chinese names and words in languages that are written with the Latin alphabet, and to enter Chinese characters with certain computer input methods.

The *pinyin* system was developed in the 1950s by a group of Chinese linguists based on earlier forms of Romanization of Chinese. It was published by the Chinese government in 1958 and was revised several times. The International Organization for Standardization (ISO) adopted *pinyin* as an international standard in 1982, followed by the United Nations in 1986.

Unlike European languages, *pinyin* is formed by the combination of initials (声母) and finals (韵母), rather than by individual consonant and vowel letters. Every Mandarin syllable can be spelled exactly with an initial followed by a final, except for the special syllable *-er* or when a trailing *-r* is considered part of a syllable. The latter case, though a common practice in some sub-dialects, is rarely used in official publications. Even though most initials contain a consonant, finals are not always simple vowels, especially in compound finals (复韵母), i.e., when a "medial" is placed in front of the final.

(Adapted from Omniglot website.)

Chapter Four

Chinese Philosophy
中国哲学

Chinese philosophy originates in the Spring and Autumn Period and the Warring States Period characterized by significant intellectual and cultural advancements. Although most of the major Chinese philosophy—Confucianism, Legalism, Taoism, Mohism, Chinese Naturalism (阴阳家), and the Logicians (名家)—began to emerge during the Warring States Period, elements of Chinese philosophy have existed for several thousand years. It was during that time that the two most influential spiritual leaders native to China, Confucius and Laozi, are thought to have lived and taught. The philosophies that they practiced, Confucianism and Taoism, coexisted in dynastic China, attracting countless numbers of followers over the past 2,500 years. The general theory of Chinese philosophy is the unity of man and heaven. This spirit of harmony between heaven and man is the characteristic of the entire history of Chinese philosophy.

4.1　Conception of the Cosmos

In ancient China, the universe was thought to be an organic system, with all parts integrated into an ordered whole. Ancient Chinese believed that there was a spiritual correspondence between the world of nature and the world of man. The meaning is also translated as "The harmony between heaven and man (天人合一)" in English.

For ancient Chinese, the universe was the totality of heaven, earth and everything in between. There was no beginning, and the world always exists. In this whole world, what is above man is heaven; what is underneath man is earth. Heaven, earth and man are the sources of all creatures. Heaven gives birth to them, earth nourishes them, and human beings complete them. Heaven endows creatures at birth with a sense of kinship loyalty; earth nourishes them with food and clothing; man completes them through ritual and music. Heaven has the power to cause proliferation; earth has the power to cause transformation; and human beings have the power to make moral distinctions.

These three aid each other like hands and feet. Each one is essential and together they form a whole. Heaven's vital energy rises, earth's vital energy descends, and man's is in the middle. The vital energy of plants and animals is born in the spring, nourished in the summer, harvested in the autumn, and stored in the winter. Hence nothing is more ethereal than vital energy, nothing is richer than earth, and nothing is more spiritual than Heaven.

The basic substance of all things is called *qi*. Everything that ever existed, at all times, is made of *qi*, including inanimate matter, humans and animals, the sky, ideas and emotions, demons and ghosts, and the world when it is teeming with different beings. *Qi* is thought to move or to operate according to a pattern that conforms to two basic modes. The Chinese names for those two modes are *yin* and *yang*.

Yin and *yang* are best understood in terms of symbolism. When the sun shines on a mountain at some time other than midday, the mountain has one shady side and one sunny side. *Yin* is the symbol of the shady side and its characteristics; *yang* is the symbol of the sunny side and its qualities. Since the sun has not yet warmed the *yin* side, it is dark, cool, and moist; plants are contracted and dormant; and water in the form of dew moves downward. The *yang* side of the mountain is the opposite of the *yin* side. It is bright, warm, and dry; plants open up and extend their stalks to absorb sunlight; and water in the form of fog moves upward as it evaporates.

This basic symbolism was extended to include a host of other oppositions. *Yin* is female, while *yang* is male. *Yin* occupies the lower position, while *yang* the higher. Any situation in the human or natural world can be analyzed within this framework. *Yin* and *yang* can be used to understand the modulations of *qi* on a mountainside as well as the relationships within a family. The social hierarchies of gender and age, for instance— the duty of the wives to serve their husbands, and the duty of younger generations to obey older ones—were interpreted as the natural subordination of *yin* to *yang*. The same reasoning can be applied to any two members of a pair.

Yin and *yang* are both competitive and complementary. On the one hand, the *yin qi* and the *yang qi* are competing forces or opposite forms of energy, which constantly work against each other. Since both are part of the totality of *qi*, when *yin* grows, *yang* declines; when *yang* strengthens, *yin* weakens. The competition is constant and the flow of *qi* is always in motion; hence, change is the constant state of *qi*. On the other hand, *yin* and *yang* complement each other, since everything relies on both of them to exist. The cooperation of *yin* and *yang* is based on their mutual competition. Things can change, grow, decline, and get reborn, exactly because *yin* and *yang* work against each other. The change of seasons is a perfect illustration of the interaction between *yin* and *yang*.

The ancient Chinese believed that the universe was simply the totality of *qi* in perpetual motion and constant alteration. In other words, the cosmos was in constant change, but there was a consistent pattern to that change discernible to human beings. Things behaved in particular ways not necessarily because of prior actions or impulsion of other things, but because of their position in the ever-moving cyclical universe. They were endowed with intrinsic natures which made such behaviour inevitable. For example, the natural disasters were seen as part of the natural development of the world, even if they posed a great risk to human survival in ancient China.

(Adapted from Asia for Educators website.)

◆ Cultural Analysis

The harmony between heaven and man is a fundamental concept in classical Chinese philosophy. Obviously, heaven is not merely the sky as viewed from the earth, nor is it the ruling gods and spirits, but rather a symbol of nature.

(1) The Connotation of Harmony

Harmony is rich in connotation and full of profound philosophy of great wisdom. There is nothing it cannot absorb and nothing it cannot cover. Harmony seeks peace, compromise, concord and unison. Harmony could be applied to many aspects of the society, such as administration, politics, economy, interpersonal relations, etc. For example, when harmony is applied in administrative field, we can coordinate various kinds of interests, synthesize different opinions and defuse complicated contradictions.

(2) Holistic Thinking

In ancient Chinese mind, man and nature are one holistic system, which brings out the holistic thinking view that the formation, development and change of everything are always the result of the movement of the whole. That is to say, the whole affects the part, and the part is the representation based on the whole.

◆ Text Comprehension

l. Judge whether the following statements are true (T) or false (F).

1) The world is an ever-moving cyclical universe and everything is made up of *qi* in ancient Chinese mind.

2) *Yin* and *yang* are two types of *qi* which are equally important in the world.

3) The social hierarchies of gender and age could also be interpreted as the natural subordination of *yang* to *yin*.

4) Heaven, earth and man are the source of all creatures and they form a holistic system in Chinese cosmology.

5) Ancient Chinese believed that there was a spiritual correspondence between the world of nature and the world of man.

2. Answer the following questions.

1) How did ancient Chinese view the cosmos?

2) Can you explain the relationship of *yin* and *yang* and their symbolic meanings?

3) What is the meaning of "heaven" in terms of "the harmony between heaven and man" in Chinese philosophy?

4.2 Confucius and Confucianism

Confucianism is the way of life advocated by Confucius in the 6th to 5th centuries BC and has been followed by the Chinese people for more than two millennia. Although it has transformed over time, it is still the substance of learning, the source of values, and the social code of Chinese society. Its influence has also extended to other countries, particularly Korea, Japan, and Vietnam.

Confucius may have initiated a cultural process known in the West as Confucianism, but he and those who followed him considered themselves part of a tradition—later identified by Chinese historians as the *rujia* (儒家)—the "scholarly tradition". Its origins can be traced back two thousand years ago, when the legendary sages Yao and Shun created a civilized world through moral persuasion.

Confucius considered himself a transmitter who consciously tried to reanimate the old in order to attain the new. He advocated revitalizing the importance of the past through a ritualized way of life. His fascination with antiquity stemmed from a profound desire to understand why certain lifestyles and institutions—such as ancestor reverence, human-centered rituals, and mourning ceremonies—had persisted for centuries. His exploration of the past was a quest for origins, which he believed were rooted in fundamental human needs for belonging and communication. For him, the fact that traditional practices had lost some of their vitality did not diminish their potential to be reborn and flourish in the future.

Confucius greatly admired Zhougong (周公), the Duke of Zhou from the 11th century BC, who was credited with consolidating, expanding, and refining the feudal ritual system. This elaborate system was built upon blood ties, marital alliances, and ancient covenants. The maintenance of both interstate and domestic harmony relied heavily on cultural values and social norms, which were grounded in the shared political belief that authority resided in universal kingship sanctified by the "Mandate of Heaven" (天命). This belief emphasized that social cohesion was achieved not through legal constraints but through the meticulous observance of rituals. As a result of this feudal ritual system, the Western Zhou Dynasty flourished in relative peace and prosperity for nearly five centuries.

Inspired by the statesmanship of Zhougong, Confucius harbored a lifelong dream to put into practice the political ideas that he had learned from the ancient sages. Although Confucius never realized his political dream, his political conception of moral persuasion became more and more influential. The Zhou Dynasty's belief in the mandate of heaven was that the virtues of the kings were essential for the maintenance of their power and authority. By Confucius' time, however, the feudal ritual system had been so fundamentally undermined that the political crises also precipitated a profound moral decline.

Confucius advocated the principle of *ren* (仁). This concept emphasizes kindness, compassion, and a sense of moral responsibility toward others, constituting the core of his ethical and political teachings. He believed that virtue, both as a personal attribute and a prerequisite for leadership, was not only essential for individual dignity, communal unity, and political stability, but also served as the foundation for fostering harmonious interpersonal relationships and social progress.

One of the fundamental Confucian values closely linked to this concept of virtue is filial piety (孝). Indeed, Confucius regarded filial piety as the first step toward achieving moral excellence and realizing the cardinal virtue of benevolence. By internalizing family values within one's mind and heart, one can develop the capacity to overcome self-centeredness. Drawing from modern psychology, filial piety helps transform the enclosed private ego into an open self. However, it is important to note that filial piety does not entail unconditional submission to parental authority. Instead, it involves acknowledging and revering the source of life, emphasizing the respect and gratitude toward one's parents and ancestors.

Confucians, moreover, are fond of applying the family metaphor to the community, the country, and the cosmos. They prefer to address the emperor as the son of heaven (天

子), the king as the ruler-father (君父), and the magistrate as the "father-mother official (父母官)", because for them the family-centered nomenclature implies a political vision. When Confucius said that taking care of family affairs was itself an active participation in politics, he had already made it clear that family ethics was not merely a private concern; the public good was realized by and through it.

Confucius believed that the smooth running of a state and its social stratification depended on the rectification of names (正名). As far as social relationship is concerned, behind each name are the responsibilities and obligations each individual should fulfill. For example, the name "emperor" represents the virtues that an ideal emperor should possess. If an emperor rules his nation according to what the name "emperor" requires, then he is worthy of the name. Confucius said, "An emperor should act in the way an emperor should be; a subject should act in the way a subject should be; a father should act in the way a father should be; a son should act in the way a son should be (君君，臣臣，父父，子子)."

Confucianism is a worldview, a social ethic, a political ideology, a scholarly tradition, and a way of life. Confucianism may be understood as an all-encompassing way of thinking and living that entails ancestor reverence and a profound human-centered ideology.

(Adapted from Britannica website.)

◆ Cultural Analysis

Confucianism has played an important role in shaping Chinese character, behavior and way of living. Its primary purpose is to achieve harmony, which is achieved by everyone having a well-defined role and treating others in a proper way.

(1) Leaving a Classic Legacy

Confucianism has left us a rich literary heritage, known as the Four Books and the Five Classics. The Four Books are: *The Great Learning* (《大学》), *The Doctrine of the Mean* (《中庸》), *The Analects of Confucius* (《论语》), and *The Works of Mencius* (《孟子》). The Five Classics are: *The Book of Poetry* (《诗经》), *The Book of Documents* (《书经》), *The Book of Rites* (《礼经》), *The Book of Changes* (《易经》), and *Spring and Autumn Annals* (《春秋》). For six centuries (1313–1905), these books became the elementary requirements of Chinese education in the feudal society and served as the basis of the civil service examination（科举考试）, through which scholars were selected for official positions at various levels of the government.

(2) Strengthening Patriarchal Society (Family-Oriented Society)

Blood relationships were emphasized, and great importance was attached to the concepts of family and filial piety in Confucianism. Within families, men enjoyed privileges superior to those of women. In society, the emperor held supreme authority, and all subjects must obey his commands.

(3) Emphasizing the Sense of Responsibility

Confucianism emphasizes that every member of society should perform their respective roles and handle relationships with others, adhering to the principle of "rectification of names" and upholding the " five constant relationships" (sovereign-subject, father-son, elder-younger brother, husband-wife, friend-friend, 五伦：君臣、父子、长幼、夫妻、朋友).

◆ Text Comprehension

1. Judge whether the following statements are true (T) or false (F).

1) Confucianism has been followed by the Chinese people for more than two millennia.

2) Confucianism began with Confucius.

3) Confucius harboured a lifelong dream to emulate Zhougong by putting into practice the political ideas that he had learned from the ancient sages.

4) Confucius saw filial piety as the first step toward moral excellence and the realization of the cardinal virtue of humanity.

5) As far as institution is concerned, behind each name are the responsibilities and obligations each individual should fulfill.

2. Answer the following questions.

1) What is Confucianism according to the text?

2) How does Confucianism apply the family metaphor to the country?

3) What are the Five Classics and what are their functions?

4.3　Laozi and Taoism

Tao Te Ching (《道德经》) was written around the sixth century BC. The author is generally believed to be Lao Dan (老聃), or Laozi—a recluse who lived during the Spring and Autumn Period. Little is known about Lao Dan, who was said to have once held a low civil position in the royal court, and was in charge of the archival records of the Zhou Dynasty. Yet because of his great knowledge, even Confucius was said to have traveled miles to consult him.

Tao Te Ching consists of just over 5,000 Chinese characters. Its 81 chapters are divided into two parts: *Tao* (the Way) and *Te* (Virtue). Short as it is, the book has played a great role in the development of Chinese culture. It has become the basis of Taoism, a school of philosophy parallel to Confucianism in ancient China.

Tao, as the fundamental concept of Taoist philosophy, first proposed by Laozi, is the ultimate source of the universe. Fundamentally speaking, *Tao* is metaphysical, indefinable, unlimited and unnameable. Laozi said, "There was something undefined and complete, existing before heaven and earth, how still it was, how formless, standing alone and undergoing no change, reaching everywhere with no danger of being exhausted. It may be regarded as the mother of all things. Truthfully it has no name, but I call it *Tao*."

In the context of cosmology, *Tao* is a life-giving force, responsible for the creation of myriad things, and stands for the cosmic order, the way things are. So an appropriate translation for *Tao* is "the Way". "The Way", used in the singular, signifies the existence of a single cosmic order or a single cosmic pattern. Under the holistic cosmic picture, the cosmic order also governs human affairs. Consequently, *Tao* takes on a moral connotation, that is, "the right way", which also stands for the "path" one ought to take. In this sense, *Tao* stands for the highest moral precepts of human beings.

Te refers to the innate nature of universal existence. As far as human beings are concerned, it means virtue, which is the nature of human beings. However, Taoism also believes human beings can be distracted from their innate virtue by their desires and excessive knowledge, thus leading to challenges in their lives.

"*Ziran* (自然 , Naturalness)" is an important concept of Laozi's philosophy. It refers to a natural state of being, an attitude of following the way of nature. Laozi emphasized that everything in the world has its own way of being and development: Birds fly in the sky, fish swim in the water, clouds float in the sky, and flowers bloom and fall. All these phenomena occur independently and naturally without following any human's will, and humans should not try to change anything that is natural. Laozi admonished people to give up any desire to control the world. Following the way of nature is the way to resolve conflicts between humans and the world.

"*Wuwei* (无为 , Non-action)" is another important concept of Laozi's philosophy. It is the guarantee of "naturalness". Laozi said, "*Tao* (the Way) acts through non-action," by which he did not mean that one should do nothing and passively wait for achievements. Neither did he deny human creativity. What he meant is that human enterprises should be built on the basis of naturalness, not on any attempts to interrupt the rhythm of nature. Human creativity should be in compliance with the way of nature.

Laozi said, "The greatest virtue is like water." He compared his philosophy of "non-contention" to water to distinguish it from the law of the jungle. He said, "Water nourishes everything but contends for nothing." To Laozi, humans tend to seek higher positions while water always flows to lower places. Driven by desire, humans like whatever they think is superior while despising whatever they think is inferior. Yet water always flows downward. As the source of life, water nourishes all living things on the earth. No life can exist without water, which contributes to the world regardless of gain or loss. Remaining low, level and tranquil, water embraces and reflects everything under the heaven. The way of water is completely different from the way of people with avid desires.

But the philosophy of Laozi is by no means weak. On the contrary, it is full of strength. According to Laozi, water accumulates great strength in its weakness and quietude. Its strength can break down all barriers in the world. He said, "Nothing in the world is weaker than water. Yet nothing is stronger than water when it comes to breaking something strong. Water is a typical example of the weak winning over the strong." Water is invincible because it desires nothing and contends for nothing.

(Adapted from Wikipedia, Stanford, and Britannica websites.)

◆ Cultural Analysis

Taoism emphasizes freedom, nature, cosmology, self-cultivation, and retirement from social life. It has had a deep and long-lasting influence in many domains of Chinese culture, including philosophy, art, literature, medicine, cuisine, and has spread widely throughout East Asia.

(1) Simple Dialectics

The core of Laozi's thought is simple dialectics, which has exerted a profound influence on the development of Chinese philosophy. In politics, it advocates the rule of doing nothing and teaching without words. In terms of self-cultivation, it emphasizes the practice of being modest and solid, not competing with others. The sentences "Everything that goes to its extreme will develop into its opposite", "Disaster hides itself behind good fortune; Good fortune leans itself against disaster" in *Tao Te Ching* can illustrate this point.

(2) Aesthetics

Taoism believes that beauty resides in natural things, transcending the material world and belonging to the spiritual realm. This philosophy values simplicity and spontaneity, emphasizing that true beauty cannot be manufactured or compelled but instead arises naturally from within. An ideal work of art should emerge naturally, like a creation of nature, through the operation of *Tao*—"the Way" of the universe.

(3) Reclusiveness (退隐)

The reclusive culture, influenced by Taoism, concentrates on the harmony between man and environment. This emphasis on harmony not only reflects a deep respect for nature but also promotes a lifestyle that seeks balance and inner peace. The Eastern Jin Dynasty (东晋) saw the rise of the great poet of reclusion—Tao Yuanming (陶渊明), whose poems vividly portrayed his peaceful rural life and charming pastoral scenes.

◆ Text Comprehension

1. Judge whether the following statements are true (T) or false (F).

1) Because of Laozi's great knowledge, Confucius was said to have traveled miles to consult him.

2) *Tao Te Ching* consists of just over 5,000 Chinese characters.

3) In the context of cosmology, *Tao* stands for the cosmic order, or the way things are.

4) All the phenomena occur dependently and humans should not try to change anything that is natural.

5) The way of water is completely different from the way of people without desires according to Taoism.

2. Answer the following questions.

1) Can you introduce Laozi briefly?

2) How do you understand *Tao*?

3) What is the connotation of "*Ziran*" and "*Wuwei*"?

◆ Exercises

1. Decide which of the following claims or works belongs to Confucianism or Taoism.

A. Retirement from social life

B. Freedom and nature

C. The Four Books and the Five Classics

D. Human-centered ideology

E. Virtue and humanity

F. Filial piety

G. *Tao Te Ching* and *Zhuangzi*

H. Non-action

Confucianism	Taoism

2. Choose the best answer to each of the following questions.

1) Which of the following is NOT true about *yin* and *yang*?

A. *Yin* represents the shady side, while *yang* represents the sunny side.

B. *Yin* symbolizes female, while *yang* symbolizes male.

   C. *Yang* occupies a lower position and is subordinate to *yin*.

   D. Humans seek a harmonious balance between *yin* and *yang*.

2) Which of the following descriptions is NOT true about the relationship among heaven, earth and man?

   A. Man has the power to cause proliferation and transformation.

   B. Heaven, earth and man aid each other like hands and feet.

   C. Man is underneath heaven and above earth.

   D. Man is above other creatures and receives destiny from heaven.

3) According to Confucius, filial piety _____.

   A. demands unconditional submissiveness to parental authority

   B. is equal to moral excellence

   C. is the attainment of humanity

   D. requires recognition of and reverence for the source of life

4) What do Confucianism and Taoism have in common?

   A. Man should live in harmony with nature and environment.

   B. Reform means a type of return to the remote past.

   C. All the subjects should obey the orders of the emperor.

   D. Taking care of family affairs is itself an active participation in politics.

5) Which of the following is NOT true about "*Ziran*"?

   A. It is usually associated with spontaneity and creativity.

   B. It means freeing oneself from selfishness and desire.

   C. It advocates maintaining a state of complexity.

   D. It is an essential characteristic that governs the *Tao*.

3. Translate the following sentences.

1) 中国哲学起源于春秋战国时期的"百家争鸣"。

2) "天人合一" 是中国古典哲学中的一个基本概念。

3) 构建和谐社会，实现和谐发展，是中国人民的梦想和愿望。

4) 儒家强调血缘关系，重视家庭观念和孝道观念。

5) 道家哲学认为宇宙按照自己的方式和谐运行。

4. Discuss the following questions.

1) How does Confucianism shape the character of Chinese people?

2) How does Taoism influence Chinese people and Chinese society?

3) Can you analyze the differences between Confucianism and Taoism?

5. Work in groups. Do research on the following Chinese philosophers and fill in the table below. Then report your findings to the class.

Philosophers	Life Stories	Major Ideas	Representative Works	Famous Sayings
Confucius				
Mencius				
Laozi				
Zhuangzi				

✦ Extended Readings

Zhuangzi《庄子》

Zhuangzi is an ancient Chinese book from the late Warring States Period (476–221 BC) which contains stories and anecdotes that exemplify the carefree nature of the ideal Taoist sage. Named for its traditional author Zhuangzi, *Zhuangzi* is one of the two foundational texts of Taoism, along with the *Tao Te Ching*. Though primarily known as a philosophical work, *Zhuangzi* is regarded as one of the greatest literary works in Chinese history, and has been called "the most important pre-Qin text for the study of Chinese literature". A masterpiece of both philosophical and literary skill, it has significantly influenced writers for more than 2,000 years, from the Han Dynasty (206 BC–220 AD) to the present.

Zhuangzi consists of a large collection of anecdotes, allegories, parables, and fables, which are often humorous or irreverent. Its main themes are spontaneity of action and freedom from the human world and its conventions. The fables and anecdotes in the text attempt to illustrate the falseness of human distinctions between good and bad, large and small, life and death, and man and nature. The stories and anecdotes of *Zhuangzi* embody a unique set of principles and attitudes, including living one's life with natural spontaneity, uniting one's inner self with the cosmic "Way" (*Tao*), keeping oneself distant from politics and social obligations, accepting death as a natural transformation, showing appreciation and praise for things others view as useless or aimless, and stridently rejecting social values and conventional reasoning. These principles form the core ideas of philosophical Taoism.

The other major philosophical schools of ancient China, such as Confucianism, Legalism, and Mohism, were all concerned with concrete social, political, or ethical reforms designed to reform people and society and thereby alleviate the problems and suffering of the world. However, Zhuangzi believed that the key to true happiness was to free oneself from the world and its standards through the Taoist principle of "non-action"—action that is not based on any purposeful striving or motives for gain—and was fundamentally opposed to systems that impose order on individuals.

Zhuangzi interpreted the universe as a thing that changes spontaneously without a conscious God or will driving it, and argued that humans can achieve ultimate happiness by living equally and spontaneously. He argued that because of humans' advanced cognitive abilities, they have a tendency to create artificial distinctions—such as good versus bad, large versus small, usefulness versus uselessness, and social systems like Confucianism—which separate themselves from the natural spontaneity of the universe. To illustrate the mindlessness and spontaneity that he felt should characterize human action, Zhuangzi most often used the analogy of craftsmen or artisans. As sinologist Burton Watson described, "the skilled woodcarver, the skilled butcher, and the skilled swimmer does not ponder or ratiocinate on the course of action he should take; his skill has become so much a part of him that he merely acts instinctively and spontaneously and, without knowing why, achieves success."

Zhuangzi vigorously opposed formal government, which he seemed to have felt was problematic at its foundation "because of the opposition between man and nature". He tried to show that "as soon as government intervenes in natural affairs, it destroys all possibility of genuine happiness." It is unclear if Zhuangzi's position amounted to a form of anarchism, as the political references in *Zhuangzi* are more concerned with what government should not do, rather than what kind of government should exist.

A master of language, Zhuangzi sometimes engaged in logic and reasoning, but then turned it upside down or carried the arguments to absurdity to demonstrate the limitations of human knowledge and the rational world. Sinologist Victor Mair compares Zhuangzi's reasoning, such as his argument with his philosopher friend Huizi（惠子）about the joy of fish, to the Socratic（苏格拉底式的）dialogue tradition, and terms Huizi's paradoxes near the end of the book strikingly like those of Zeno of Elea（芝诺）.

(Adapted from Wikipedia website.)

Mencius 孟子

Mencius (372 BC–289 BC) was a Chinese Confucian philosopher who has often been described as the "Second Sage（亚圣）", that is, after Confucius himself. He is part of Confucius' fourth generation of disciples. Mencius inherited Confucius' ideology and developed it further. Living during the Warring States Period, he is said to have spent much of his life travelling around the states offering counsel to different rulers. Conversations with these rulers formed the basis of *The Mencius*（《孟子》）, which was later canonized as a Confucian classic.

One primary principle of his work is that human nature is righteous and humane（性本善）. The response of citizens to the policies of rulers embodies this principle, and a state with righteous and humane policies will flourish by nature. The citizens, with freedom from good rule, will then allocate time to take care of their wives, brothers, elders, and children, and be educated with rites and naturally become better citizens.

Mencius expounded on the concept that the human is naturally righteous and humane. It is the influence of society that causes bad moral character. Real improvement results from educational cultivation in favorable environments. Likewise, bad environments tend to corrupt the human will. This, however, is not proof of innate evil because a clear-thinking person would avoid causing harm to others. The four beginnings (The feeling of commiseration definitely is the beginning of humanity; the feeling of shame and dislike is the beginning of righteousness; the feeling of deference and compliance is the beginning of propriety; and the feeling of right or wrong is the beginning of wisdom. 四端：恻隐之心，仁之端也；羞恶之心，义之端也；辞让之心，礼之端也；是非之心，智之端也。) could grow and develop, or they could fail. In this way, Mencius synthesized integral parts of Taoism into Confucianism. Individual effort is needed to cultivate oneself, but one's natural tendencies are good to begin with. The object of education is the cultivation of benevolence, otherwise known as *Ren* (仁). This position of Mencius put him between Confucians such as Xunzi (荀子) who thought people were innately bad, and Taoists who believed humans did not need cultivation, but only to accept their innate, natural, and effortless goodness.

According to Mencius, education must awaken the innate abilities of the human mind. He denounced memorization and advocated active interrogation of the text, saying, "One who believes all of a book would be better off without books (尽信书则不如无书)". One should check for internal consistency by comparing sections and debate the probability of factual accounts by comparing them with experience.

Mencius emphasized the significance of the common citizens in the state. While Confucianism generally regards rulers highly, he argued that it is acceptable for the subjects to overthrow or even kill a ruler who ignores the people's needs and rules harshly. This is because a ruler who does not rule justly is no longer a true ruler.

All relationships should be beneficial, but each has its own principle or inner logic. A ruler must justify his position by acting benevolently before he can expect reciprocation from the people. In this view, a king is like a steward. Although Confucius admired kings of great accomplishment, Mencius clarified the proper hierarchy of human society. Although a king has presumably higher status than a commoner, he is actually subordinate to the masses of people（民贵君轻）and the resources of society. Otherwise, there would be an implied disregard of the potential of human society heading into the future. One is significant only for what one gives, not for what one takes.

Mencius distinguished between superior men who recognize and follow the virtues of righteousness and benevolence and inferior men who do not. He suggested that superior men considered only righteousness, not benefits（君子喻于义，小人喻于利）. To secure benefits for the disadvantaged and the aged, he advocated free trade, low tax rates, and a more equal sharing of the tax burden.

Mencius' interpretation of Confucianism has generally been considered the orthodox version by subsequent Chinese philosophers, especially by the Neo-Confucians of the Song Dynasty.

(Adapted from Wikipedia website.)

Chapter Five

Ancient Chinese Education
中国传统教育

The education system in ancient China, dating back to the inception of Chinese civilization, profoundly shaped the lifestyle, social structure, shared values, and ideologies of the Chinese people. During the protracted feudal era, the imperial examination system, known as *keju* (科举考试), played a pivotal role in facilitating the transition from an aristocratic form of governance to a meritocratic one. This comprehensive educational framework encompassed not only the intricate school system but also the rigorous examination system and the underlying educational ideology.

5.1   School System in Ancient Chinese Society

In primitive society, knowledge was transmitted orally from elders to their children. With the emergence of hieroglyphic writings approximately 3,000 years ago, specialized institutions were established to impart knowledge. During the Xia Dynasty, formal schools were introduced, referred to as *Xiao* (校) in that era, *Xiang* (庠) in the Shang Dynasty and *Xu* (序) in the early Zhou Dynasty.

Generally speaking, education in ancient China was divided into official school education and private school education, which complemented each other to train talents for the ruling class.

Ancient official school education comprised a comprehensive set of educational systems sponsored by the central and local governments in slave and feudal societies. Its primary aim was to train a diverse range of talents to meet the needs of the ruling class, which played a pivotal role in shaping the social and political landscape of ancient China.

It is said that official school education emerged during the Western Zhou Dynasty. According to historical documents, however, the central official school education was only initiated in the Western Han Dynasty, and it waxed and waned during the Wei, Jin, and Northern and Southern Dynasties, owing to changes in political situation. It was not until the Tang Dynasty that the central official school education reached its peak with the advocacy and encouragement of the ruling class. As an instrument of the national examination system, official school education was established during the Northern Song Dynasty. By the Qing Dynasty, it existed only in name.

The highest institutions of learning were called *Taixue* (太学 , Imperial Colleges) or *Guozijian* (国子监 , Imperial Academies). *Taixue* taught Confucianism and Chinese literature, among other things, to gain access to high level civil service positions, although a civil service system based upon competitive examination rather than recommendation was not introduced until the Sui Dynasty and did not become a mature system until the Tang Dynasty. In addition, a number of professional academies were established by the government to train specialized talents for the ruling class, such as the History Academy of the Northern and Southern Dynasties, the Calligraphy Academy of the Tang Dynasty, the Law Academy of the Song Dynasty and the Painting Academy of the Ming Dynasty.

Ancient local official schools started with Shujun Academy (蜀郡书院) established by Wen Weng (文翁, 156–101 BC) in the Shu Prefecture (presently Sichuan Province) during Emperor Jing's (汉景帝) reign of the Western Han Dynasty. Other prefectures across the country soon opened their own schools. The local official school system was completely established in the first year of Emperor Ping's (汉平帝) reign of the Western Han Dynasty, but during the Wei, Jin, and Northern and Southern Dynasties, it gradually declined due to unceasing wars. Local official schools developed on an unprecedented scale during the early Tang Dynasty, and were inherited and developed on a larger scale during the Song, Liao, Jin, Yuan, Ming and Qing dynasties.

As with the ancient official school education, the ancient private school education also played an important part in the history of Chinese education. It was first initiated by Confucius in the Spring and Autumn Period and had a great influence on the Chinese people.

The Spring and Autumn Period and the Warring States Period were periods of transition from slavery society to feudal society, during which education went through dramatic changes along with the prevailing economic and political situations. Ancient private schools emerged under such circumstances. Scholars served different rulers and created various schools of thought, among which the most famous included Confucianism, Mohism, Taoism and Legalism, leading to the contention of a hundred schools of thought.

However, Emperor Qin Shi Huang forbade private schools, burned books and even buried Confucian scholars alive. Emperor Wu of the Western Han Dynasty carried out a policy of proscribing all non-Confucian schools of thought and espousing Confucianism as the orthodox state ideology, but private schools were permitted during his reign. Private schools outnumbered official ones during the later Eastern Han Dynasty, and a number of Confucian-classics masters, such as Ma Rong (马融) and Zheng Xuan (郑玄), recruited disciples widely and trained lots of talents. The study of Confucian classics emphasized textual research of names and objects, later known to the world as Sinology.

Although official school education was on the wane, private school education prospered during the Wei, Jin, and Northern and Southern Dynasties. Private education broke out of the mold of traditional Confucianism, incorporating metaphysics, Buddhism, Taoism and technology. Private schools existed throughout rural and urban areas during the Tang Dynasty, and there emerged great Confucian masters such as Yan Shigu (颜师古) and Kong Yingda (孔颖达). Private schools took two forms in the Song, Yuan, Ming and Qing dynasties: academies (书院) sponsored by country gentlemen and private elementary schools (私塾) run by scholars.

(Adapted from China Highlights website.)

◆ Cultural Analysis

Generally speaking, schools in ancient China fell into two categories: official schools run by the government and private schools, which influenced Chinese society differently.

(1) The Influence of Official Schools

The characteristics and functions of the official schools are class-based, and the purpose is to cultivate various ruling talents for the court. The educational content is mainly based on Confucian classics, with the Four Books and the Five Classics as the main teaching materials. The central government educational system has played a very important role in cultivating outstanding talents, inheriting Chinese cultural heritage, and prospering scientific and academic undertakings.

(2) The Influence of Private Schools

Private schools provided opportunities for ordinary people to receive education, which broke the official education system of the integration of politics and education, and made education an independent activity. The private schools brought new teaching contents and methods, accumulated rich educational experience, and promoted the development of pre-Qin educational theories.

✦ Text Comprehension

1. Judge whether the following statements are true (T) or false (F).

1) The official schools are usually sponsored by the central governments.

2) The central official school education reached its peak in the Tang Dynasty.

3) Shujun Academy established by Wen Weng is the earliest local official school.

4) Emperor Qin Shi Huang encouraged the development of private schools, though he burned Confucian books and even buried Confucian scholars alive.

5) Throughout Chinese history, there were more official schools than private schools.

2. Answer the following questions.

1) What are the two categories of schools in ancient China?

2) How did private schools develop? What are the contributions of private schools in the history of China?

3) What are the differences between the official school and private school?

5.2　The Imperial Examination System

The imperial examination system, also known as *keju*, was an official recruitment system in which scholars took examinations covering various disciplines and categories. The most talented were selected and awarded official positions. It was an essential part of the Chinese government administration in the Han Dynasty (206 BC–220 AD) until it was abolished when the Qing attempted to modernize in 1905. The examination system was systematized in the Sui Dynasty as an official method for recruiting bureaucrats. The civil-service system reached its summit during the Song Dynasty, and the Ming and Qing dynasties adopted it.

The first centralized Chinese empire emerged during the Qin Dynasty. Appointments to the positions in Qin government were based on recommendations from prominent aristocrats and existing officials, and it was widely accepted that candidates must come from the aristocracy. However, the introduction of the imperial examination ensured that the appointments to civil service positions were no longer based on favoritism or inherited privilege, but on the capabilities of the individual candidates, as demonstrated by their performance in the civil service examinations.

The examinations were categorized into local, provincial and national levels. Those who passed the local exams earned the title of *xiucai* (秀才 , cultivated talent) and the exams assessed candidates on their knowledge of the Confucian classics and their proficiency in composing poetry on assigned topics using prescribed poetic forms and calligraphy. The provincial level examinations tested candidates on the breadth of their knowledge of the classics. A candidate who passed the provincial level exam was termed *juren* (举人 , recommended man) and became eligible to participate in the national level. At the national level, candidates were examined on their ability to analyze contemporary political problems, in addition to the usual examinations based on the classics. An individual who succeeded in the national examination was raised to the level of *jinshi* (进士 , presented scholar). Occasionally, highly prestigious special examinations were held by imperial decree. Passing the *jinshi* exam was the requirement for holding high office. The subject matter of the examinations was confined to the Four Books and the Five Classics of Confucianism. In the Ming and Qing dynasties, the form for an examination paper became the stylized *baguwen* (八股文 , the eight-legged essay), which had eight main headings, consisted of 700 characters or less, and addressed topics in a prescribed manner.

The examination system distributed its prizes according to provincial quotas, which meant that imperial officials were recruited from the whole country, in numbers roughly proportional to each province's population. Elite individuals all over China, even in the disadvantaged peripheral regions, had a chance to succeed in the examinations and achieve the rewards of holding office. Furthermore, anyone passing the exams would be given privileges such as exemption from labor service and corporal punishment, government stipends, and admission to upper-gentry status. The clans or families of those who rose through these examinations also rose in social prestige and wealth, which strengthened the concept in feudal China—Learning is more valuable than anything else (万般皆下品，唯有读书高).

The passing rate of the imperial examinations was low and restricted by regional quotas, for example, the passing rate was about two percent during the Tang Dynasty. The personal suffering undergone by individuals in preparing for and taking the examinations has become part of Chinese folklore. Many candidates failed repeatedly, and some committed suicide because of the disgrace that their failure brought upon their families. Others continued to take exams even when they became old and gray-haired men. Fortunately, frustration with the examination system could lead individuals to contribute to society. The Tang Dynasty poet Du Fu is a case in point; his failure in the Imperial Examinations divorced him from the scholarly tradition, and propelled him on an itinerant career as a poet. Similarly, the great Chinese novelist, Cao Xueqin (曹雪芹), wrote *The Dream of the Red Chamber* (《红楼梦》) after his hopes of a civil service career ended in failure.

(Adapted from New World Encyclopedia website.)

Cultural Analysis

The imperial examination system, which lasted for 1,300 years, left an indelible mark on traditional Chinese society, profoundly shaping its values, beliefs, and societal structures.

(1) Facilitating the Unification of Fundamental Values

The examination system upheld cultural unity and consensus on fundamental values by standardizing the content of the exams. This ensured that local elites and political aspirants across China were all imbued with the same values, thereby facilitating the socialization of individuals through the study of Confucian classics.

(2) Promoting the Stability of Society

The imperial examination system sparked a spirit of learning, creativity, and progress among its participants, vitalizing society and driving its development. Although only a small fraction of candidates succeeded in passing the exams and earning titles, the process of studying, self-education, and the hope of future success sustained the enthusiasm of those who participated. Even those who failed the exams could positively contribute to society by serving as teachers, patrons of the arts, and managers of local projects, without the need for official state appointments.

Text Comprehension

1. Judge whether the following statements are true (T) or false (F).

1) The imperial examination system was an official recruitment system which lasted 1,300 years in China.

2) Learning the Confucian classics was essential for success in the imperial exams.

3) The candidates who passed the local exams would be called *juren*.

4) The civil examinations strengthened the concept in feudal China—Learning is more valuable than anything else.

5) The great poet Du Fu never failed in the imperial examination.

2. Answer the following questions.

1) What are the contents of the imperial examination?

2) What are the three main stages of the imperial examination system?

3) What are the functions of the imperial examination in feudal society?

5.3 Comparison Between Ancient Chinese and Western Education

The term "education", with its connotations of nurturing the mind and fostering knowledge, first appeared in the writings of Mencius in ancient China. Meanwhile, Western education can be traced back to the ancient Greek era, where the foundations of philosophy, logic, and the sciences were established.

In ancient times, China cultivated the ruling class through education, while Western education paid more attention to the improvement of personal knowledge. Consequently, Western institutions of education were relatively scattered, whereas Chinese education was more concentrated and somewhat cliquish due to the need of the government. The formal education in ancient China was characterized by its distinctively secular and moral orientation. Its paramount purpose was to develop a sense of moral sensitivity and duty towards people and the state. Even in the early stages of schooling, the curriculum consisted of harmonious human relations, rituals, and music. However, the primary goal of ancient Western education was to prepare students at low-cost private schools for citizenship, democracy, oratory, and ethical decision-making. Education focused on the mind, the body, and the sense of aesthetics. Students learned the seven liberal arts: grammar, logic, rhetoric, arithmetic, geometry, music, and astronomy. Following this foundational education, they could then continue to study philosophy or one of the practical arts, such as medicine or architecture.

The ancient Chinese educational thought began with Confucius and Mencius, the most important representatives of Confucianism during the Spring and Autumn Period and the Warring States Period. They were also early educators, whose thought influenced China for more than 2,000 years.

Confucius believes that education is necessary for all people, regardless of class and status in society. Confucius saw education as a process of constant self-improvement and held that its primary function was to cultivate the *junzi* (君子). He regarded public service as the natural consequence of education and sought to revitalize Chinese social institutions, including the family, school, community, state, and kingdom. Confucius' educational thoughts are concentrated in the *Analects of Confucius*. Starting from the discussion of human nature, Confucius believed that there was little difference between humans in their innate nature, and personality differences were mainly formed after birth. Therefore, he attached great importance to postnatal education and advocated "teaching without distinction (有教无类)". Mencius' teaching ideology was an inheritance and development of Confucius', both in terms of educational purpose and teaching methods. In terms of teaching principles, Mencius proposed teaching students by their aptitude.

The ancient Greek Socrates (469–399 BC), Plato (427–347 BC), and Aristotle (384–322 BC) are the "three sages" of the West, who have had a profound influence on the development of Western educational thought for more than two thousand years.

Socrates' thought on education is grounded in teleology, morals, and intellect. The teleological aspect of education focused on training talents with virtue and talent to run the country; moral education theory proposed that the primary purpose of education is to cultivate morality through the imparting of knowledge; the theory of intellectual education emphasized that the ruler must have a wide range of knowledge, including astronomy, geometry, arithmetic, and other practical courses of the teaching system.

Plato thinks that "to learn is to remember", which means to learn is not to get something from the outside, but to recall the knowledge already in the soul. Plato's book *The Republic* (《 理想国 》) constructs an educational system to cultivate philosophical kings. In the preschool education stage, education should be controlled by the state by setting up early childhood education institutions and providing public care for children, and children should be taught mainly by playing games and telling stories.

Aristotle's educational thought is based on his theory of the human soul. He divided the human soul into vegetal, animal, and rational parts. Among them, the vegetal soul is at the lowest level, which is manifested in the human body, referring to the body's nutrition, growth, and development; the animal soul expresses the human instinct, emotion and desire. The rational soul is at the highest level, which is mainly manifested in people's thinking, understanding, and judgment. By his theory of the human soul, Aristotle put forward the educational thought of harmonious development of the body, morality, intelligence, and beauty.

There are some differences in education theories and methods between ancient China and ancient Greece. However, both ancient Chinese and Western educators attached great importance to the education of human morality and human nature, and education itself and the essence of education are all the same.

(Adapted from Atlantis Press website.)

◆ Cultural Analysis

Ancient Western education and Chinese education have been influenced by many factors, such as the economy, war, politics, and so on. Therefore, there are differences in educational theories and methods.

(1) Different Educational Concepts

Western educators, such as Plato and Aristotle, advocated universal education; Chinese scholars, led by Confucius, advocated education for all people without discrimination. Western education aimed at raising national quality and national defense power, while Chinese education aimed at improving people's wisdom and strengthening social stratification.

(2) Different Educational Focus

Ancient Western education placed greater emphasis on individuals' development, specifically focusing on morals, intelligence, sports, and aesthetics. Its aim was to cultivate well-rounded individuals who possessed not only academic knowledge but also moral virtue, physical fitness, and artistic appreciation. In contrast, Chinese education has traditionally prioritized the cultivation of moral character and the promotion of social harmony. It emphasizes ethics above all other aspects of personal development.

◆ Text Comprehension

1. Judge whether the following statements are true (T) or false (F).

1) The word "education" first appeared in the literature of Confucius in China.

2) The formal education in ancient China was distinguished by its secular and moral character.

3) Confucius thought that education should be necessary for all people, regardless of class and status in society.

4) The primary goal of ancient Western education was to prepare students solely for ethical decision-making.

5) According to Plato, to learn is not to get something from the outside, but to recall the knowledge already in the soul.

2. Answer the following questions.

1) What are the curriculums of early schooling in ancient China and Greece?

2) What is the educational thought proposed by Confucius mentioned in the text?

3) What is Socrates' thought on education? How did Plato explain his educational ideas?

◆ Exercises

1. Match the following concepts to the educators.

Educators	Concepts
1) Confucius	a) Teaching students by their aptitude
2) Mencius	b) Knowledge is morality
3) Socrates	c) Dividing human soul into vegetal, animal, and rational parts
4) Aristotle	d) Cultivating the philosophical king
5) Plato	e) Teaching without distinction

2. Choose the best answers to each of the following questions. You may choose MORE THAN ONE answer.

1) The highest institutions of learning were called _____ in feudal China.

A. *Xiao*

B *Taixue*

C. *Guozijian*

D. Academies

2) Private schools outnumbered official ones during the _____ Dynasty.

A. Han Dynasty

B. Eastern Jin Dynasty

C. Tang Dynasty

D. Song Dynasty

3) To obtain a civil service post, a candidate had to pass through several stages of Imperial Examination. They are _____.

A. county examination

B. district examination

C. provincial examination

D. palace examination

4) In the West, the "three sages" have had a profound influence on the development of Western educational thought, they are _____.

A. Socrates

B. Plato

C. Aristotle

D. Nietzsche

5) What are the main subjects on the curriculum for most private schools in ancient China?

A. history

B. harmonious human relations

C. rituals

D. music

3. Translate the following sentences.

1) 三人行，必有我师焉。

2) 早在 2600 多年前，管仲就说过，一年之计，莫如树谷；十年之计，莫如树木；终身之计，莫如树人。

3) 中国第一部教育学专著《学记》中也提出了"教学为先"的思想，认为国家的首要任务就是教育。

4) 春秋时期，孔子在他的家乡开办私学，并提出人无论贫贱还是富贵，都有受教育的权利。

5) 中国民间有许多尊师的说法，如"一日为师，终身为父"。

4. Discuss the following questions.

1) What is the significance of private schools in Chinese history?

2) What are the functions of Imperial Examination System in ancient China?

3) Can you find out some differences between Chinese education and Western education in modern time and try to analyze the cultural differences?

5. Work in groups. Do research on the following educators and fill in the table below. Then report your findings to the class.

Educators	Achievements	Educational Thoughts
Confucius		
Mozi		
Dong Zhongshu		
Zhu Xi		

◆ Extended Readings

Educational Thought of Mozi 墨子的教育理念

Mozi was a great thinker, educator and scientist in the Spring and Autumn Period and Warring States Period. Before he turned 30, Mozi founded the first comprehensive civilian school in human history, offering subjects such as liberal arts, science, military, and engineering. This school had cultivated a large number of talents, known to "fill the world" (弟子弥丰充满天下). Mozi's educational thought emphasized practice and discipline, with the purpose of "promoting the benefits of the world and eliminating the evils of the world (兴天下之利，除天下之害)".

Based on the political ideals of Mohism, Mozi advocated "universal love" and "non-aggression". He trained the Mohist disciples in ideology, wisdom, and willpower to form an action team to benefit the world, restore order and rebuild the country. Mozi's educational thought takes into consideration people's livelihood and individual development, as well as the economic concepts of mutual benefit and sharing, which provides a lasting enlightenment. The Mohist education, which attaches great importance to physical labor and practical skills, is the fundamental training for survival ability, and the basic guarantee for solving people's livelihood problems.

Mozi believed that "Officials are not permanently noble and commoners are never always humble (官无常贵而民无终贱)". Mozi's school was intended to break down the noble and aristocratic hereditary system, and to build a political system in which the country is governed by the wise, thus opening the door for the social sages to become officials. Therefore, in order to establish a government of wise men and to realize the fair flow of social strata, Mozi advocated reforming the unitary and monopolistic system of the Western Zhou Dynasty, eliminating the restrictions based on country, region, origin and age, popularizing education for all. Mozi trained not only the virtuous sages and chivalrous men, but also the military, science and technology talents, farmers and personnel from all walks of life. He embraced students from a wide variety of backgrounds, including those from farms and workshops, even straw shoes makers and mattress craftsmen.

Mozi's educational thought has obvious utilitarian orientation and extreme pragmatism, because he realized that labor was not only a means of creating material wealth, but also a way to develop human body, mind and spirit. Therefore, Mozi emphasized the labor of farming, harvesting and storing. Only those who are able to work hard, endure, and faithfully execute the "moral" of Mohism can become disciples of Mohism.

According to Mozi, the minimum right to survival of lower-class workers can only be guaranteed by cultivating an awareness of striving for wealth, practicing simplicity and selflessness, preventing the rich from being arrogant, and ensuring that the poor do not go hungry. In this regard, Mozi personally acted as an example for his disciples: "lived diligently but died poor (勤生薄死)" and "took self-suffering to the extreme (以自苦为极)". Mozi encouraged his disciples to follow their own business, divide their careers, and strive for self-support. As for the teaching methods of Mohism, some researchers said, "Mohism's teachings are not only about principles, but also about techniques."

The *Mohist Classic* (《墨经》) and *Classic Theory* (《经论》) are the teaching guidelines of the Mohist School. The training of Mohist involves not only theoretical study, but also practical content such as hands-on operation and field exercises.

(Adapted from Atlantis Press website.)

Women's Education in Ancient China 中国传统女性教育

Before the end of the Qing Dynasty, women's education was different, not only from that of today but also from that of men at that time.

The aim of traditional women's education was limited to teaching social ethics and family traditions with an emphasis on how to become a virtuous wife and good mother. As early as the Western Zhou Dynasty, great difference between men and women's education was obvious. By the age of 10, girls were mostly confined to their boudoirs and brought up by their parents to be subservient to the men. In fact, a girl's entire upbringing would be centered around learning the most important virtue of being docile and obedient. Hence, the education of women at that time was no more than cooking, sewing, knitting, weaving and housekeeping. These skills were acquired through their female elders or nannies if the girls came from a wealthy background, and not as a result of formal schooling. Women would be unable to paint or write and, above all, they would be barred from politics. It was customary for young girls to be "betrothed at fifteen and married at twenty", and marriage for a woman always meant serving her parents-in-law and taking care of her husband and children.

It was not until the Tang Dynasty that the status of women improved slightly under the influence of the Hu people (胡人) who had migrated from the north to the south on a massive scale. This development prompted a steady increase in the number of women working in writing.

However, women's status suffered a setback with the coming of the Song Dynasty, when Confucianism was prevalent in society. As Lü Kun (吕坤) of the Ming Dynasty said, "Few people teach their daughters to read and write nowadays for fear that they might become over ambitious." Again, in *Wen's Book of Mother Indoctrination* (《温氏母训》), it was stated that "It is sufficient for women to know a few hundred words such as fuel, rice, fish and meat for their daily use. To know more can do more harm than good." Therefore, the concept that "a virtuous woman is one who has no talent" was widely accepted at that time and also brought a return to the teachings aiming to prepare virtuous wifehood and motherhood in women.

People in the Ming Dynasty were generally abhorred by the thought of women reading and writing since female literacy was associated with the idea of moral corruption in women. This was because of the fact that courtesans and female singers who were looked upon virtually as prostitutes were mainly from the rank of literate women. Moreover, the opposition to women's intellectual promotion was founded on the conviction that a woman's only commitment in life was to marry and to bear children, and that literacy was seen as a moral stigma for women. Therefore, women's education was critically frowned on by Confucians; Lü Kun pointed out that parents were reluctant to allow their daughters to study because they thought it might corrupt their children.

This concept of "ignorance as virtue" for women reached its peak at the end of the Ming Dynasty when almost all educated and gifted women were treated as though they were loose-living. This belief was first publicly challenged by intellectuals during the Qing Dynasty. The May Fourth Movement in 1919 posed a significant threat to the entire traditional system. Of course women's emancipation won support from most Chinese youth, marking a new chapter in the history of Chinese women's education.

(Adapted from Taylor & Francis Online website.)

Chapter Six

Chinese Literature
中国文学

Chinese literature, including poetry, historical writing, drama, and various forms of fiction, is one of the major literary heritages of the world, with an uninterrupted history of more than 3000 years. Many works of Chinese literature are themed around real life, reflecting the experiences, emotions, and wisdom of countless generations. Numerous great literati are still remembered today not only for their brilliant literary talents but also for their profound insights into life and society. Their masterpieces, which have withstood the test of time, have achieved enduring fame and continue to inspire readers worldwide.

6.1　Classical Poetry

One of the earliest and most influential poetic anthologies was *Chuci* (《楚辞》), composed primarily of poems by Qu Yuan (屈原) and Song Yu (宋玉). The poems in this collection, marked by their lyrical and romantic qualities, represent a tradition distinct from the earlier *Book of Songs* (《诗经》). During the Han Dynasty, the poetic style of *Chuci* evolved into *fu* (赋), a form characterized by rhymed verse interspersed with introductory and concluding passages, which set it apart from folk ballads and poems known as *yuefu* (乐府诗). Following the Han Dynasty, the subsequent era of political disunity witnessed the emergence of literary works imbued with romantic sentiment and heavily influenced by Taoism.

Classical poetry reached its peak during the Tang Dynasty. The early Tang poetry was best known for its *lüshi* (律诗), an eight-line poem with five or seven words in each line; and *jueju* (绝句), a four-line poem with five or seven words in each line. Over 48,900 poems from the Tang Dynasty, spanning more than 300 years, have been passed down and remain widely known today. Famous poets of the Tang Dynasty included Wang Wei, Bai Juyi, Li Shangyin, to name just a few. The best two were Li Bai and Du Fu, who are very prestigious in the whole world. Therefore, later generations referred to them as "Li Du (李杜)".

Widely praised as the "Poet-Immortal (诗仙)", Li Bai endeared himself to readers as a free spirit, distinguished by his uninhibited and unique persona. His poems, filled with lofty sentiments and powered by a boundless imagination, painted vivid pictures of the magnificent mountains and mighty rivers of his beloved motherland, capturing the essence of nature in every verse. More than 900 poems by Li Bai have been preserved, among which the most famous are "Invitation to Wine" (《将进酒》), "The Sichuan

Road" (《蜀道难》), and "Watching the Waterfall at Lushan" (《望庐山瀑布》). These poems have been intonated by people for generations, inspiring countless souls and leaving a lasting impact on Chinese literature.

Du Fu is revered as "Poet-Sage (诗圣)" by posterity for his profound insight into human nature and society. When he was young, Du Fu visited many places of interest and historical sites, immersing himself in the beauty and wisdom of his surroundings. However, his later life was full of frustrations, including political exile and personal hardships, which gradually deepened his understanding of people's suffering and social injustices. In his poems, Du Fu boldly exposed the corruption of the feudal society and profoundly portrayed people's miserable lives, and expressed his compassion and longing for a better world. More than 1,400 of his poems have been preserved till today, and the best-known ones, such as "Spring Outlook" 《春望》 and "Ballad of the Army Carts" (《兵车行》), continue to resonate with readers and inspire people to reflect on the human condition.

Even today, the Chinese people are still very fond of the Tang poetry, some of which can be recited even by children, for example, "Quiet Night Thoughts" (《静夜思》) by Li Bai and "Delightful Rain on Spring Night" (《春夜喜雨》) by Du Fu. Famous verses like "You can enjoy a great sight; by climbing to a greater height (欲穷千里目，更上一层楼)" and "Do you not see the Yellow River come from the sky (君不见黄河之水天上来)" are often quoted by many. The book *Three Hundred Tang Poems* (《唐诗三百首》) is a bestseller both at home and abroad. Currently in China, the quote "Familiarity with 300 Tang poems will enable you to compose poetry yourself (熟读唐诗三百首，不会写诗也会吟)" has been popular.

The subsequent writers of classical poetry lived in the shadow of their great Tang predecessors. Although there were many fine poets in subsequent dynasties, none reached the level of this period. As the classical style of poetry lost its prominence, a more flexible poetic medium, *ci* (词), emerged. The *ci*, a poetic form based on the tunes of popular songs, was developed to its fullest by the poets of the Song Dynasty. In the course of its development, many outstanding *ci* composers, such as Su Shi, Li Qingzhao, Xin Qiji and Lu You appeared. Like Tang poetry, the *ci* in the Song Dynasty held a very important position in the history of Chinese literature.

Su Shi enriched Tang poetry by incorporating its elements into his own poems, thereby broadening its scope and elevating its status. His style is exuberant and spontaneous, reflecting his virile quality and unrestrained nature. His philosophy represents a combination of Confucianism and Taoism. To "serve the crown and to attain great renown" is his Confucian ideal and to "retire as times require" and to be detached from personal gain and loss is his Taoist ideal. Su Shi's poems are marked by passion, refreshment and mellifluence. His poems are rich in subject, ranging from expressing his patriotism, to describing scenes of country, to depicting the grievance of lovers parting.

Li Qingzhao was an outstanding *ci* poetess who lived in the transition between the Northern and Southern Song dynasties. Her works are exquisite, refined and full of true feeling, nostalgically recalling her happy life in the north and revealing her distress in the south. She expressed her understanding and pursuit of true love, described the impact of changing seasons on human sentiment, and reflected the misery of the people suffering from the decline of their country and families. Many of her moving verses, such as "Can't you see? / Can't you see? / The green leaves are fresh but the red flowers are fading! (知否？知否？应是绿肥红瘦！)" and "How can such sorrow be driven away forever? / From eyebrows kept apart, / Again it gnaws my heart. (此情无计可消除，才下眉头，又上心头)" show her poetic gifts.

As *ci* gradually became more literary and artificial after the Song Dynasty, *sanqu* (散曲), a more informal and colloquial form of verse based on dramatic arias, emerged in China. The incorporation of *sanqu* into drama marked an important step in development of vernacular literature.

(Adapted from World History website.)

◆ Cultural Analysis

Chinese poetry, written in classical Chinese and characterized by certain traditional forms, such as the *yuefu* of the Han Dynasty, the poetry of the Tang Dynasty and the *ci* of Song Dynasty, holds an important place in Chinese culture.

(1) The Combination of Confucianism and Taoism

Confucianism and Taoism, as the core of Chinese culture, have influenced Chinese scholars and their works. Some poets were more influenced by Confucianism, such as Du Fu, and some were more influenced by Taoism, such as Li Bai in the Tang Dynasty. However, many poets were influenced by both. Generally speaking, they were inspired by Confucianism during times of success in their careers, and they comforted themselves with Taoist ideas during difficult times, such as Su Shi and Tao Yuanming.

(2) The Coexistence of Realism and Romanticism

The Book of Songs covers many aspects of worldly life such as farming, feasting, war, marriage, and love; it is considered the representative of realism. *Chuci* tends to use mythological imagery and symbolic meaning of plants to express the enthusiastic pursuit of an ideal world with passionate language and magnificent imagination. Both of the earliest anthologies have been integrated in the literary history and have had a profound impact on future generations.

✦ Text Comprehension

1. Judge whether the following statements are true (T) or false (F).

1) *Chuci,* primarily consisting of poems ascribed to Qu Yuan and Song Yu, is more lyrical and romantic than the poems in *The Book of Songs.*

2) The era of disunity following the Han Dynasty saw the rise of realistic nature poetry heavily influenced by Taoism.

3) Many Tang poems can be recited even by children in modern China.

4) Su Shi created the *ci* based on the style of Song poetry, thereby broadening its scope and elevating its status.

5) The incorporation of *sanqu* in drama marked an important step in development of vernacular literature.

2. Answer the following questions.

1) What are the differences between *The Book of Songs* and *Chuci* ?

2) What are the characteristics of the poems written by Li Bai and Du Fu respectively?

3) What are your different feelings when reading the works of Su Shi and Li Qingzhao?

6.2 Historical Books

The Book of Documents is the first collection of ancient historical documents and one of the Five Classics, and it served as the foundation of Chinese political philosophy for over 2,000 years. The *Spring and Autumn Annals* is among the earliest surviving Chinese historical texts arranged in annalistic form. Both works are traditionally ascribed to Confucius. The *Zuo's Commentary on the Spring and Autumn Annals* (《左传》), attributed to Zuo Qiuming (左丘明) in the 5th century BC, is the earliest Chinese work of narrative history covering the period from 722 to 468 BC. The anonymous *Strategies of Warring States* (《战国策》) is a renowned ancient historical work containing varied materials on the political, military, and diplomatic struggles of the Warring States period between the 3rd and 1st centuries BC.

The Records of the Grand Historian is the first systematic historical text in China and it sets the history-biography format. Completed around 94 BC by historian Sima Qian (司马迁) in the Western Han Dynasty, it was initially conceived by his father, Sima Tan (司马谈), a historian who held an official position related to astronomy at the court. It presents a monumental history of ancient China from the age of the legendary Yellow Emperor to the reign of Emperor Wu of Han (汉武帝) in the author's own time.

Sima Qian organized the chapters into five sections: "Basic Annals (本纪)", "Tables (表)", "Treatises (书)", "Hereditary Houses (世家)", and "Biographies (列传)". The "Basic Annals" make up the first 12 chapters, which are largely similar to the records from the ancient Chinese court chronicle tradition. This section includes information on the Five Emperors (五帝：黄帝、颛顼、帝喾、唐尧、虞舜), the emperors of the Xia, Shang, and Zhou dynasties, the first emperor of Qin and other actual rulers of China, such as Xiang Yu (项羽), while excluding rulers without real power. The "Tables" consist of one genealogical table and nine other chronological tables. They show reigns, important events, and royal lineages. The "Treatises", sometimes called "Monographs", record the development of various systems, including ritual and music, astronomy and military law, social economy, geography of rivers and canals, etc. The "Hereditary Houses" describe the historical traces of the hereditary princes and the deeds of particularly important people. The "Biographies" are the life stories of representatives from various aspects other than emperors and princes and the biographies of ethnic minorities.

The Records of the Grand Historian has been called a "foundational text in Chinese civilization" and regarded as the forerunner of Chinese historical writing and literature. It established the model for historical writing in subsequent dynasties in China. In contrast to Western historical works, *the Records of the Grand Historian* does not treat history as "a continuous, sweeping narrative", but rather breaks it down into smaller, overlapping units that focus on famous leaders, individuals, and major topics. In all, *the Records of the Grand*

Historian, with 526,500 Chinese characters, is four times longer than Thucydides' (修昔底德) *History of the Peloponnesian War* (《伯罗奔尼撒战争》) and longer than *the Old Testament* (《旧约》).

Unlike subsequent official historical texts that proclaimed the divine rights of the emperors, and degraded those who were defeated in their quest for power, Sima Qian's more liberal and objective prose has been renowned and followed by poets and novelists. Most volumes of "Biographies" are vivid descriptions of events and people. Sima Qian sought out stories from individuals with closer knowledge of certain historical events to ensure the reliability and accuracy of his records. For instance, the record of Jing Ke's (荆轲) attempt to assassinate the King of Qin incorporates an eye-witness report by Xia Wuju (夏无且), a physician to the King of Qin who happened to be present at the diplomatic ceremony for Jing Ke, and this account was passed on to Sima Qian by those who knew Xia.

Sima Qian has a tactful way of accentuating the positive aspects of rulers in the "Basic Annals", while incorporating negative information into other chapters. Therefore, his work must be read as a whole to obtain a comprehensive understanding. For example, the account of Liu Bang's (刘邦) desperate attempt to escape the chase of Xiang Yu's men by pushing his own children off the carriage to make it lighter was not included in the emperor's biography, but found in the biography of Xiang Yu. He is also careful to balance the negative and positive portrayals, for example, in the biography of Empress Lü (吕太后) which contains startling accounts of her cruelty. He pointed out at the end that despite her personal life, her rule brought peace and prosperity to the country.

In the Song Dynasty, another great Chinese historiography known as *The Comprehensive Mirror to Aid in Government* (《资治通鉴》) was ascribed to Sima Guang (司马光). It narrates the history of China from 403 BC to the beginning of the Song Dynasty in 959 AD chronologically.

(Adapted from Wikipedia website.)

◆ Cultural Analysis

The Chinese civilization has been meticulously recorded by historians, as the Chinese nation always attaches great importance to the preservation of its history. Generally speaking, Chinese historical texts are rich and diverse, with a continuous narration.

(1) Significant Historical Achievements and Literary Value

Lu Xun praised *Records of the Grand Historian* as "the masterpiece of historians, and the *Li Sao* without rhyme（无韵之离骚）". Many stories in *The Records of the Grand Historian* have also become idioms still in use today, and passed down through generations by word of mouth, such as "besieged on all sides（四面楚歌）", "establish a set of rules（约法三章）", "fight with one's back to the river（背水一战）", etc. These idioms and allusions have greatly enriched Chinese culture and represent a precious cultural heritage for future generations.

(2) The Idealism of Chinese People

The Records of the Grand Historian has depicted a group of benevolent and righteous individuals who adhere to morality, including patriotic people who uphold righteousness for the country, virtuous people who devote themselves to defending benevolence, and chivalrous people who repay kindness with death. The moral spirit embodied in these figures not only serves as the foundation for the author's ideal personality and life values, but also represents the relentless pursuit of the Chinese nation.

(3) The Golden Mean（中庸之道）

The Chinese nation embraces the concept of the golden mean, emphasizing moderation and impartiality, which is also reflected in *The Records of the Grand Historian*. For instance, Sima Qian did not judge the characters by their success or failure, but comprehensively restored the historical facts from an objective perspective, such as his portrayal of the outstanding yet cruel monarch Qin Shi Huang, and Liu Bang, a powerful but unscrupulous individual.

◆ Text Comprehension

l. Judge whether the following statements are true (T) or false (F).

1) The *Book of Documents,* attributed to Zuo Qiuming in the 5th century BC, is the earliest Chinese work of narrative history.

2) The "Tables" present reigns, important events, and royal lineages in table format.

3) Sima Qian's sources for writing materials are all from archives and imperial records.

4) Sima Qian is also careful to balance the negative and positive portrayals of historical figures.

5) *The Records of the Grand Historian* is the forerunner of Chinese narrative literature.

2. Answer the following questions.

1) What are the characteristics of the "Biographies" in *The Records of the Grand Historian*?

2) Why is *The Records of the Grand Historian* also considered a work of narrative literature? How did it influence later Chinese narrative literature? Can you explain it with examples?

3) How did Sima Qian acquire the writing materials for *The Records of the Grand Historian*?

6.3 Classical Novels

Throughout history, Chinese writers have preferred the historical genre to tell stories about people, while poetry has been favored for expressing personal emotions. Chinese fiction, with its roots in narrative classics such as *A New Account of the Tales of the World* (《世说新语》), *Soushen Ji* (《搜神记》), *Wenyuan Yinghua* (《文苑英华》), *Great Tang Records on the Western Regions* (《大唐西域记》), *Miscellaneous Morsels from Youyang* (《酉阳杂俎》), *Taiping Guangji* (《太平广记》) and official histories, developed into the novel form as early as the Song Dynasty. This transformation was driven by the emergence of a money-based economy and urbanization during the Song Dynasty, which led to the professionalization of entertainment. This process was further accelerated by the spread of printing technology, rising literacy rates, and improved educational opportunities. Consequently, Chinese novels gradually became more realistic, delving deeper into social, moral, and philosophical issues. From the 14th to the 18th centuries, they evolved into extended prose narratives that realistically depicted a believable world.

By the late Ming Dynasty and early Qing Dynasty, Chinese fiction had diversified, gained self-awareness, and become experimental, marking a pinnacle of classical

Chinese fiction. *Outlaws of the Marsh* (《水浒传》), *Journey to the West*, *Romance of the Three Kingdoms* (《三国演义》) and *Dream of the Red Chamber*, these four novels form the core of classical Chinese literature and enjoy a high reputation throughout the world. Similar to the works of Dante (但丁) or Shakespeare (莎士比亚) in Europe, these works serve as touchstones that Chinese literary culture continually revisits for new relevance and fresh insight.

Outlaws of the Marsh

Outlaws of the Marsh is a novel that chronicles a peasant rebellion. Written by Shi Nai'an (施耐庵), who lived during the late Yuan and early Ming dynasties, the novel is based on popular stories of a peasant uprising led by Song Jiang (宋江) in the later years of the Song Dynasty. It depicts the rise and fall of the rebellion in the Liangshan (梁山) region, revealing the social realities that drove civilians to rebel against official oppression. The novel vividly portrays 108 heroes and heroines from Liangshan, praising their fearless deeds. Episodes such as *Wu Song Strikes a Tiger* (《武松打虎》) and *Lu Zhishen Pulls Out a Willow Tree* (《鲁智深倒拔垂杨柳》) remain memorable to this day. The novel has inspired numerous modern adaptations and continues to resonate with its themes of rebellion, repression and subservience.

Journey to the West

Journey to the West was written in the 16th century by Wu Cheng'en (吴承恩), which depicts the pilgrimage of the Buddhist monk Xuanzang (玄奘) to India, along with his travels through western regions of China accompanied by his three disciples. While based on Buddhism, the novel draws on Chinese folk tales, mythology, pantheism and Taoism to create its fantastical cast of characters and creatures. These creatures include various demons encountered by Xuanzang during his travels, and a variety of animal-spirits who assume human form. The novel also includes three disciples characterized as a monkey, a pig and a river ogre who are bound to accompany Xuanzang as they attempt to atone for their past sins. *Journey to the West* was an early example of the *Shenmo* (神魔) genre, which incorporated fantastical fiction focusing on gods or demons. It played an important role in shaping vernacular Chinese literature during the Ming Dynasty.

Romance of the Three Kingdoms

Romance of the Three Kingdoms is a historical novel which recounts the political intrigue and deceit during the Three Kingdoms Period of Chinese history. It combines history, legend and mythology to tell the tumultuous story of this era. Written by Luo Guanzhong（罗贯中）, this epic tale incorporates hundreds of characters and weaves a multitude of complicated plotlines in its portrayal of the disintegration of a unified China into three warring kingdoms: Cao Wei（曹魏）, Shu Han（蜀汉）, and Eastern Wu（东吴）. The novel also depicts their eventual reconciliation and unification. The belief in the cyclical nature of history is succinctly expressed in the opening line of the novel: "It is a general truism of this world that anything long divided will surely reunite, and anything long united will surely divide（话说天下大势，分久必合，合久必分）". Due to its complexity, epic length and density, reading *Romance of the Three Kingdoms* can be quite challenging.

Dream of the Red Chamber

Written in the mid-18th century during the Qing Dynasty, *Dream of the Red Chamber* was the last of the four great novels of Chinese literature to gain prominence. It is a semi-autobiographical work that focuses on the financial and moral decay of the author Cao Xueqin's（曹雪芹）family and, by extension, reflects the broader decline of the Qing Dynasty. Recognized for its formal beauty and innovation, *Dream of the Red Chamber* has spawned a scholarly field of its own, known as "Redology（红学）", which remains a vibrant academic subject in China. The novel is markedly more nuanced and precise than its fellow classics, offering an incredibly detailed rendering of 18th-century Chinese aristocratic life while paying particular attention to the complexities of social conventions in this esoteric world. The novel is thus a repository for those interested in Chinese culture, providing insight into religious, social and political aspects of upper-class life in China. It also offers insight into a wide variety of facets of Chinese culture, from medicine to mythology and art, all of which continue to influence contemporary culture in China.

(Adapted from Wikipedia and The Culture Trip websites.)

• Cultural Analysis

The creation and dissemination of these four works marked the emergence of the novel form in China as a counterpart to more refined philosophical and poetic works.

(1) Mythological and Historical Sources

Diverse myths and numerous historical events serve as the primary source of novel creation. These sources, including tales of gods, ogres, battles, and heroes, provide a solid foundation for novelists to construct intricate narratives that transport readers to fantastical realms and deeply immerse them in the complexities of human experience.

(2) The Transformation of Language

These novels use vernacular Chinese, departing from the previously dominant Classical Chinese. While they maintain the elegance of poetry and rhyme, they also employ simple and easy-to-understand popular language. This departure from the subtlety and obscurity of Tang poetry and Song *ci* allows for an integration of their elegance while creating a different charm through vernacular language.

◆ Text Comprehension

1. Judge whether the following statements are true (T) or false (F).

1) Chinese fiction, with its roots in narrative classics and official histories, developed into the novel form as early as the Song Dynasty.

2) The novel in China gradually became more autobiographical and delved deeper into the exploration of social, moral, and psychological issues.

3) *Journey to the West* played a significant role in the emergence of vernacular Chinese literature during the Ming Dynasty, as the centuries-old folk tales were written and disseminated for the first time.

4) *Romance of the Three Kingdoms* combined history, legend and mythology to narrate the turbulent story of feudal society.

5) Renowned for its formal beauty and innovation, *Dream of the Red Chamber* has spawned a scholarly field known as "Redology".

2. Answer the following questions.

1) What led to the emergence of classical Chinese novels?

2) What genre do *Outlaws of the Marsh* and *Romance of the Three Kingdoms* belong to?

3) What is the theme of *Journey to the West*? Can you explain it with some examples from the novel?

4) What cultural significance can be derived from *Dream of the Red Chamber*?

◆ Exercises

1. **Match the literary genres and features with the books. (Each book may correspond to more than one feature.)**

Literary Genres	Books	Features
1) Classical poetry	A) *The Records of the Grand Historian*	a) The use of *fu*, *bi* and *xing*
	B) *The Spring and Autumn Annals*	b) Fiction of gods and demons
	C) *The Book of Songs*	c) Biographical history books
	D) *Romance of the Three Kingdoms*	d) Ballad in Chu state
2) Historical books	E) *Journey to the West*	e) Adversity as a tool for growth
	F) *The Comprehensive Mirror to Aid in Government*	f) Five characters / seven characters
		g) Chronicles
	G) *Three Hundred Tang Poems*	h) Delivering a belief that anything long divided will surely reunite
3) Novels	H) *Chuci*	i) Confucian classics
		j) The use of vernacular language

2. **Choose the best answer to each of the following questions.**

1) _____ is the earliest anthology.

   A. *The Book of Songs*

   B. *Chuci*

   C. *The Spring and Autumn Annals*

   D. *Tianwen*

2) _____ endeared himself to readers as a free spirit with a unique persona characterized by wildness.

   A. Li Bai

   B. Du Fu

   C. Wang Wei

   D. Li Qingzhao

3) Which one is NOT the characteristic of *The Records of the Grand Historian*?

A. It is the first systematic Chinese historical text and sets the history-biography format.

B. It is started and completed by Sima Qian.

C. It presents a monumental history of ancient China from the age of the legendary Yellow Emperor to the reign of Emperor Wu of Han in the author's own time.

D. It accentuates the positive aspects of rulers in the "Basic Annals", while incorporating negative information into other chapters.

4) Which one is NOT the characteristic of the four great novels?

A. They are rooted in narrative classics.

B. They represent a pinnacle of classic Chinese fiction.

C. It is challenging to read because of the complexity, epical length and density.

D. They articulate the vast multitude of voices that constitute the Chinese populace.

5) Which one is NOT the characteristic of *Dream of the Red Chamber*?

A. It is a semi-autobiographical work.

B. It offers an incredibly detailed rendering of 18th-century Chinese aristocratic life.

C. It provides insight into a wide variety of facts of Chinese culture, from medicine to mythology and art, but all of which continued to influence contemporary culture in China.

D. It continues to be relevant today with its prototypical tale of rebellion, repression and subservience.

3. Translate the following sentences.

1)《诗经》中有先祖创业的颂歌，有祭祀鬼神的乐章，更有劳动人民的真实生活写照。

2) 李清照的词以怀旧的笔调回忆她在北方的幸福生活，同时表露出她在南方生活的悲伤心情。

3) 司马迁善于将人物放到激烈的对抗环境中，让人物的言行来说话，从而使人物的性格更生动、鲜活、真实，具有强烈的艺术感染力。

4) 话本的出现引起了正统文学向通俗文学的转变，这一转变为后来明清小说与元代戏剧的繁荣打下了坚实的基础。

5)《西游记》描写了孙悟空、猪八戒、沙和尚保护唐僧去西天取经的故事。他们一路上降妖除魔，经历了八十一难，终于取回了真经。

4. Discuss the following questions.

1) What is the significance of *The Book of Songs* and *Chuci* in Chinese literature?

2) What are the influences of *The Records of Grand Historian* on Chinese literature?

3) Which one are you more interested in among the four classical novels? Why?

5. Form groups of three or four. Do research on the following classic Chinese literature and fill in the table below. Then report your findings to the class.

Classic Chinese Literature	Themes	Idioms
The Book of Songs		
The Records of the Grand Historian		
The Comprehensive Mirror to Aid in Government		
Romance of the Three Kingdoms		

◆ Extended Readings

The Book of Songs《诗经》

The Book of Songs (《诗经》), one of the "Five Classics", marks the beginning of Chinese literature and lays the foundation for subsequent Chinese poetic forms, including Pre-Qin poetry, Han Yuefu songs, Wei and Jin folk songs, Tang poetry, Song lyrics, and Yuan opera. It is one of the earliest artistic forms, originated from folk songs before the advent of written Chinese. The collection comprises 305 poems composed over a period of approximately 500 years, from the early Western Zhou Dynasty to the middle of the Spring and Autumn Period. *The Book of Songs* consists of three parts: *Feng* (《风》), *Ya* (《雅》), and *Song* (《颂》).

Feng (folk songs) includes 160 folk ballads from 15 vassal kingdoms. These ballads are typically short lyrics in simple language, primarily ancient folk songs that capture the voices of the common people. They often address themes such as love and courtship, longing for an absent lover, soldiers on campaign, farming and housework, and political satire, exemplified by "Fat Rats" (《硕鼠》) from the Wei kingdom. This section is the most vibrant and popular part of the book, marking the beginning of the vernacular tradition in Chinese poetry.

Ya (odes) , which is subdivided into *Da Ya* (*The Major Odes*,《大雅》) and *Xiao Ya* (*The Minor Odes*,《小雅》), contains dynastic hymns or ceremonial odes written by court officials and aristocrats. *Da Ya* includes poems and epics depicting court life, banquets, and harvest celebrations. *Xiao Ya* describes army life and the lives of nobles. These odes best reflect the stable Chinese social system.

Song (eulogies) includes 40 songs for sacrificial ceremonies and ceremonial occasions, praising deceased emperors and often accompanied by dance performances. An exemplary piece from the Song Dynasty is *Qingmiao* (《清庙》), which extols the virtues and deeds of the deceased emperor through solemn and reverent language, reflecting the grandeur and reverence of ancient Chinese sacrificial rituals.

Regardless of whether the various poems in *The Book of Songs* were originally folk songs, they exhibit an overall literary polish and a degree of stylistic consistency. Approximately 95% of the lines in these poems are written in a four-syllable meter, featuring a slight pause between the second and third syllables. Lines typically occur in syntactically related couplets, with occasional parallelism, and longer poems are generally divided into similarly structured stanzas.

One characteristic of the poems in *The Book of Songs* is their use of "repetition and variation". This creates a pattern of similarities and differences in the formal structure: in successive stanzas, some lines and phrases are repeated verbatim, while others vary from stanza to stanza. By the time of Tang poetry, disallowing verbal repetition within a poem became one of the rules distinguishing old-style poetry from the new, regulated style.

Another characteristic of *The Book of Songs* is the direct expression of true feelings. Many texts reflect the real life of that period and express authors' thoughts and feelings naturally and straightforwardly without artificial modality. This reality results in a high degree of integration between ideological connotations and artistic charm within *The Book of Songs*, which also exerts a far-reaching influence on Chinese poetic styles throughout later ages.

In terms of writing techniques, poems can be classified into *fu* (赋), *bi* (比), *xing* (兴), i.e. narration, metaphor, and evocation. The perfect combination of these three techniques can be seen in "Guan Ju" (《关雎》):

An osprey cooing tender,	关关雎鸠，
On an islet under the sky.	在河之洲。
A fair maiden so slender,	窈窕淑女，
Ideal for a good young guy.	君子好逑。
Long or short grows the cress,	参差荇菜，
The water flows left and right.	左右流之。
The fair maiden in nice,	窈窕淑女，
Pursued by him day and night.	寤寐求之。
...	……

Xing is like the prelude of a song, using natural images to set the scenes for the poem so as to evoke the mood. "Guan Ju" begins with the description of cooing osprey on an islet for a romantic atmosphere, which represents a characteristic of Chinese poetry—a fusion of emotions with natural surroundings.

Bi employs implicit comparisons and analogies, which are used in "Guan Ju" to compare the difficulty of picking cress to the difficulty of pursuing his lover. In Chinese culture, *bi* is considered the best way to express romantic love.

Fu employs straightforward narration and description. For example, in "Guan Ju", it describes the poet's perseverance in pursuing his lover by saying "He misses her day and night, For long he cannot fall asleep (悠哉悠哉，辗转反侧)". This reflects the natural, simple and unaffected nature of Chinese folk culture.

The clever juxtaposition of *fu*, *bi*, and *xing* helps create a complete picture: from meeting to chasing and finally marrying his lover. It begins with a beautiful picture and ends in happiness, conveying the Chinese pursuit of completeness (圆满).

(Adapted from Wikipedia and Young's China Travel websites.)

Tao Yuanming 陶渊明

Tao Yuanming (365–427), also known as Tao Qian (陶潜), was one of the most well-known poets during the Six Dynasties period.

Tao Yuanming's great-grandfather, Tao Kan (陶侃), was an esteemed general and governor of the Eastern Jin Dynasty. His grandfather and father both served as government officials, rising to the level of county governor. However, the family circumstances into which Tao Yuanming was born were marked by moderate poverty and lacked significant political influence. Unfortunately, his father passed away when he was just eight years old. In order to support his family, Tao Yuanming took on a minor official post in his 20s. After about 10 years at that post and a brief term as county magistrate, he resigned from official life due to its excessive formality and widespread corruption. Together with his wife and children, he retired to a farming village south of the Yangtze River. Despite the hardships of a farmer's life and frequent food shortages, Tao was contented in writing poetry, cultivating chrysanthemums, and drinking wine. Disregarding thoughts of gain or loss, he lived his life purely according to his own values.

During Tao Yuanming's time, there was a preference for an elaborate and artificial style in poetry. However, his poetry stands out for its plain and unpretentious language, which captures the essence of life. He integrates daily scenes, such as chrysanthemum-picking, wine-drinking, and farming, into his works. For example, the line "Picking chrysanthemums, I see the Southern Mountain" succinctly portrays the harmony between man and nature. His tone is casual yet refined, conveying deep contemplation on life. His works not only demonstrate his respect for nature and aversion to court corruption but also showcase his creative versatility. Unfortunately, his simple and straightforward approach wasn't fully appreciated until the Tang Dynasty.

One of Tao Yuanming's most renowned works is his prose poem "Peach Blossom Spring" (《桃花源记》). This narrative poem tells the story of a fisherman who discovers a hidden paradise full of peach blossoms, clear streams, and friendly people. The fisherman is amazed by the beauty and tranquility of the place and decides to stay there. The poem has been interpreted as a metaphor for a utopian society or as a symbol of the poet's desire for a simple and peaceful life. In addition to "Peach Blossom Spring", Tao Yuanming's other notable works include "Returning to the Farm to Dwell" (《归园田居》), "Wine-Drinking Song" (《饮酒》), and "Biography of Mr. Five Willows" (《五柳先生传》). These works further showcase his literary talent and philosophical insights.

The following is Tao's poem—"Wine-Drinking Song V" (《饮酒其五》).

结庐在人境，而无车马喧。

问君何能尔？心远地自偏。

采菊东篱下，悠然见南山。

山气日夕佳，飞鸟相与还。

此中有真意，欲辨已忘言。

In people's haunt I built my cot,

Of wheel's and hoof's noise I hear not.

How can it leave on me no trace?

Secluded heart makes secluded place.

I pick chrysanthemums at will,

Carefree, I see the Southern Hill.

The mountain air is fresh day and night,

Together birds go home in flight.

What revelation at this view?

Words fail me if I try to tell you.

(Translated by 许渊冲 .)

I built a cottage right in the realm of men,

Yet there was no noise from wagon and horse.

I ask you, how can that be so?—

When mind is far, its place becomes remote.

I picked a chrysanthemum by the eastern hedge,

Off in the distance gazed on south mountain.

Mountain vapors glow lovely in twilight sum,

Where birds in flight join in return.

There is some true significance here:

I want to expound it but have lost the words.

(Translated by Stephen Owen.)

(Adapted from Wikipedia website.)

Chapter Seven

Chinese Performing Arts
中国表演艺术

Chinese performing arts, ranging from martial arts like kung fu to folk songs and dances, are numerous and varied, embodying the spirit of "a hundred flowers bloom and a hundred schools contend (百花齐放，百家争鸣)", which may date back to the tribal era long before the culture became well developed. These art forms have continuously evolved, developed, and changed throughout history while the essence of their original forms has been kept. This chapter will introduce some well-known performing arts.

7.1　Chinese Opera

Traditional Chinese opera or *xiqu* (戏曲), is a form of musical theatre in China that has its roots going back to the early periods in China. It is an amalgamation of various art forms that existed in ancient China, and gradually evolved over more than a thousand years, reaching its mature form in the 13th century during the Song Dynasty. Early forms of Chinese theater were simple, but over time various art forms such as music, song and dance, martial arts, acrobatics, costume and make-up art, as well as literary art forms, were incorporated to form traditional Chinese opera. Performers had to practice for many years to gain an understanding of their roles. Exaggerated features and colors made it easier for the audience to identify the roles portrayed.

Emperor Taizong in the Tang Dynasty (唐太宗) established an opera school with the poetic name *Liyuan* (梨园, Pear Garden). From that time on, the performers of Chinese opera were referred to as "disciples of the Pear Garden (梨园弟子)". There are over a hundred regional branches of traditional Chinese opera today. In the 20th century, the Peking Opera emerged in popularity and came to be known as the "national theatre" of China. However, other genres like Shaoxing Opera (越剧), Henan Opera (豫剧), Kunqu Opera (昆曲), Shaanxi Opera (秦腔), Huangmei Opera (黄梅戏), Pingju (评剧), and Sichuan Opera (川剧) are also performed regularly before dedicated fans. Their differences are mainly found in music and dialect; the stories are often shared and borrowed. The vast majority of Chinese operas are set in China before the 17th century, whether they are traditional or newly written.

One feature of Chinese opera is the different styles of facial make-up (脸谱). Originally, the designs are painted on each performer's face to emphasize or exaggerate their natural complexion. However, over time, they came to symbolize a character's personality, role, and fate. So the audience can understand the story by observing the facial painting as well as the costumes. In general, red represents loyalty and courage; purple signifies wisdom, bravery and steadfastness; black symbolizes loyalty and integrity; watery white denotes cruelty and treachery; oily white represents an inflated and domineering person; blue conveys valor and resolution; green embodies chivalry; yellow indicates brutality; dark red portrays a loyal and time-tested warrior; while gray depicts an old scoundrel. Gold and silver are used on the faces and bodies of Buddhas, spirits, and demons, because their shining color can create a supernatural effect. Besides color, lines also serve as symbols. For example, a figure can be painted either all white on his face, or just around the nose. The larger the area painted white, the more viperous the role it represents. Although these symbolic meanings are fairly well established, there is still flexibility allowed in the use of color.

For centuries, Chinese opera was the main form of entertainment for both urban and rural residents in China, as well as the Chinese diaspora. However, its popularity sharply declined in the second half of the 20th century due to political and market factors. For young people, Chinese opera is no longer a part of the everyday popular music culture, but it remains attractive to many older people who see it as a representation of national or regional identity.

Peking Opera (京剧) is the most dominant form of Chinese opera, which combines music, vocal performance, mime, dance and acrobatics. Originating in Beijing during the mid-Qing Dynasty (1644–1912), it became fully developed and recognized by the mid-19th century. The art form was extremely popular at the Qing court and has been regarded as one of China's cultural treasures. Major performance troupes are based in Beijing, Tianjin and Shanghai.

Peking Opera is characterized by four main role types: *sheng* (生 , gentlemen), *dan* (旦 , women), *jing* (净 , rough men), and *chou* (丑 , clowns). With their elaborate and colorful costumes, performers are the only focal points on Peking Opera's characteristically sparse stage. They skillfully use speech, song, dance and combat in movements that are symbolic and suggestive rather than realistic. Above all else, the skill of performers is evaluated according to the beauty of their movements. Performers also adhere to a variety of stylistic conventions to help audiences follow the plot of the production. Each movement must convey layers of meaning in harmony with music. The music of Peking Opera can be divided into the *xipi* (西皮) and *erhuang* (二黄) styles. Melodies include arias, fixed-tune melodies and percussion patterns. The repertoire of Peking Opera includes over 1,400 works based on Chinese history, folklore and, increasingly, contemporary life.

Peking Opera performers use four main skills. The first two are song and speech. The third is dance-acting, which includes pure dance, pantomime, and various other types of dances. The final skill is combat, which includes both acrobatics and fighting with a variety of weaponry. Performers can spray fire out of their mouths or act as a dwarf while squatting. All of these skills are expected to be performed effortlessly, in line with the spirit of the art form. This reflects a saying among actors: "One minute's performance on the stage takes ten years' practice behind the scenes (台上一分钟，台下十年功)."

Peking Opera shares similarities with other traditional Chinese arts by prioritizing meaning over accuracy. The ultimate goal for performers is to infuse beauty into every movement. Great emphasis is placed on tradition within this art form. Gestures, settings, music, and character types are all determined by long-standing conventions. This includes conventions of movement (动作程式), which serve to convey particular actions to the audience. For example, walking in a large circle always signifies traveling a great distance, while a character straightening his or her costume and headdress indicates that an important character is about to speak.

(Adapted from Wikipedia website.)

◆ Cultural Analysis

Traditional Chinese opera is an important part of traditional Chinese culture, often referred to as the essence of Chinese culture. Its artistic features encompass integration and virtuality.

(1) Integration

Chinese opera is an integration of various artistic forms, incorporating elements such as music, dance, acting, mime, comedy, tragedy, acrobatics and martial arts. An aspiring opera performer must master the skill of singing (唱), reciting (念), acting (做) and fighting (打).

(2) Virtuality

Chinese opera, presented in the form of poetry, music and dance, is more virtual than realistic. It has developed a set of artistic techniques to convey a virtual world on stage through exaggerated makeups, expressive voices and fixed gesture patterns. This virtuality transcends the limitations of time and space on stage to depict a broader spectrum of life. For example, traveling on the river can be symbolized by an oar; horse-riding by a horsewhip; troops by several soldiers, etc., aiming for spiritual resemblance rather than physical likeness (求神似而非形似).

◆ Text Comprehension

1. Judge whether the following statements are true (T) or false (F).

1) Chinese opera is an amalgamation of various art forms in China.

2) The performers of Chinese opera were also called "disciples of the Pear Garden".

3) In general, the white color in facial makeup symbolizes loyalty and courage.

4) Peking Opera, like other traditional Chinese arts, places emphasis on accuracy rather than meaning.

5) Walking in a large circle on the stage of Peking Opera always symbolizes traveling a long distance.

2. Answer the following questions.

1) What are the symbolic meanings of different facial makeups? Can you give some examples?

2) What are the main roles in Peking Opera?

3) What are the artistic characteristics of Chinese opera ?

7.2   Chinese *Quyi*

Quyi is a general name for a wide variety of speaking and singing art forms, deeply rooted in Chinese history and culture. In ancient times, both storytelling and comic performances were not only widespread and popular among common people, but also enjoyed in the palaces and the mansions of nobility. During the Tang Dynasty, many stories were created; some of them were from Buddhist scriptures and some were accompanied by folk songs. During the Song Dynasty, trade prosperity, urban growth and population expansion speeded up the development and flourishing of storytelling and other *quyi* forms.

There are about 400 forms of *quyi*, all centered around speaking and singing as their major expressions. Therefore, the language used must be lively, simple, vivid yet colloquial, and easy to memorize and recite. Moreover, the artists have to try their best to stimulate the audience through words and songs that inspire them to conjure up images. Unlike dramas or operas, *quyi* usually needs only one or two performers who may play several roles. In addition, the contents of *quyi* are shorter and more down-to-earth than other art forms, and the artists usually compose, compile and design by themselves. Characterized by its talking-singing arts (说唱艺术), *quyi* can be roughly classified into singing form and talking form. Major singing forms, such as *Jingyun dagu* (京韵大鼓), normally tell short stories through brief songs. Some combine singing with speaking, such as *Suzhou pingtan* (苏州评弹), and these performances are often lengthy. Others feature a combination of singing and speaking, such as *Shandong kuaishu* (山东快书).

Er'renzhuan or Song-and-Dance Duet (二人转) is the most direct and vivid representation of the local culture of Northeast China. It reflects the Northeasterners' simple, frank and optimistic traits. This performance art is a mixture of operas, songs, dances and acrobatics. It is usually performed by one clown and one positive female role, hence comes the name. The dancing is inspired by the celebratory dances of local farmers during sowing and planting. It also features the folk dance techniques such as waving fans or handkerchiefs. It is very popular for its interesting stories, rhythmical melodies, humorous language and peculiar local style.

Talking forms include *pingshu* (评书) and *pinghua* (评话), which are used to tell long stories that may span over several months. The *pingshu* performer, dressed in a gown, sits behind a table with a folded fan and a gavel (醒木). The gavel is used as a prop to strike the table, either as a signal for the audience to be quiet or to capture their attention and enhance the performance, especially at the beginning or during intervals. The art of storytelling, with its wide appeal, has contributed to the development of other art forms and has nurtured many talented artists. Famous novels such as *Romance of the Three Kingdoms* and other serialized novels (章回小说) were created under the influence of the storytelling artists.

One form of *quyi* that remains very popular today is crosstalk (相声). It is a language art that combines four basic artistic skills—speaking, imitating, teasing and singing (说、学、逗、唱). The language is rich in puns and allusions. It is typically performed in the Beijing dialect or in Mandarin with a strong Northern Chinese accent. Crosstalk can be performed in different forms. Monologue comic talk（单口相声）is performed by one person that mainly tells jokes; dialogue comic crosstalk（对口相声）, the most popular form, features two actors, with one person acting as the leading comedian called *dougen*（逗哏）and the other as the supporting role called *penggen*（捧哏）; and a multi-player show, otherwise known as multilogue crosstalk（群口相声）, is played by three or more people. Currently, crosstalk covers a wide range of subjects. Apart from works in traditional ironic style, there are creations that celebrate new heroes and events, reflecting real life. The classic works include "Operas and Dialects"（《戏剧与方言》）, "A Nighttime Tour"（《夜行记》）, "Buying Monkeys"（《买猴儿》）, etc.

Although there are different kinds of *quyi*, most of it contains the following six techniques of expression: talking（说）, singing（唱）, acting（演）, commenting（评）, using humor（噱）and imitating（学）. Talking is required to be clear and vivid. In *quyi*, talking skills are more significant than singing skills, as the saying goes, "talking is the monarch and singing is its subject（说为君唱为臣）". *Quyi* artists hone their skills over the years, mastering clear articulation（吐字）, expressive performance（传神）, humor（使噱）, dialects（变口）, fluent delivery（贯口）, vocal imitation（口技）, and insightful commentary（批讲）. Singing should be melodious, captivating and story-related. As for acting, *quyi* actors may perform in factories, fields, or sentry posts for the audience, so they need to use vivid intonations and facial expressions, as well as distinctive body languages and props, in order to convey the theme of their performance. Moreover, performers usually make insightful and thought-provoking comments on the characters and events within the story to impress the audience. *Quyi* artists also give interesting and incisive jokes or provide laughter to enliven the atmosphere and entertain the audience. They can also imitate dialects, accents, different characters, or some natural sounds as needed for storytelling and characterization. This skill not only achieves effective results but also creates an authentic atmosphere.

(Adapted from Baidu Baike website.)

◆ Cultural Analysis

Quyi has a broad mass appeal and a strong Chinese flavor. Many excellent *quyi* performances reflect Chinese people's thoughts, ideals and moral aspirations. Due to its diverse nature of performance, *quyi* continues to thrive in modern entertainment.

(1) The Heritage of Chinese History and Literature

Quyi has played a significant role in preserving the history and culture of many ethnic groups. As a result, *quyi* has retained the features of primitive art in singing and storytelling. Many epics, folk songs and narratives of ethnic groups from different historical periods in China have been passed down through *quyi*.

(2) The Origin of Classical Chinese Novels and Opera

There are about 400 forms of *quyi,* all using speaking and singing as their main expressions. This requires the language to be lively, simple, vivid, colloquial, and easy to memorize and recite, which led to the development of opera and long novels.

◆ Text Comprehension

1. Judge whether the following statements are true (T) or false (F).

1) In ancient times, storytelling and comic performances were despised in the palaces and the mansions of nobility.

2) Speaking and singing are the major forms of expression in *quyi*.

3) *Er'renzhuan* is the most direct and vivid representation of the local culture of Southwest China.

4) *Quyi* artists may imitate dialects, accents, different characters, or some natural sounds as needed for storytelling and characterization.

5) Monologue comic talk is performed by one person who mainly tells jokes.

2. Answer the following questions.

1) What are the four basic skills in crosstalk? Can you give some examples to illustrate its characteristics?

2) What are the differences between Chinese opera and q*uyi* performance?

3) What are the techniques of expression in q*uyi*? Which one is considered the most important, and why?

7.3   Chinese Acrobatics

Acrobatics, also known as Chinese Variety Show, is pronounced "*zaji*（杂技）" in Chinese. *Za*（杂）means variety, and *ji*（技）means art and skill. Acrobatics is a performance art that shows extraordinary feats of balance, agility and motor coordination. Acrobatics is often associated with activities that make extensive use of gymnastic skills, such as circus and gymnastics, and it can also be found in many other athletic activities, such as martial arts, ballet and diving.

Chinese Acrobatics can be dated back to Neolithic times when primitive man showcased their labor skills, kongfu skills and special skills for amusement during breaks or celebrations. As one of the traditional art forms, acrobatics has long been popular among the Chinese people for more than 2,000 years. As early as the Warring States Period, there appeared rudiments of acrobatics. During the Qin and Han dynasties, *juedi*（角抵）or *baixi*（百戏）variety shows were enjoyed by common people. *Juedi* was originally an entertainment that involved men wearing horns charging at each other like bulls, but became a general term used interchangeably with *baixi* to describe popular entertainment during the Han Dynasty. These shows consisted of a variety of acts such as conjuring, acrobatics, wrestling, musical performances, dance, martial arts, horsemanship and juggling. In the Eastern Han Dynasty, Zhang Heng（张衡）was one of the first scholars to describe the acrobatic theme shows in royal palaces in his *Ode to the Western Capital*（《西京赋》）. Zhang's descriptions included men swallowing knives and spitting fire, costumes transforming into different creatures, as well as children performing acrobatics on high poles. The performances became more elaborate and during the Tang Dynasty, the performing arts became popular in the emperor's court, with acts becoming more refined. Eventually, the performing arts lost favor in the imperial court and returned to the common people, with most performers taking to the streets. During the Song Dynasty, the variety shows were performed in entertainment centers called *washe*（瓦舍）, meaning "tiles". Towards the end of the Ming Dynasty, the performers started performing on stage. By the end of the Qing Dynasty, Chinese Acrobatics regained popularity with the imperial court and has remained a popular art form to this day.

Handstands on Stacked Chairs（高空叠椅）is one of the classic performances. Chairs are simple pieces of furniture, but they can become stage props with which acrobats perform graceful and precipitous feats. After much practice, the feats have become more diverse and impressive. This act is divided into two parts: first, a single acrobat performs handstand stunts on stacked chairs; and when performed by a group, the acrobats do various stunts on one stack, two stacks, or even three stacks of chairs. The chairs are stacked precipitously one on top of another, and the acrobats perform in symmetry from bottom to top. The whole scene looks like a splendid peacock displaying its fine feathers.

Performances that imitate animals' movements are called "Imitation Performances", and the Lion Dance (舞狮) is the best known of these. In recent years, this act, along with other acrobatic acts, has also evolved to include new characteristics. For example, the "lion" may tread on a rolling ball across a seesaw, walk on stakes, or stand on a pile of stools. The Lion Dance displays the brave, lively and playful character of the animal and is worth watching repeatedly.

Plate-Spinning (转盘) is another classic performance. As the stage curtain rises slowly to the tune of melodious sounds, a group of lovely girls come out spinning plates on long sticks. In recent years, this performance has broken new ground. Apart from the basic spinning, acrobats have created a number of intricate patterns. For instance, in performing the "backflip in mid-air", an acrobat holds sticks with spinning plates in both hands while making a swift backflip from table to ground. In performing the "stand on the head", two acrobats work together, with one resting upside down on the head of the other and then rolling down the latter's back to the ground. During the process, both acrobats keep their plates spinning steadily on their sticks.

The Pagoda of Bowls (顶碗) is also one of the classics in acrobatics, with a history dating back over 2,000 years. A brick carving from a tomb of the Han Dynasty shows a figure performing a handstand with a pagoda of bowls, providing evidence of its ancient origins. In recent years, this performance has become more specialized. Previously, it is performed by a single acrobat on a stool, but now it is done in cooperation by two people. One acrobat stands on top of the other and performs various feats with a pagoda of bowls. These feats include standing with one foot on the other's head, doing a one-hand stand, and passing the bowls from head to foot or vice versa. While the upper member is giving his/her performance, the lower one also showcases his/her skills by pushing up the acrobat with one hand or sitting on the ground and turning himself/herself. At the end of the show, the upper performer makes a forward somersault in mid-air, throwing off the bowls and landing steadily on the ground. Simultaneously, the lower performer catches any falling bowls in his/her hand.

(Adapted from China Travel and Wikipedia websites.)

◆ Cultural Analysis

In general, the focus of acrobats' training is placed on their head, waist, and legs. However, the conceptual basis, training techniques, and acrobatic practice are also influenced by traditional Chinese martial arts.

(1) The Emphasis on Balance and Harmony

Acrobatics is the performance of extraordinary feats of balance, agility and motor coordination. Acrobats strive to appear calm and steady on the tightrope while maintaining balance between light and heavy in feet-balancing acts. There is a great deal of skills involved in stability during dangerous movements and quietness during agile actions. There is also a pursuit of surprise in routine performance and a demonstration of strength in suppleness.

(2) The Use of Farming Tools or Household Items

Elements of ancient acrobatics originated from people's daily life and work. Tools of labor like tridents and wicker, and household items such as tables, chairs and bowls were widely used in performances. During festivals, people often performed "flying trident", "balancing on chair", "jar tricks", "hoop-diving", and "lion dance" in the market places or on the streets of town, which shows people's emphasis on enjoying life.

◆ Text Comprehension

1. Judge whether the following statements are true (T) or false (F).

1) Chinese *zaji* can be dated back to as early as the Han Dynasty.

2) During the Han Dynasty, the performing arts of *zaji* became more refined.

3) *Zaji* has never been shown in the imperial court.

4) The place for the variety shows was called *washe*, meaning "tiles" in ancient time.

5) The conceptual basis, training techniques, and acrobatic practice of *zaji* are also influenced by traditional Chinese martial arts.

2. Answer the following questions.

1) Why is *zaji* a reflection of Chinese realistic daily life?

2) Can you give a brief account of the historical development of *zaji* in China and its cultural peculiarity?

3) What is the Pagoda of Bowls?

◆ Exercises

1. Match the Chinese performing arts with their types and features.

Chinese Performing Arts	Types	Features
1) Chinese opera	A) Crosstalk	a) *Sheng, dan, jing, chou*
	B) *Er'renzhuan*	b) Speaking, imitating, teasing and singing
2) *Quyi*	C) Peking Opera	c) Facial makeup
	D) Lion Dance	d) Horsemanship
3) *Zaji*	E) *Qinqiang*	e) Circus
	F) The Pagoda of Bowls	f) Standing on the head

2. Choose the best answer to each of the following questions.

1) _____ is(are) used on the faces and bodies of Buddhas, spirits, and demons.

   A. Black

   B. White

   C. Yellow

   D. Gold and silver

2) The _____ is a male clown role.   .

   A. *sheng*

   B. *dan*

   C. *jing*

   D. *chou*

3) Singing form includes the following EXCEPT _____.

   A. *Jingyun dagu*

   B. *Suzhou pingtan*

C. *Er'renzhuan*

D. *pingshu*

4) Acrobatics is most often associated with activities that make extensive use of the following EXCEPT _____.

A. gymnastics

B. circus

C. *martial arts*

D. singing

5) An acrobat holds sticks with spinning plates in both hands while making a swift backflip from table to ground. This is the performance of _____.

A. Lion Dance

B. Plate-Spinning

C. The Pagoda of Bowls

D. none of the above

3. Translate the following sentences.

1) 京剧表演的四项基本功为唱、念、做、打。

2) 京剧脸谱与角色性格特点关系密切。

3) 相声是一种民间曲艺，以说、学、逗、唱为突出特点。

4) 杂技指柔术、车技、口技、顶碗、走钢丝、变戏法、舞狮子等。

5) 二人转由一男一女表演，表演时手拿扇子、手绢，边唱边舞。

4. Discuss the following questions.

1) What are the similarities and differences between Chinese crosstalks and Western talk shows?

2) What national values can be found in Chinese Acrobatics?

3) What are the common characteristics of Chinese opera and Western opera? Can you also compare the cultural connotations between the two?

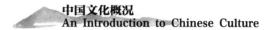

5. Form groups of three or four. Do research on the following Chinese performing arts and fill in the table below. Then report your findings to the class.

Chinese Performing Arts	Definition	Features	Cultural Analysis
Kunqu Opera			
Conjuring			
Monologue Crosstalk			
Pingshu			

◆ Extended Readings

◢ **Chinese Shadow Puppetry 皮影戏**

Shadow puppetry, also known as Shadow Play, was very popular during the Tang and Song dynasties in many regions of China. Shadow puppets were first made of paper cuttings, but later they were made from the leather of donkeys or oxen. That's why they are called *piying* (皮影) in Chinese, which means "shadows of leather".

More than 2,000 years ago, a favorite concubine of Emperor Wu of the Han Dynasty died of illness. The emperor missed her so much that he lost his desire to reign. One day, a minister happened to see children playing with dolls and noticed their vivid shadows on the floor. Inspired by this scene, the smart minister hit upon an idea. He made a cotton puppet of the concubine and painted it. As night fell, he invited the emperor to watch a rear-illuminated puppet show behind a curtain. The emperor was delighted and took to it from then on. This story is recorded in the official history book and is believed to be the origin of shadow puppetry.

Shadow puppetry wins the heart of the audience by its lingering music, exquisite sculptures, brisk colors and lively performances. "One mouth tells stories of thousands of years; a pair of hands operates millions of soldiers." This is how the shadow puppeteer works. Known as the "business of the five", a shadow puppet troupe is made up of five people: one operates the puppets, one plays a *suona* horn (唢呐), one plays *banhu* fiddle (板胡), one is in charge of percussion instruments, and one sings. The singer plays all the roles in the puppet show, which of course is very difficult. Additionally, the singer also plays several of the over 20 kinds of musical instruments in a puppet show. These ancient musical instruments enhance this traditional folk art.

The stage for the play is a white cloth screen, on which the shadows of flat puppets are projected. Shadow puppets look similar to paper-cut figures except that their joints are connected by thread so that they can be operated freely. The scene may be simple and primitive, but it is the consummate performance that attracts the audience. For example, a puppet can even smoke and blow out a smoke ring with operator's help. In one drama, as a maid sits in front of a mirror, her reflection matches her actions. The operator manages to handle five puppets at the same time, each controlled by three threads. No wonder the operator is compared to the 1000-hand Kwan-yin (千手观音).

To enhance the limited visibility of puppets, shadow puppets use exaggeration and heavy dramatization. The faces and the costumes of the puppets are vivid and humorous. The flowery color, elegant sculpting and smooth lines make the puppets not only props but also artworks. It takes as many as 24 procedures and more than 3,000 cuts to create each figure.

The figures all have a large head and a small body that tapers down. For example, a man has a big head with a square face, broad forehead and a tall strong body without being too masculine. On the other hand, a woman has a thin face, a small mouth and slim body without being too plump. Effeminacy and tenderness are considered the standard of Chinese beauty.

The design of the figures follows traditional moral evaluation and aesthetics. The audience can tell a figure's character by seeing its mask. Like the masks used in Peking Opera, a red mask represents uprightness, a black one symbolizes fidelity, and a white one signifies treachery. The positive figure has long narrow eyes, a small mouth and a straight bridge of nose, while the negative one has small eyes, a protruding forehead and sagging mouth. The clown has a circle around his eyes, which conveys an air of humor and frivolity even before he begins performing.

Lavish background pieces, including architecture, furniture, vessels and auspicious patterns, are featured in the shadow play. This earthly form of art impresses audiences by its vividness and refinement.

In addition to the necessary figures for a shadow play, the shadow puppets also include heroes from folklore and history, such as the four ancient beauties: Xi Shi, Wang Zhaojun, Diao Chan, and Yang Guifei; or other characters like the Monkey King and Emperor Qin Shi Huang. Shadow puppetry in Shaanxi Province is believed to be the most typical form of this art.

(Adapted from Travel China Guide website.)

Kunqu Opera

Kunqu Opera is one of the oldest forms of opera still existing in China. It evolved from the local melody of Kunshan, and subsequently came to dominate Chinese theaters from the 16th to the 18th centuries. The style is originated in the Wu cultural area. It has distinguished itself by the virtuosity of its rhythmic patterns and has exerted a dominant influence on more recent forms of opera in China, such as Sichuan Opera and Peking Opera. In 2001, UNESCO proclaimed Kunqu Opera as a masterpiece of the Oral and Intangible Heritage of Humanity.

Kunqu Opera, known as the mother of all Chinese operas, has its origin in the late Yuan Dynasty, dating back some 600 years ago to the lower Yangtze River Valley. This traditional performing art was named after its birthplace, Mt. Kunshan, located near the city of Suzhou in today's Jiangsu Province, East China.

The development of Kunqu music went through several stages. In the early days, the songs were composed of long and short lines. The singer sang solo, and the orchestra came in at the end of each line. In the chorus sections, only percussion instruments were used.

In the Ming Dynasty, reformed by Wei Liangfu (魏良辅) under the reign of Emperor Jiajing, Kunqu Opera became mild, smooth, and graceful. The performers attached great importance to clear recitation, correct singing, and pure tunes. Meanwhile, the composers wrote the musical scores after working out the tunes, and the songs were written in seven- or ten-character lines. Accompaniment was provided by three types of musical instruments: stringed instruments, bamboo flutes, and drums and clappers. In addition, Kunqu Opera had 12 roles, and the *Jing* and *Chou* roles were no longer limited to portraying foolish, awkward, or stingy people exclusively.

Kunqu Opera is acknowledged as an elegant opera in terms of music, recitation, and the performers' movements. The lyrics are usually written by scholars, poets and writers with very high aesthetic and artistic competence, and are advocated also by officials. It is foremost acclaimed as "watermill songs (水磨调)" because of its soft arias and the graceful movement of its performers. By carrying forward the tradition of ancient poetry and common speech, this art form also holds high literary value.

Kunqu Opera has a comprehensive system of acting, and its wide-ranging repertoire has many delicate and elegant tunes. The musical instruments used in Kunqu Opera are distinguished from those used in Peking Opera. In order to perfectly match the poetic style of the performance, the flute is widely used as the accompanying instrument instead of stringed instruments. The orchestra consists of traditional instruments such as the *dizi* (笛子), a horizontal bamboo flute which plays the leading part; the *xiao* (箫), a vertical bamboo flute; the *sheng* (笙), a mouth organ; and the *pipa* (琵琶), a plucked string instrument with a fretted finger board.

However, Kunqu Opera, acknowledged as an elite opera, has experienced some decline since the 18th century because it requires a high level of technical knowledge from the audience. Its refined language and elegant lyrics may be too sophisticated to understand for ordinary people, while its lingering tunes and slow-paced rhythms cannot be appreciated by modern audience. Today, it faces competition from mass culture and lacks interest among the young people.

Throughout its 600-year history, Kunqu Opera has accumulated a repertoire of more than 400 *zhezixi* (折子戏). Some of these scripts were written by outstanding playwrights. Guan Hanqing (关汉卿), for instance, wrote more than 60 *zaju* (杂剧 , poetic dramas), including *The Injustice to Dou E* (《窦娥冤》) (also known as *Snow in the Summer*). Other masterpieces include *The West Chamber* (《西厢记》) by Wang Shifu (王实甫), *The Peony Pavilion* (《牡丹亭》) by Tang Xianzu (汤显祖), *The Palace of Eternal Youth* 《长生殿》 by Hong Sheng (洪昇), and *The Peach Blossom Fan* 《桃花扇》 by Kong Shangren (孔尚任).

The most famous among them is *The West Chamber*, which depicts a romance set against the ancient feudal society. It tells the story of a young man and woman who strive for the freedom of marriage. This poetic drama attained an extremely high artistic level in terms of its lyrics, music, plot and performing skills. Today, it stands as a classic among Chinese dramas.

Unlike Peking Opera, which is popular among the ordinary people, Kunqu Opera reflects the tastes of the scholar-bureaucrat, and belongs to the high culture of ancient poetic and aesthetic life. It represents the highest achievement in Chinese Opera and embodies a harmonious combination of classical music, poetry and dance. In classical Chinese culture, poetry and music have always been closely intertwined as two important artistic forms. Many ancient Chinese musicians are also scholars and poets. Kunqu Opera is a perfect example of the harmonious blend of Chinese music and poetry.

Actually, other schools of Chinese opera all consider Kunqu Opera as their ancestor and benefit a lot from it. There is no denying that Kunqu Opera represents the highest artistic achievements in traditional Chinese opera, thus holding a unique position in the history of world culture.

(Adapted from *China Daily* website.)

Chapter Eight

Chinese Architecture
中国建筑

Traditional Chinese architecture has a history as long as Chinese civilization itself. Generally speaking, Chinese architecture is characterized by various features such as bilateral symmetry, the use of enclosed open spaces, the incorporation of *fengshui*, etc. Due to China's vast land, the architectural styles of different regions and ethnic groups may vary in characteristics and functions, all of which can reflect the culture in different areas. The architecture can also be classified according to whether it was built for royals, commoners, or religious purposes. In this chapter, we will explore the beauty of Chinese architecture, including civilian housing, imperial palaces and classical Chinese gardens.

8.1 Civilian Housing

Siheyuan（四合院）refers to a courtyard surrounded by buildings on all four sides. It is a historical type of residence that was commonly found throughout China, particularly renowned in Beijing and rural Shanxi Province. In ancient times, a spacious *siheyuan* would be occupied by a single, usually large and extended family, signifying wealth and prosperity. *Siheyuan*, a traditional building style that has endured for over 2,000 years, can be dated back to as early as the Western Zhou Dynasty. The different types of *siheyuan* across China are the template for most Chinese architecture styles which exhibit outstanding and fundamental characteristics of Chinese architecture. *Siheyuan* were built according to the traditional concepts of the five elements（五行）that were believed to compose the universe, and the eight diagrams of divination（八卦）. The gate was positioned at the southeast corner which was the "wind" corner, and the main house was built on the north side which was believed to belong to "water" element, used to prevent fire.

Siheyuan serves as a cultural symbol of Beijing and a window into its old ways of life. When the new capital city Dadu（大都）of the Yuan Dynasty was constructed, Beijing *siheyuan*, a distinctive style of residential house, emerged and developed during this period. The great Italian traveler, Marco Polo, once praised the ingenious and elegant design of this highly original house style created by ancient Chinese people as beyond description in any language.

Siheyuan mostly consists of outer and inner yards. The outer yard is horizontal and long, and its main door opens to the southeast corner, ensuring the privacy of the residents and adding to the spatial change of the residence. The entrance gate is usually painted vermilion and decorated with copper door knockers. Normally, there is a screen wall (影壁) inside the gate for privacy as well as to protect the house from evil spirits according to superstition. A pair of stone lions are often placed outside the gate. In some large *siheyuan* compounds, private gardens are attached, symbolizing wealth and status in ancient times.

After entering the main door and turning westward into the outer yard, one will find guest rooms, a servant's room, a kitchen and a toilet. Going northward from the outer yard through an exquisitely shaped and quite beautiful floral-pendant gate, one will enter the square and spacious main yard. The principal house, situated in the northern part of the compound, is the largest structure. It is typically inhabited by senior family members and serves as a venue for family ceremonies and the reception of honored guests. Inside the principal house, a plaque inscribed with the words "Heaven, Earth, Sovereign, Parents, and Teacher" (天地君亲师) is usually displayed, emphasizing the family's deep reverence for tradition. Adjacent to the pricipal house on its left and right sides are side rooms (耳房), connected by corridors, which may accommodate elderly family members. In front of these corridors, there is a small and tranquil corner where a study is often located. On both sides of the main yard, there are wing rooms serving as living rooms for the younger generations. Both the principal room and the wing rooms face the yards, which have front porches. Verandas link the floral-pendant gate and the three houses, so that one can move along or sit and enjoy the flowers and trees in the courtyard. Behind the principal room, there is often a long row of *houzhaofang* (后罩房 , backside building), which serves as either a utility room (杂物间) or a living room for unmarried daughters and female servants. In traditional Chinese culture, unmarried girls were not allowed to be exposed directly to the public, so they occupied the most secluded buildings in the *siheyuan*. The layout of a simple courtyard reflects traditional Chinese morality and Confucian ethics.

With no steel or concrete, *siheyuan* is built of bricks and wood. It is believed that when people live in a timber house rather than one made of cement or stone, they maintain a constant connection with nature and achieve harmony between nature and human beings. The walls of *siheyuan* provide security as well as protection against dust and storms. Adorned with plants, rocks, and flowers, the yard also functions as a garden, and serves as an open-air living room that brings heaven and earth closer to people's hearts. The veranda divides the courtyard into several big and small spaces that are not very distant from each other. Family members gather here to talk with each other, creating a cordial atmosphere.

Siheyuan's modest square courtyards are conducive to take in sunshine in winter. However, in areas south of Beijing, the setting sun in summer is quite strong, so the courtyards are designed to be narrower and longer on the north-south side to reduce excessive sunshine. In contrast, in the northwest regions such as Gansu and Qinghai provinces, where dust storms are very strong, courtyard walls tend to be higher. In the northeast where land is abundant but the weather is cold, courtyards are built broad and large to increase exposure to sunlight, and there are more open areas inside the walls.

(Adapted from Wikipedia website.)

◆ Cultural Analysis

Residential houses, as a product of human civilization, have been designed and built according to human needs, and they also embody the Chinese social and ethical values.

(1) The Harmony Between Heaven and Man

The courtyard, designed as a square of appropriate size, is meticulously landscaped with a variety of colorful flowers and strategically placed rocks. This thoughtful arrangement creates a serene and inviting atmosphere, perfect for outdoor relaxation. The carefully designed space fosters a harmonious connection between nature and humanity, drawing heaven and earth closer to people's hearts.

(2) Family Hierarchy

The design of *siheyuan* follows the Confucian tenets of order and hierarchy that were highly valued in traditional Chinese society. According to traditional Chinese customs, buildings with doors facing the front of the property are considered more important than those facing the sides. Buildings located in the rear and more private sections are held in higher esteem and reserved for elder members of the family or the display of ancestral plaques, whereas those near the front are typically designated for servants and hired help.

(3) Centripetal and Cohesive Atmosphere

The centripetal and cohesive atmosphere displayed by *siheyuan*, with its strict rules and forms, is a typical expression of the character of most Chinese residences. The design of the courtyard, which is closed off from the outside while open to the inside, can be seen as an integration of two conflicting mindsets. On one hand, it reflects the desire of feudal families to maintain a certain level of separation from the outside world. On the other hand, the mindset deeply-rooted in the mode of agricultural production makes the Chinese particularly inclined to connect with nature.

◆ Text Comprehension

1. Judge whether the following statements are true (T) or false (F).

1) *Siheyuan* serves as a cultural symbol of Beijing and a window into its old ways of life.

2) The layout of *siheyuan* embodies the concept of *fengshui*.

3) The courtyard is an open-air living room for family members to talk with each other, creating a cordial atmosphere.

4) In the northwest regions such as Gansu and Qinghai provinces, where storms are very strong, courtyard walls tend to be higher.

5) The family hierarchy can be observed from the layout of *siheyuan* in ancient China.

2. Answer the following questions.

1) What are the reasons behind the name *siheyuan*?

2) Why is *siheyuan* considered to be a structurally sound and well-engineered building?

3) How do *siheyuan* differ in various regions of China?

8.2   Classical Chinese Gardens

The Chinese garden, a distinctive landscape architectural style, has evolved over 3,000 years. The earliest recorded gardens can be dated back to the Shang Dynasty, a period marked by the emergence of sophisticated architectural practices. These gardens served as symbols of power and wealth. During subsequent dynasties, including the Zhou, Qin, and Han, Chinese gardens adopted more intricate designs while incorporating elements of Taoism, Buddhism, and Confucianism. These philosophical influences shaped their layouts, plant selections, and water features, creating serene and harmonious environments. By the Tang and Song dynasties, Chinese gardens had evolved into not only havens for leisure and contemplation but also centers for cultural and artistic exchange.

Classical Chinese gardens include both the vast gardens of the Chinese emperors and members of the imperial family, built for pleasure and to impress, and the more intimate gardens created by scholars, poets, former government officials, soldiers and merchants, made for reflection and escape from the outside world. People create an idealized miniature landscape, which is meant to express harmony between man and nature.

A typical Chinese garden is enclosed by walls and includes one or more ponds, rock works, trees and flowers, and an assortment of halls and pavilions within the garden connected by winding paths and zig-zag galleries. By moving from structure to structure, visitors can view a series of carefully composed scenes that unfold like a scroll of landscape paintings. Rocks, water, architecture and plants are the four essential elements of the Chinese garden.

Mountains serve as an indispensable element in garden landscape design. Although royal gardens frequently incorporate natural mountains to create scenery, artificial mountains still play a crucial role in garden design. The man-made hills in the gardens are not high, but they beautifully match the buildings, pavilions and everything else in the gardens, creating a harmonious and serene atmosphere. Looking at the hills, people feel as if they live in a mountainous area and enjoy the beauty and tranquility of nature, far removed from the hustle and bustle of city life. In traditional Chinese culture, the mountain peak was a symbol of virtue, stability and endurance, embodying qualities that were highly esteemed in ancient times. It also holds significance in the legend of the Isles of the Immortals (蓬莱仙岛), making it a central element in many classical gardens.

In classical gardens, there are various water features such as artificial lakes, ponds, rivers, streams, springs, deep pools and waterfalls. A pond or lake serves as the central element of a Chinese garden. The main buildings are usually placed beside it, with pavilions scattered around the lake to offer visitors different perspectives. The garden often has a pond for lotus flowers and goldfish, along with pavilions over the water for viewing them. The water, another central element of the garden, complements the mountain and represents dreams and the boundlessness of spaces. The shape of the garden pond often hides its edges from viewers on the other side, creating the illusion that it extends to infinity. The softness of water contrasts with the solidity of rocks. The water reflects the ever-changing scenery, and even a gentle breeze can soften or erase these reflections.

The buildings within the garden are diverse, including halls, pavilions, terraces, marble boats, corridors, bridges and towers. They blend with the natural environment and serve as viewpoints for enjoying the scenery both within and beyond the garden. Therefore, careful consideration should be given to the orientation of the buildings, as well as the placement of doors and windows to maximize viewing angles and routes. It is important that garden buildings are aesthetically pleasing and complement their surroundings. Attention to detail, such as intricately carved decorative guardrails featuring floral motifs, patterned windows that cast beautiful shadows with sunlight, and grilles adorned with traditional designs, significantly enhances the overall charm and aesthetic appeal of the garden architecture. Classic garden architectures often feature calligraphy or paintings that further enhance their beauty and endow them with a sense of history and culture. Ultimately, the garden architecture should both meet practical needs and contribute to the overall landscaping of the garden.

Flowers and trees represent nature in its most vivid form, and provide a beautiful contrast to the straight lines of the architecture and the sharp edges and immobility of the rocks. Their vibrant colors and delicate textures create a sense of warmth and vitality amidst the cold, hard surfaces of built structures. They continuously change with the seasons, providing both sounds—such as rain on banana leaves or wind through bamboo—and aromas to delight visitors. Each flower and tree in the garden carries its own symbolic meaning. For instance, the pine, bamboo and plum blossom are revered by scholars who designed classical gardens as the "Three Friends of Winter" (岁寒三友). These plants are highly valued for their ability to remain green or bloom even in winter, symbolizing resilience and enduring beauty.

Taoism had a strong influence on the classical garden. After the Han Dynasty, gardens were frequently built as retreats for government officials who had lost their positions or who wanted to escape the pressures and corruption of court life in the capital. They chose to pursue the Taoist ideals of disengagement from worldly concerns. The gardens were designed to evoke the idyllic feeling of wandering through a natural landscape, to feel closer to the ancient way of life, and to appreciate the harmony between man and nature.

(Adapted from Wikipedia website.)

◆ Cultural Analysis

While the Chinese house reflects the Confucian idea of regulating human society, the Chinese garden follows the Taoist principle of harmony with nature. Similar to how Taoism provides a means of escape from Confucian constraints, the design of a garden allows for the release of creative imagination.

(1) Emphasis on Naturalness

Chinese garden architecture takes advantage of its surroundings to blend natural scenes and human interests, eschewing symmetry along an axis in favor of an irregular and intricate layout in both large and small spaces. The inclusion of trees beside hills, ponds, streams, and various buildings creates a more natural scenery within the garden. It is a true expression of the concept that an ideal garden was "made by men but seems natural (虽为人造，宛若天成)".

(2) Pursuit of Spiritual Realm

As a special shelter for people, private gardens were designed to provide a utopian space where individuals could connect intimately with nature and return to their inner selves or ancient idealism. Some private gardens served as places for solitude, meeting people's need to retreat from officialdom's strife and worldly affairs. They sought a return to nature and cultivation of temperament.

◆ Text Comprehension

1. Judge whether the following statements are true (T) or false (F).

1) The earliest recorded Chinese gardens were large enclosed parks where the kings and nobles hunted, or where fruit and vegetables were grown.

2) People create an idealized miniature landscape in classical gardens, which is meant to express harmony between man and nature.

3) In classical Chinese gardens, both the orientation of the buildings and the placement of doors and windows should be taken into consideration to maximize viewing angles and routes.

4) The water in the garden complements the building and represents dreams and the infinity of spaces.

5) Taoism has a strong influence on the classical garden.

2. Answer the following questions.

1) What are the functions of buildings in classical Chinese gardens?

2) What are the symbolic meanings of the mountain and the water in classical Chinese gardens?

3) What is the purpose of scholars and retired officials to build gardens in ancient China?

8.3 Imperial Palaces

The Forbidden City, an imperial palace complex, is located at the heart of Beijing, China. Commissioned in 1406 by Emperor Yongle of the Ming Dynasty, it was first officially occupied by the court in 1420. The name "Forbidden City" originated from the fact that access to the area was barred to most subjects of the realm. Only the emperor had unrestricted access to any section, while high-ranking government officials and even members of the imperial family were granted limited access. The 178-acre compound was designated a UNESCO World Heritage site in 1987 in recognition of its importance as the centre of Chinese power for five centuries, as well as for its unparalleled architecture and its current role as the Palace Museum of dynastic art and history.

The architecture of this walled complex adheres rigidly to the traditional Chinese geomantic practice of *fengshui*. The orientation of the Forbidden City, as well as all of Beijing, follows a north-south line. Within the compound, the most important buildings, especially those along the main axis, face south to honour the sun. The arrangement of buildings and ceremonial spaces conveys an impression of great imperial power while reinforcing the insignificance of the individual. This architectural concept is evident in even the smallest details—the relative importance of a building can be judged not only from its height or width but also by the style of its roof and the number of figurines perched on the roof's ridges.

Some of the most notable landmarks in the Forbidden City include the Meridian Gate (午门), the Hall of Supreme Harmony (太和门), and the Imperial Garden (御花园). The Meridian Gate is an imposing formal southern entrance to the Forbidden City. Its auxiliary wings, which flank the entryway, are outstretched like the fore-paws of a guardian lion. The gate is also one of the tallest buildings in the complex, standing 125 feet high at its roof ridge. One of its primary functions was to serve as a backdrop for imperial appearances and proclamations. Beyond the Meridian Gate lies a large courtyard, 140 metres deep and 690,210 metres wide, through which the Golden River（金水桥）runs in a bow-shaped arc. The river is crossed by five parallel white marble bridges, which lead to the Gate of Supreme Harmony.

North of the Gate of Supreme Harmony lies the Outer Court（外朝）, heart of the Forbidden City. Here, the three main administration halls stand atop a three-tiered marble terrace, overlooking an immense plaza. The area encompasses about three hectares, providing enough space to accommodate tens of thousands of subjects who come to pay homage to the emperor. Towering above this space stands the Hall of Supreme Harmony （太和殿）, where the throne of the emperor is located. This hall, measuring 64 by 37 metres, is not only the largest single building in the compound, but also one of the tallest (being approximately the same height as the Meridian Gate). It was the centre of the imperial court. To the north, on the same triple terrace, stand the Hall of Central Harmony （中和殿）and the Hall of Preserving Harmony（保和殿）, both of which are important government function locations.

Further to the north lies the Inner Court（内廷）, which encompasses the three halls that comprised the imperial living quarters. From south to north, these are: Palace of Heavenly Purity（乾清宫）, Hall of Union（交泰殿）and Palace of Earthly Tranquility （坤宁宫）. Smaller than the Outer Court halls, the three halls of the Inner Court were the official residences of the emperor and the empress. The emperor, representing *yang* and the Heaven, would occupy the Palace of Heavenly Purity. The empress, representing *yin* and the Earth, would occupy the Palace of Earthly Tranquility. In between them was the Hall of Union, where *yin* and *yang* mixed to produce harmony. To both west and east sides of the three main halls in the Inner Court are located the Western Palaces（西六宫）and the Eastern Palaces（东六宫）. These palaces were the residences of the imperial consorts. Adjacent to these palaces, at the northernmost limit of the Forbidden City, is the 1.2-hectare Imperial Garden. Its organic design seems to deviate from the rigid symmetry of the rest of the compound. The garden was designed as a place of relaxation for the emperor, with a fanciful arrangement of trees, fish ponds, flower beds, and sculptures.

The design of the Forbidden City, from its overall layout to the smallest details, was meticulously planned to reflect philosophical and religious principles, and above all to symbolize the majesty of imperial power. The color yellow is associated with the emperor, hence almost all roofs in the Forbidden City bear yellow glazed tiles. The main halls of the Outer and Inner courts are all arranged in groups of three—mimicking the shape of the *qian* trigram (乾卦), which represents the Heaven. The residences of the Inner Court are arranged in groups of six—mimicking the shape of the *kun* trigram (坤卦), which represents the Earth. The sloping ridges of building roofs are decorated with a line of statuettes led by an immortal riding a phoenix and followed by an imperial dragon. The number of statuettes represents the status of the building. For instance, a minor building might have three or five while the Hall of Supreme Harmony has ten—the only building in the country to be permitted this honor in imperial times.

(Adapted from Britannica website.)

◆ Cultural Analysis

The design and decoration of imperial palaces are deeply influenced by Confucianism, reflecting several key principles.

(1) Balance and Harmony

Imperial palaces are usually arranged in a strict symmetrical layout along a north-south central axis, symbolizing balance and harmony. The Outer Court, where the emperor rules the country, is located at the front, and the Inner Court, where the emperor and his consorts live, is situated at the back area. This layout of Forbidden City embodies *yin-yang* philosophy precisely.

(2) Architectural Hierarchy

The hierarchy has been emphasized in imperial palaces because they are the symbol of the government and the center of the whole empire. The number of zoomorphic statuettes on the eaves, along with other elements such as layers of terrace, roof styles, and width and depth of building, collectively manifest the hierarchy of each building in the imperial palace complex.

(3) Combination of Aesthetics and Practicality

The zoomorphic animals decorated on the eaves and the colorful paintings on wooden structures exemplify Chinese philosophy's fusion of aesthetics with practicality. For instance, these zoomorphic ornaments not only add a sense of mystery to the palace, but also serve a practical purpose by fastening roofs and keeping water out.

◆ Text Comprehension

1. Judge whether the following statements are true (T) or false (F).

1) The Forbidden City was the former Chinese imperial palace and winter residence of the emperor of China from the beginning of the Ming Dynasty to the end of the Qing Dynasty.

2) The Forbidden City was designed to be the centre of the ancient, walled city of Beijing.

3) The Hall of Supreme Harmony is the largest surviving wooden structure in China.

4) Traditionally, the Forbidden City is divided into two parts: Outer City and Inner City.

5) The number of statuettes on the ridge of roof represents the status of the building in the Forbidden City.

2. Answer the following questions.

1) What was the function of the Forbidden City in ancient China?

2) What are the major halls on the north-south axial line in the Forbidden City?

3) How does the layout of the Forbidden City embody the *yin-yang* theory?

◆ Exercises

1. Label the names of the constructions and the family members who live in the buildings on the map of *siheyuan*.

A. Senior family members	a. Principal house（正房）
B. The elder's wife	b. Eastern wing house（东厢房）
C. Servants	c. Western wing house（西厢房）
D. The eldest son and his wife	d. Side rooms（耳房）
E. The younger son and his wife	e. Opposite house（倒座房）
F. Unmarried daughters	f. Backside building（后罩房）
G. Female servants	g. Screen wall（影壁）

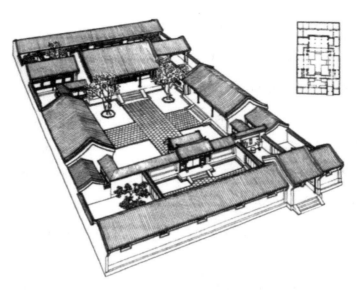

2. Choose the best answer to each of the following questions.

1) Which of the following is NOT true about the courtyard in a *siheyuan*?

   A. The layout of the courtyard symbolizes Chinese morality and Confucian ethics.

   B. The courtyard reflects feudal families' need to maintain separation from the outside world.

   C. The courtyard offers a place to escape from the pressures and corruption of the capital.

   D. The courtyard is an open-air, large living room for the family to talk and relax.

2) What do the designs of *siheyuan* and classical gardens have in common?

   A. They are both cultural symbols of Beijing.

   B. They both follow Confucian tenets of order and hierarchy.

   C. They both reflect people's desire to get close to nature.

   D. They both showcase the aesthetic taste of the owner.

3) Which of the following is true about the four essential elements of Chinese gardens?

   A. Flowers and trees hold symbolic meanings.

B. Architecture occupies a large part of the space.

C. Mountain symbolizes dreams and the infinity of spaces.

D. Water represents lightness and flexibility.

4) Which of the following is NOT true about the function of each hall in the Forbidden City?

   A. The Outer Court was used for ceremonial purposes, while the Inner Court served as the residence.

   B. The Hall of Central Harmony was used for the final stage of the Imperial Examination.

   C. The Palace of Heavenly Purity was the official residence of the emperor, representing *yang*.

   D. The Western Palaces and the Eastern Palaces were the residences of the imperial consorts.

5) How does the design of the Forbidden City symbolize the majesty of imperial power?

   A. The Outer Court is enclosed by the Inner Court.

   B. The main halls of the Outer and Inner courts represent the Heaven.

   C. The residences of the Inner Court represent the Earth.

   D. Almost all the roofs in the Forbidden City bear yellow glazed tiles.

3. Translate the following sentences.

1) 中国的住宅根据人的需要设计和建造，体现了中国社会的伦理价值观。

2) 中国的住宅反映了儒家规范人类社会的思想，而中国的园林遵循了道家与自然和谐相处的原则。

3) 从金碧辉煌的宫殿，到多姿多彩的民居；从诗情画意的亭台楼阁，到奇妙别致的宝塔古桥，千百年来，中国人创造了一个又一个的建筑奇迹。

4) 中国古典园林的另一个特点是巧妙地将诗画艺术和园林风景融为一体。

5) 佛教寺庙记载了古代社会文化的发展，具有重要的历史价值和艺术价值。

4. Discuss the following questions.

1) How does the design of Chinese houses reflect the Confucian idea of regulating human society?

2) How does classical Chinese gardens follow the Taoist principle of living in harmony with nature?

3) Are there any similarities in the architectural design between civilian housing and imperial palaces?

5. Work in groups. Do research on the following flowers or trees in Chinese gardens and fill in the table below. Then report your findings to the class.

Flowers and Trees	Major Characteristics	Symbolic Meaning	Relevant Poetry
Pine			
Bamboo			
Plum Blossom			
Orchid			
Lotus Flower			
Peony			

◆ Extended Readings

Humble Administrator's Garden 拙政园

Listed as a World Heritage Site in 1997 by UNESCO, the Humble Administrator's Garden in the city of Suzhou is one of the top four classical gardens in China [the other three are Summer Palace (颐和园), Chengde Mountain Resort (承德避暑山庄) and Lingering Garden (留园)]. Located in the northeastern corner of Suzhou, the Humble Administrator's Garden was originally built in 1509 by Wang Xianchen (王献臣), a former imperial censor during the Ming Dynasty. From then on, the garden has been changed and reconstructed several times. Repaired and extended in the early 20th century, it is now a key cultural relic under state protection.

The Humble Administrator's Garden is a representation of Jiangnan(江南 , south of the Yangtze River) classical garden, and is now the largest classical garden in Suzhou, covering an area of 5.2 hectares. The whole garden features water scenery, green hills, delicate pavilions and lush flowers and trees to create a poetic picture of classic Jiangnan. It can be divided into three parts: Eastern Garden, Central Garden and Western Garden; each with different characteristics.

The Eastern Garden is the largest of the three, covering an area of 21,000 square meters. Its style is more vivacious than the other two, featuring wild and idyllic scenery. There is only one pond, one hill, two halls and four pavilions in the eastern part. The pond is extremely large and rectangular in shape, with an ear-shaped islet standing in its center, upon which sits the Far Away Looking Pavilion (放眼亭). The rest of the halls and pavilions are spread around the pond and hill in a wild arrangement that exudes a pure simple style.

The Central Garden is the essence of the Humble Administrator's Garden. Covering an area of about 23,000 square meters, the garden features watery scenery with one-third of its total area covered by water. The large pond is surrounded by trees; all architectures and artificial hills by the pond are strewn at random. The overall pattern still retains the simple and vigorous style of the Ming Dynasty. The Drifting Fragrance Hall (远香堂) is the main architecture of Central Garden as well as the whole Humble Administrator's Garden. As a place for receiving guests, it has windows in the four directions, so that guests can see the surrounding scenery in the hall. Other main attractions include Fragrant Isle (香洲), Pavilion in Lotus Breezes (荷风四面庭), Small Canglang

(小沧浪) and Snow-like Fragrant Prunus Mume Pavilion (雪香云蔚庭), etc. Most architectures' names in this garden are related to lotus—a symbol of noble characteristics in China.

Tracing back to the years of Emperor Qianlong of the Qing Dynasty, the original bluestone foundation of the Drifting Fragrance Hall has survived. It usually attracts tourists with its unique architecture, featuring delicate panoptic windows on all four walls. The Drifting Fragrance Hall was built facing the water on three sides. The north platform is rather spacious, acting as a wonderful deck for admiring the beautiful lotus in the pond. When it breezes, the scent of lotus wafts into the hall, giving rise to its name.

Located in the Central Garden as well, Secluded Pavilion of Phoenix Tree and Bamboo Pavilion (梧竹幽居) is an ingeniously designed pavilion which deserves its poetic name. Backing against a corridor and pond, it is flanked by dense phoenix trees and bamboos on either side, creating a strong atmosphere of elegance and quietness. Adding to its charm are four round doorways in surrounding walls that resemble moons hanging over the pavilion. With good daylight, visitors can enjoy amazing framed scenes from different angles of these overlapping circles. On the horizontal tablet of the pavilion, there are four Chinese characters " 梧竹幽居 " written by Wen Zhengming (文徵明), who was a great painter and the designer of the Humble Administrator's Garden.

Covering an area of 8,000 square meters, the Western Garden is centered on a winding pond that connects to the big pond in the Central Garden. The Western Garden is famed for its delicately decorated architectures. The most famous one is the Mandarin Duck Hall (鸳鸯厅) in the southern part. The quadrate hall is divided into the northern part and the southern part by partition board and hangings. The northern part is called the Hall of 36 Pairs of Mandarin Ducks (卅六鸳鸯馆), which is used for admiring lotus in summer. The southern part is called the Hall of 18 Camellias (十八曼陀罗花馆) which is used for appreciating the artificial hills and camellias (山茶) in winter.

The Whom-to-Sit-With Pavilion (与谁同坐轩) is laid out in the Western Garden with an interesting name that derives from a poem of Sushi (苏轼)—"With whom shall I sit? Bright moon, gentle breeze and myself (与谁同坐？明月清风我)." This pavilion shapes like an unfolded fan. Its roofs, window-openings, stone tables, stone benches and horizontal tablets all look like unfolded fans, so it is also called the Fan Pavilion (扇亭). When looking out from the window-opening at the back wall towards the Hat Pavilion (帽亭), which resembles a picture painted on a fan, one must admire the wisdom of the skilled gardener. Whether standing in the pavilion or looking into distance allows one to appreciate endless beauty.

(Adapted from China Discovery website.)

Chinese Temples 中国寺庙

Temples symbolize the long history and rich culture of China, and are regarded as valuable art treasures. There are many different religions in China, such as Buddhism, Christianity and Islam introduced from other regions, as well as Taoism and Confucianism, the native-born religions. Each religion has its own temples or houses of worship. For example, Buddhist temples consist of a temple, pagoda and grotto, which are called *si* (寺), *ta* (塔), and *shiku* (石窟) in Chinese respectively. Taoist architecture is referred to as *gong* (宫), *guan* (观) or *an* (庵) in Chinese. Confucian temples, such as *Kongmiao* (孔庙) and the Temple of Heaven (天坛) are called *miao* (庙), *gong* (宫), or *tan* (坛) in Chinese. An Islamic house of worship is referred to as a Mosque (清真寺).

Chinese temples are well-preserved cultural artifacts from every dynasty. And temple culture has influenced every aspect of Chinese people's life, such as painting, calligraphy, music, sculpture, architecture, temple fairs, folk customs and many others. The following are typical religious architectural styles in China.

The European churches often use exquisite spires (尖顶), arched domed roofs and stained glass windows to convey religious morals. Every detail of the buildings is intended to express the striking contrast between the promised land in Heaven (天国福地) and the miserable world on Earth (悲惨人世). However, in a different way, Chinese temples aim to express the concept of the integration of heaven and humanity, emphasizing that human beings are a part of nature. Following this idea, many temples actively embrace themselves into nature. This explains why many Chinese temples are located in mountains and forests.

Furthermore, like a beautiful picture which is made up of lines of different lengths and thicknesses, Chinese temples use various pillars, beams and arches interlaced with each other to create an architecture complex. Each building does not stand alone; for example, the Hall of Mahavira (大雄宝殿) should stand out against the mountain forests, with side halls highlighting its elegance and artistic conception.

A Chinese Taoist temple is a holy hall where Taoists perform their religious ceremonies. It blends Taoist taste and ideas on construction with traditional Chinese thoughts and traditional construction methods. It thus has formed a unique style among many different types of ancient Chinese architecture. Taoist temples of different scales, from palace-like temples, to simple huts or caves can be found throughout China. The Taoist trinity, known as the San Qing (Three Pure Gods), is worshiped in Taoist temples. They are Jade Pure (玉清), Upper Pure (上清) and Great Pure (太清). The themes of statue and murals in Chinese Taoist temples are familiar to common people and the religious atmosphere is not as intense as in Buddhist temples.

Taoism pursues a prolonged and fruitful life, which is greatly reflected in the decorations used in temple construction. Windows, doors, eaves, and girders of Taoist constructions are carved with Chinese characters meaning blessing (福), longevity (寿) and auspiciousness (吉). Cypress, tortoise, bamboo, kylin (麒麟), dragon and phoenix are symbols of friendship, long life, honor, protection from evilness, and auspicious signs. Similarly, the fan, fish, narcissus, bat and deer represent kindness, abundance, immortality, blessings and prosperity. The images of sun, moon, star and cloud signify glorious sunshine illuminating all things. Taoism has had a significant influence on Chinese folk culture, as many ordinary people have decorated their homes with pictures depicting stories from Taoism, such as "The Eight Immortals Cross the Sea (八仙过海)".

Taoism encourages human beings to live harmoniously with nature. Most Taoist temples are built along a mountain side. Many of them are wooden-framed, which is believed to be beneficial to health.

(Adapted from Travel China Guide website.)

Chapter Nine

Traditional Chinese Festivals
中国节日

Rich in cultural significance and with a lengthy history, traditional Chinese festivals form an important and splendid part of Chinese culture. Most traditional festivals took shape during the Qin Dynasty, which was the first unified and centrally administered dynasty of China. By the Han Dynasty, China had undergone a period of great development, leading to the establishment of major traditional festivals. During the prosperous Tang Dynasty, traditional festivals evolved from their primitive roots of sacrifice, taboo, and mystery to become more entertaining. As a result, festive occasions became livelier and more exciting, giving rise to an array of folk customs. While some festivals and customs are still celebrated today, others have faded over time.

9.1　The Spring Festival

The Chinese New Year is now popularly known as the Spring Festival because it starts from the Start of Spring (立春). The celebration was traditionally highlighted with a religious ceremony in honor of Heaven and Earth (天地), the gods of the household and the family ancestors. Offering sacrifices to ancestors, the most vital ritual, united the living members with those who had passed away. Departed relatives were remembered with great respect for their role in laying the foundations for the fortune and the glory of the family.

One legend about the origin of the Spring Festival goes that the beast *Nian* (年兽) had a very big mouth that could swallow many people in one bite. People were very scared. One day, an old man came to their rescue, offering to subdue *Nian*. To *Nian* he said, "I have heard that you are very capable, but can you swallow other beasts of prey instead of people who are by no means your worthy opponents?" With the guidance of the old man, it did swallow many of the beasts that also harassed people and their domestic animals from time to time. After that, the old man disappeared while riding on the back of *Nian*. He turned out to be an immortal god. Now that *Nian* was gone and other beasts of prey were also scared into forests, people began to enjoy their peaceful life. Before leaving, the old man told people to put up red paper decorations on their windows and doors at the end of each year to scare away *Nian* in case it sneaked back again, as red was the color that frightened the beast the most.

From then on, the tradition of observing the conquest of *Nian* has been carried on from generation to generation. The term " 过年 ", which originally meant "survive the year", has evolved into today's "celebrate the (New) Year". This is because the word "*guo*（过）" in Chinese carries both the meanings of "pass-over" and "observe". Actually, the Chinese character 年 (*nian*) itself means that crops are ready to be harvested. It is a combination of two single characters, "grains"（禾）and "thousand"（千）, so the blend of the two characters（秊）means a very rich harvest. In the old days, after a year's hard work, people would prepare liquor and delicious food for a rich feast to celebrate the year's harvest and the arrival of a new year. Therefore, this day was considered the most important and happiest day in the year.

More food is consumed during the New Year celebrations than at any other time of the year. A large amount of traditional food is prepared for family and friends, as well as for those who have passed away. On New Year's Day, the Chinese family enjoy dishes with symbolic meanings, such as a whole fish to represent togetherness and abundance, and a chicken with its head and feet to symbolize completeness and chances. The uncut, long noodles are a typical dish often enjoyed during the festival, symbolizing a wish for a long and prosperous life. In south China, one of the favorite and most typical dishes is *niangao* （年糕）, a sweet steamed glutinous rice（糯米）pudding. However, in the north, steamed-wheat bread（馒头）and small meat dumplings are preferred. The tremendous amount of food prepared at this time symbolizes abundance and wealth for the household.

A few days before the New Year, every corner of the house must be swept and cleaned. This tradition is believed to help wipe away the old and evil spirits. On New Year's Eve, decorations like red paper-cuttings, lanterns, or spring couplets are put up. Written in black ink on large vertical scrolls of red paper, spring couplets are put up on door frames, windows, or other gateways. These couplets mainly contain short poems written in classical Chinese, which express good wishes for the family in the coming New Year. Lucky money（压岁钱）put in the red envelopes（红包）is often given to the younger generation by adults or elders, symbolizing the warding off or suppression of evil. On the covers of the red envelopes are usually icons representing what year it belongs to or common greetings like "Happy New Year（新年快乐）" and "Wish everything goes well for you（吉祥如意）".

Dragon dances and lion dances are very popular and commonly performed during the Chinese New Year. From the first day of the New Year to the 15th day of the first lunar month, streets are filled with these traditional performances. They are performed by a group of people, some of whom manage the "dragon" and "lion", while others beat the drums. It is believed that the loud sound created by the drums, combined with the presence of the dragon and lion, serves to scare away evil spirits.

(Adapted from *China Daily* and China Culture Tour websites.)

◆ Cultural Analysis

The Spring Festival is the oldest traditional festival for Chinese people, which originated from the primitive sacrifice. It is a great occasion for family reunions, similar to Christmas in the West when family members and relatives get together to maintain harmonious relationships.

(1) Seasonal Characteristics

The time of celebration falls during the deep winter, when all agricultural crops have disappeared from the earth. It is a time when primitive people offered sacrifices to the supernatural power—Heaven asking for the return of crops and vitality. This period serves as both a preparing time of agriculture and a time following the harvest.

(2) Family-Oriented Society

The Spring Festival is a festival that strengthens the bond among family members, which echoes the core values of traditional Chinese culture since family has always been attached importance to in China. All family members come back home during the Spring Festival to express sincere good wishes and communicate with each other to maintain good relationships through visiting, exchanging auspicious words, sharing delicious food and giving red envelopes, etc.

◆ Text Comprehension

1. Judge whether the following statements are true (T) or false (F).

1) The Chinese New Year is known as the Spring Festival because it starts from the Start of Spring.

2) The term "过年", which originally meant "survive the year", has evolved into today's "celebrate the (New) Year". This is because the word "*guo*" in Chinese having both the meaning of "pass-over" and "observe".

3) During the Spring Festival, a chicken must be presented with its head and feet to symbolize completeness, and noodles should be uncut to represent long life.

4) Red envelopes are used to put money in, known as lucky money, symbolizing the warding off or suppression of evil.

5) The ancient Chinese believed that the dragon and lion could scare away evil spirits.

2. Answer the following questions.

1) What is the origin of the Spring Festival ?

2) How do people usually celebrate the Spring Festival and why?

3) Why do Chinese people prepare more food during the Spring Festival than on usual days?

9.2　The Qingming Festival

The Qingming Festival, also called Tomb Sweeping Day, is a traditional Chinese festival and an important day for most people to sweep tombs and commemorate their ancestors. It usually falls on April 4th or 5th. On May 20th, 2006, the festival was listed as one of the first national intangible cultural heritage events.

Qingming is one of the twenty-four solar terms in the traditional Chinese solar calendar. Originally, it had no connection with tomb sweeping or showing respect to ancestors; instead, it was associated with climate and nature. In Chinese, "Qingming" means "clearness and brightness", indicating the period in early April when the weather becomes noticeably warmer and brighter, and nature awakens in northern and central China (this occurs earlier in southern China). During this time, people begin to wear lighter clothing and walk outdoors to savor the burgeoning spring.

The tradition of honoring ancestors in China has been practiced since ancient times, as the Chinese people believed that the spirits of their deceased ancestors watched over the family. To keep them happy, offerings of food and burning paper ghost money were made, with the belief that this would bring prosperity to the family through good harvests and more children. For a long time, ancient Chinese visited the tombs of their ancestors throughout the year. During the Tang Dynasty, the practice gradually became associated with the Qingming Festival, which fell on the day after Hanshi Festival (寒食节). On this day, no fire or smoke was allowed and people only ate cold food. The Qingming Festival then became a designated time for people to sweep tombs and show respect for their deceased ancestors before focusing on growing crops.

The legendary story of the Hanshi Festival is usually associated with Jie Zitui (介子推), a loyal defender of Duke Wen of Jin (晋文公). In his earlier years, he was known as Chong'er (重耳), a prince in exile. One day in 655 BC, Jie Zitui secretly cut a piece of flesh from his thigh and cooked it into a meat soup to serve chong'er, which moved the prince so much that he promised to reward him one day. Nineteen years later, Prince Chong'er returned to his kingdom and took power as Duke Wen of Jin. However, he forgot Jie Zitui when he greatly rewarded and honored all of his followers. It was only when others mentioned Jie Zitui that Duke Wen of Jin remembered him and felt ashamed.

Then, the duke decided to visit Jie Zitui personally and confer a title on him. Jie refused to meet the prince and hid on a nearby mountain with his aged mother. Duke Wen of Jin set fire to the mountain to force Jie Zitui out of hiding. Tragically, three days later, the duke and his people found two dead bodies—those of Jie Zitui and his mother—in a cave under a willow tree on the mountain. In honor of Jie Zitui, a man who never sought fame and profit, Duke Wen of Jin respectfully buried him and his mother, held a memorial ceremony for their tomb, and ordered his subjects not to use fire and only to eat cold food on that day.

There are various activities for the Qingming Festival. The most popular ones include sweeping and repairing tombs, going on spring outings, flying kites, and putting willow branches on gates.

Tomb sweeping is the most important custom of the Qingming Festival. People commemorate and show respect to their ancestors by visiting their graves, offering food, tea or wine, burning incense, burning or offering joss paper (representing money), etc. They sweep the tombs, remove weeds, and add fresh soil to the graves. They may stick willow branches, flowers, or artificial plants on the tomb. They pray before their ancestors' graves in hope of receiving blessings for their families. However, the custom has been greatly simplified today, especially in cities where many people simply put flowers at their dead relatives' tombs.

During the Qingming Festival, some people wear soft willow branches and place them on gates and front doors. It is believed that this custom helps ward off wandering evil spirits during the Qingming Festival. This custom is believed to have originated from Buddhist influence. Traditional depictions of the Goddess of Mercy (观音菩萨) often portray her seated on a lotus flower, with a willow branch placed in a vase of water at her side, which she used to ward off demons.

The Qingming Festival is a good time to feel the breath of spring. It is also called the *Taqing* (踏青) Festival because it typically occurs shortly before everything turns green in the north and during the peak of the spring flower season in the south. It marks the beginning of spring, when people spend more time outside as the weather warms up.

Different places have different foods for the Qingming Festival. Traditional Qingming festival foods include *qingtuan* (青团), peach blossom porridge, crispy cakes, river snails (田螺), and eggs. These foods are usually prepared a day or two before the arrival of the Qingming Festival, so people can enjoy them during the holidays. *qingtuan* is a popular Qingming food made of glutinous rice powder and green vegetable juice, stuffed with sweet bean paste. They are jade-green in color, glutinous in taste, and sweet in aroma.

(Adapted from China High Lights website.)

✦ Cultural Analysis

The Qingming Festival, a traditional festival with a history spanning over 2,500 years, is an occasion of unique characteristics, combining mournful tributes to the deceased with the joyful celebrations of spring outings.

(1) Seasonal Characteristics

The Qingming Festival is one of the 24 solar terms in traditional Chinese lunar calendar. People often engage in a sport to ward off the cold and anticipate the arrival of spring. From that date on, temperature begins to rise and rainfall increases, indicating that it is a crucial time for plowing and sowing in the spring. Therefore, the festival has a close relationship with agriculture.

(2) Chinese Cosmology

In ancient times, people viewed man and nature as a holistic system; therefore, they would embrace nature and feel its rhythm, especially during the turning points of each season. This is why people enjoy going on spring outings to appreciate the beauty of nature.

(3) Chinese Moral Value

Respecting and honoring those who are older than you is an important aspect of traditional Chinese moral values. This attitude extends towards those who have passed away. It reinforces filial piety in the Chinese community by encouraging them to make special efforts to visit graves, columbaria or temples to pay their respects.

◆ Text Comprehension

1. Judge whether the following statements are true (T) or false (F).

1) The origin of the name *Qingming* was related to climate and nature in this season. Originally, it wasn't related to tomb sweeping or showing respect to ancestors.

2) Jie Zitui, who lived in the Warring States Period helped Chong'er a lot in dealing with political affairs.

3) People show respect to their ancestors by visiting their graves. At the same time, they pray before their ancestors' graves and beseech them to bless their families.

4) The Qingming Festival is also called the Taqing Festival. *Taqing* means a spring outing when people go out and enjoy the spring blossoms.

5) The Qingming Festival is an occasion that integrates moments of mourning with periods of joyful celebration.

2. Answer the following questions.

1) What are the characteristics of the Qingming day in terms of climate and weather?

2) What did Chong'er do to Jie Zitui? What do you think of the Duke Chong'er?

3) What world views and moral values are reflected in the Qingming Festival?

9.3　The Dragon Boat Festival

The Dragon Boat Festival, also called the Double Fifth Festival, is celebrated on the 5th day of the 5th month of the Chinese lunar calendar.

One possible explanation for the origins of the festival is linked to superstitions about the date on which it falls. Traditionally, the fifth lunar month was considered to be an unlucky time. In certain regions of China, people believed that during this month, the dreaded five poisonous animals started to come out of their winter hiding places. These animals were referred to as *wudu*（五毒）including centipedes, poisonous snakes, scorpions, lizards and toads. To safeguard themselves during this time, ancient people practiced rituals such as poking pictures of the five poisonous animals with pins, which was believed to render their real-life counterparts harmless.

In addition to the threat posed by the reemergence of poisonous animals, it was also believed that people were more prone to falling ill around this time. Over the years, various traditions emerged to help ensure that people were protected from illness and bad luck during the dreaded Double Fifth. One such tradition that has survived to today is the custom of hanging wormwood and calamus branches on one's door to ward off evil spirits.

There are some legends related to the origin of the festival, among which the most widely circulated is the story of Qu Yuan—a patriotic poet and loyal official during the Warring States Period. Qu Yuan was the top adviser to the Kingdom of Chu, and dedicated his whole life to assisting the King in strengthening the state. He advised the King to ally with the State of Qi to fight against the powerful State of Qin. However, he was slandered by jealous officials and accused of treason, and the King dismissed and exiled him. During his exile, the Qin State took the capital of Chu. On hearing of the defeat, Qu Yuan in great despair committed suicide by drowning himself in the Miluo River on the 5th day of the 5th lunar month.

When the local people heard of Qu Yuan's death, they were very sad. They rowed out on the river to search for his body but were unable to find him. To preserve his body, the locals paddled their boats up and down the river, hitting the water with their paddles and beating drums to scare away evil spirits. They threw lumps of rice into the river to feed the fish, so that they would not eat Qu Yuan's body. An old Chinese doctor poured realgar wine into the river to poison monsters and protect Qu Yuan. Gradually, these commemorations evolved into festival customs, such as dragon boat racing, eating *zongzi*, and drinking realgar wine.

Dragon boat racing is one of the popular activities in the Dragon Boat Festival. A dragon boat is long and narrow with a carved dragon head at the prow of the boat. Although the size of the boats and their crews may vary, in most cases, a crew consists of 20 paddlers who sit side-by-side in pairs facing the bow. There is also a drummer who sits at the bow of the boat, facing the paddlers. During a race, the drummer leads the paddlers by rhythmically beating on a drum. Furthermore, there is a steerer who sits at the back of the boat and helps steer it using a long oar.

Official races organized by the International Dragon Boat Federation are held in many parts of the world. In China, there are also various informal races organized by local villages and communities. Many of these informal races are held in communities where people have a close relationship with nearby bodies of water, and most families have their own boats. In these settings, instead of watching from the bank, villagers sometimes row their family boats out into the river to get a closer look at the dragon boats during the race.

It is a tradition for the Chinese to eat *zongzi* during the Dragon Boat Festival. *Zongzi* is usually a pyramid-shaped dumping made of glutinous rice wrapped in bamboo or reed leaves. People in the north enjoy *zongzi* with dates, while those in the south prefer mixed ingredients, such as meat, sausage, and eggs. This custom is very popular not only in China but also in Korea, Japan, and other countries in Southeast Asia.

It is believed that many contagious diseases and plagues originate in the fifth lunar month during the Dragon Boat Festival. Chinese people, especially children, make fragrance bags to wear around their necks to avoid catching these contagious diseases and to keep evil spirits away. Fragrance bags are made from a variety of sewn bags and contain the powders of calamus, wormwood, realgar, and other fragrant items.

During the Dragon Boat Festival, people often put calamus and wormwood leaves on their doors and windows to repel insects, flies, fleas, and moths from their houses. Hanging these plants on doors or windows is also believed to dispel evil, and bring health to the family, especially the kids.

(Adapted from China Highlights and CLI websites.)

◆ Cultural Analysis

The Dragon Boat Festival may have originated from the early totem worship and has been associated with relieving the symptoms of illness, preventing epidemic and warding off evil spirits due to the seasonal characteristics in China. Additionally, it is also a way to show respect for Qu Yuan and convey the national beliefs and values.

(1) Seasonal Characteristics

The festival is held close to the Summer Solstice (夏至), a time when pests, poisonous animals, and germs become active. As a result, people take measures to prevent diseases and epidemics. Over time, the practice of warding off evil spirits has also been incorporated into the festival's traditions.

(2) Totem Worship

The boats used for racing during the festival are intricately crafted into the awe-inspiring shape of dragons, a design deeply rooted in ancient totemic worship. This reflects the significance of the dragon as a totem in Chinese culture.

(3) National Values

Qu Yuan is commemorated on this day for his beautiful literary works, outstanding political ability and patriotism, which are deeply valued by the Chinese people. Therefore, it reflects the national values of patriotism and respect for outstanding achievements in China.

◆ Text Comprehension

1. Judge whether the following statements are true (T) or false (F).

1) Traditionally, the fifth lunar month was considered to be an unlucky time.

2) According to legendary stories, when Qu Yuan got the news that the Qin State took the capital of Chu, he, in great despair, committed suicide by drowning himself in the Yangtze River on the 5th day of the 5th lunar month.

3) There is a drummer who sits at the stern of the boat facing the paddlers.

4) In some informal races organized by local villages and communities, villagers sometimes row their family boats out into the river so that they can get a closer look at the dragon boats during the race.

5) During the fifth lunar month, Chinese people may make fragrance bags and hang them on their necks.

2. Answer the following questions.

1) What did ancient Chinese think of the fifth month? What did they usually do?

2) How do Chinese people celebrate the Dragon Boat Festival? Please list some detailed activities.

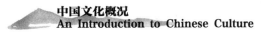

3) What the differences between the international dragon boat race and those held by local villages?

◆ Exercises

1. Match the traditional foods and activities with the festivals.

Festivals	Foods	Activities
1) The Spring Festival	A) *Niangao*	a) Tomb sweeping
	B) *Zongzi*	b) House sweeping and cleaning
	C) Peach blossom porridge	c) Spring outing
	D) Whole fish	d) Putting up spring couplets
2) The Qingming Festival	E) Uncut noodles	e) Dragon boat racing
	F) *Qingtuan*	f) Dragon dances and lion dances
		g) Putting willow branches on gates
3) The Dragon Boat Festival		h) Hanging calamus and wormwood leaves
		i) Giving red envelopes
		j) Wearing fragrance bags

2. Choose the best answer to each of the following questions.

1) Traditional Chinese festivals took shape during the _____ Dynasty and became more entertaining during the _____ Dynasty. (Multiple choice question)

A. Spring and Autumn Period

B. Qin Dynasty

C. Han Dynasty

D. Tang Dynasty

2) Traditional New Year foods include all the following EXCEPT _____.

A. small meat dumplings

B. chicken feet

C. a whole fish

D. sweet steamed glutinous rice

3) The traditional Chinese Hanshi Festival _____.

   A. was the day after Tomb Sweeping Day

   B. was declared to commemorate Duke Wen of Jin

   C. featured using fire to cook food in history

   D. was part of the Qingming Festival nowadays

4) What is the common practice during both the Spring Festival and the Qingming Festival?

   A. Burning or offering joss paper.

   B. Paying homage to ancestors.

   C. Wearing fragrance bags.

   D. Putting up red paper decorations.

5) What did the locals do to preserve Qu Yuan's body?

   A. Putting willow branches on the banks of the river.

   B. Putting calamus and wormwood leaves on their boats.

   C. Throwing lumps of rice into the river.

   D. Beating on a drum at the bow of the boat.

3. Translate the following sentences.

1) 人们在春节贴春联，在元宵节放烟花。

2) 寒食节的由来，是晋文公重耳为了纪念忠臣介子推。

3) 在清明节扫墓、祭祀祖先是遵守孝道的典范。

4) 挂艾草和佩香囊是为了辟邪驱毒。

5) 赛龙舟不仅限于端午节，龙舟文化活动已经扩展至世界很多地方，甚至演变为重要的赛事。

4. Discussing the following questions.

1) How can the Spring Festival help strengthen family bonds? Can you provide some examples of celebratory activities that contribute to this?

2) What aspects of Chinese culture are reflected in the traditions of the Qingming Festival? Are there any notable literary and artistic works about the Qingming Festival?

3) Please compare traditional Chinese festivals and Western festivals, and identify the similarities and differences between these two systems of celebrations.

5. Form groups of three or four. Do research on the following traditional Chinese festivals and fill in the table below. Then report your findings to the class.

Festivals	Origins	Common Practices	Spirit & Emotion Conveyed	Relevant Poems
The Lantern Festival				
The Double Seventh Festival				
The Mid-Autumn Festival				
The Double Ninth Festival				

◆ Extended Readings

The 24 Solar Terms 二十四节气

The 24 Solar Terms were developed by farmers in ancient China through observation of the sun's annual motion. These terms are used to mark the changing seasons, weather patterns, and natural variations. The year is divided into 24 equal periods providing a time frame for farmers to plan crop production and farming, as well as daily life and festivals. In 2016, the Twenty-Four Solar Terms were listed on the *Representative List of the Intangible Cultural Heritage of Humanity* by UNESCO (联合国教科文组织《人类非物质文化遗产代表作名录》).

As early as the Spring and Autumn Period, the Chinese established two major solar terms: Summer Solstice and Winter Solstice, which mean "the sun is at the northernmost point" and "the sun is at the southernmost point" respectively. Near the end of the Warring States Period, they distinguished the four seasons: Start of Spring and Spring Equinox; Start of Summer and Summer Solstice; Start of Autumn and Autumnal Equinox; Start of Winter and Winter Solstice. Eight key solar terms were established according to the moving positions of the sun and the moon at the beginning and middle of a month, as well as the climate and natural phenomena. During the Western Han Dynasty, the 24 solar terms were completed and officially designated; most of them refer to the climate of Xi'an, the capital at that time.

The 24 Solar Terms are divided based on the sun's annual motion in the ecliptic plane (黄道面 , the earth's orbit around the sun). They are an integral part of the traditional Chinese calendar zodiac. The calendar takes into account the longest and shortest days of the year, as well as the two days when the length of the day is the same as the night. The significant seasonal changes are marked by the Spring Equinox, Summer Solstice, Autumn Equinox, and Winter Solstice.

Seasons	Solar Terms	Implications
Spring	Start of Spring 立春	It marks the beginning of spring.
	Rain Water 雨水	Rainfall increases from then on.
	Awakening of Insects 惊蛰	Hibernating insects start to awaken with spring thunder.
	Spring Equinox 春分	The mid-spring, when day and night are approximately equal in length.

(Continued)

Seasons	Solar Terms	Implications
Spring	Qingming 清明	It is warm and bright (when not raining) and vegetation turns green.
	Grain Rain 谷雨	Rainfall increases greatly and helps the growth of grain.
Summer	Start of Summer 立夏	It marks the beginning of summer.
	Grain Buds 小满	Grain gets plump but is not yet ripe.
	Grain in Ear 芒种	Grain grows ripe and summer farming begins.
	Summer Solstice 夏至	The longest day and the shortest night of the year.
	Minor Heat 小暑	The weather becomes noticeably hotter.
	Major Heat 大暑	The hottest time of the year, when rainfall is the greatest.
Autumn	Start of Autumn 立秋	It marks the beginning of autumn.
	End of Heat 处暑	It marks the end of hot summer days.
	White Dew 白露	Temperatures begin to drop and it turns quite cool.
	Autumn Equinox 秋分	The mid-autumn, when day and night are approximately equal in length again.
	Cold Dew 寒露	It turns a bit cold.
	Frost's Descent 霜降	It turns colder and frost appears.
Winter	Start of Winter 立冬	It marks the beginning of winter.
	Minor Snow 小雪	It starts to snow.
	Major Snow 大雪	The snow becomes heavy.
	Winter Solstice 冬至	The shortest day and the longest night of the year.
	Minor Cold 小寒	The beginning of the coldest days of the year.
	Major Cold 大寒	The coldest time of the year.

The Solar Terms are given meaningful titles. Some of them reflect the changes of seasons, such as Start of Spring, Start of Summer, Start of Autumn, and Start of Winter; some indicate the changing weather conditions like Rain Water, Grain Rain, White Dew, and Cold Dew; some indicate changes in temperature such as Minor Heat, Major Heat, End of Heat, Minor Cold and Major Cold. Some embody the recurring natural phenomena like Awakening of Insects, Qing Ming, and Grain Buds.

Originating in the Yellow River Valley, the Solar Terms reflect the knowledge about climate changes acquired by the Chinese ancestors during their farming activities. Over the years, the Solar Terms have played an important role in China's agricultural and animal husbandry production.

(Adapted from China Travel website.)

The Chinese Zodiac

The Chinese zodiac, known as *sheng xiao* (生肖) or *shu xiang* (属相), features 12 animal signs in the following order: Rat, Ox, Tiger, Rabbit, Dragon, Snake, Horse, Goat, Monkey, Rooster, Dog and Pig. With its origins in ancient zoolatry and a history of more than 2,000 years, the 12 Chinese zodiac animals form a cycle that represents years in China and hold significant importance in Chinese culture.

Chinese zodiac is an imaginary belief based on the zodiac animals' temperament, and combines traditional Chinese religions, philosophy, astrology, and numerology (命理学). In ancient times, it was believed to decide people's destiny, control a year's harvest and even influence the fortune of the whole nation. Nowadays, Chinese people still believe that zodiac signs affect their personality, ideas, behavior, fortune, and marriage compatibility to some extent.

The excavated ancient bamboo books have proved the existence of the Chinese zodiac before the Qin Dynasty, and the complete 12 animals' cycle was established before or during the Eastern Han Dynasty. The popular totem saying is related to animal worship.

According to an ancient folk story called "Great Race", the Jade Emperor decreed that each year on the calendar would be named after an animal in the order they reached where he was.

To get there, the animals had to cross a river. The Cat and the Rat decided that the best and fastest way was to hop on the back of the Ox. The Ox, kindhearted and naive, agreed to carry them both across. As they were about to reach the other side, the Rat pushed the Cat into the water, and then jumped off the Ox, rushing to the Jade Emperor. It was named as the first animal of the zodiac calendar. The Ox had to settle in the second place. The third one to come was the Tiger. Even though it was strong and powerful, it struggled against strong currents pushing him downstream.

Next arrived Rabbit, explaining how it crossed the river by jumping from one stone to another in a nimble fashion. Halfway through, it almost lost the race, but it was lucky enough to grab hold of a floating log that washed it ashore. In fifth place came the flying

Dragon. The Jade Emperor wondered why such a swift airborne creature did not come in first. The Dragon explained that it had to stop at a village and brought rain for all the people, so it was held back. Then, on its way to the finish line, it saw the helpless Rabbit clinging onto a log. In an act of kindness, the Dragon gave a puff of breath to help the poor creature land on the shore. The Jade Emperor was astonished by the Dragon's good nature, and thus named it as the fifth animal.

Meanwhile, the Horse arrived. The Snake, however, was hiding in the Horse's hooves, and its sudden appearance frightened the Horse and made it fall back. As a result, the Snake ended up in sixth place while the Horse came in seventh. The Goat, Monkey, and Rooster worked as a team to reach the other side. The Rooster found a raft, and the Monkey and the Goat tugged and pulled, trying to get all the weeds out of the way. The Jade Emperor was pleased with their teamwork and decided to name the Goat as the eighth animal followed by the Monkey and then the Rooster. The eleventh animal placed in the zodiac cycle was the Dog. Although it was a strong swimmer and runner, it wasted time playing in water and almost did not finish the race.

Just when the Jade Emperor was about to end the race, an "oink" sound was heard: it was the Pig. The Pig felt hungry in the middle of the race, so it stopped to eat and then fell asleep. It finished the race in twelfth place, becoming the last animal to arrive. The cat eventually drowned and failed to be in the zodiac. It is believed that this is why cats always hunt rats and also hate water.

(Adapted from Travel China Guide and Wikipedia websites.)

Chapter Ten

Chinese Food and Drinks
中国饮食

China's long history, vast territory and rich culture have given rise to the distinctive art of Chinese cuisine. Over thousands of years of creative and accumulative efforts, the selection of ingredients, cooking techniques and serving styles have been developed to the highest level and Chinese cuisine has become increasingly popular among more and more overseas gourmets. Originating from different regions and ethnic groups of China, Chinese cuisine can be divided into many categories, such as the eight famous Chinese cuisines, local snacks, ethnic foods, and so on. Rooted in the traditional Chinese philosophy, Chinese food represents the harmony and balance of nature. It not only satisfies gourmets' appetites, but also keeps them healthy.

10.1　Chinese Food Culture

Chinese food serves as an excellent manifestation of culinary culture, encompassing diverse elements such as food resources, cooking techniques, dietary therapy, and dining utensils. Savoring delicious Chinese dishes is not merely a sensory pleasure but also a profound exploration into the philosophical principles that guide the Chinese way of life.

"The masses regard food as their heaven (民以食为天)." This saying vividly illustrates that Chinese cuisine is of great significance in the life of the Chinese people. Whenever a full month has passed since a baby was born, or when there is a birthday, wedding, New Year's Eve, or other major festivals, a banquet is held to celebrate. When someone passes away, a meal is also arranged after the funeral as an expression of gratitude to those who attended the funeral. The significance of these banquets and meals lies in providing an opportunity for people to come together and share both happiness and sadness in life. As a result, there is always a warm atmosphere on these occasions that reflects harmonious relationships within families and communities.

The foods in a meal are divided into *fan* (饭 staple food) and *cai* (菜 accompanying dishes). The staple food mainly refers to a carbohydrate or starch—typically rice, noodles or steamed buns, and the accompanying dishes include vegetables, fish, meat, or other items.

Yin and *yang* principles are also applied in Chinese food. Most vegetables and fruits are considered *yin* foods, which are generally moist or soft and have a cooling effect, nurturing the feminine aspect of our nature. *Yang* foods—such as fried, spicy dishes, or those with red meat—are warming and nourish the masculine side of our nature. A well-balanced meal should not only harmonize a variety of tastes, but also provide a balance between cooling and warming foods.

Chinese dishes focus on color, aroma, taste, and presentation. Each element is essential in making a good dish. Color refers to the harmonious blending of ingredients and seasonings, resulting in a visually pleasing appearance. Aroma refers to the smell of the dish, which is intended to stimulate the appetite. The aroma of Chinese dishes is achieved by using the right spices, such as dried mushrooms, sesame oil, pepper, cinnamon (桂皮), star anise (八角茴香), rice wine, chili pepper, garlic, fresh ginger, and scallions. Taste is the essence of Chinese cuisine and is achieved through the perfect balance of ingredients and seasonings like soy sauce, salt, sugar, vinegar, and spicy peppers which create flavors that are salty, sweet, sour or hot. It's important to preserve the natural taste and juices of food while cooking each dish. In addition to taste, the beauty of Chinese cuisine also lies in its presentation with finely cut ingredients, colorful combinations, and decorative vegetable sculptures on plates creating an elegant dining experience. Only when all four elements—color, aroma, taste, and presentation—come together can a dish be considered well-made and a true work of art.

Therefore, a Chinese dish is usually made up of more than one ingredient. This is because when a single item is cooked on its own, it often lacks contrast and therefore harmony. A dish's distinctive appearance, taste, and flavor do not rely on the exact number of ingredients or any single item in most cases. To achieve the perfect combination of color, aroma and taste, cooks usually pay great attention to selecting and matching the ingredients.

According to the saying in *Huangdi Neijing* (《黄帝内经》, *Yellow Emperor's Internal Canon of Medicine*), "The five grains provide nourishment. The five fruits provide support. The five domestic animals provide enrichment. The five vegetables provide filling." All grain crops serve as the staple food that provides basic nutrition for the body and is necessary for human health. But that is not enough; people should eat different kinds of fruits, meats and vegetables. Only by consuming a balanced diet can we be healthy and energetic. Making good use of the medicinal properties of food can turn a tasty dish into effective medication, which is known as therapy by diet. For example, pear, persimmon, olive, turnip and white jelly fungus are among the best foods for moistening the lungs.

(Adapted from Cchatty website.)

◆ Cultural Analysis

In China, food is an integral part of daily life, strongly influenced by Taoism and Confucianism. The Taoist school has developed the hygienic and nutritional science of food, while Confucianism emphasizes the art of cooking and the importance of people eating together.

(1) Food and Bond

Eating is not just about filling the stomach and enjoying delicious food; it also serves as a powerful medium for communication, offering opportunities to connect and engage with others. Through shared meals, we strengthen the bonds between family members, fostering deeper understanding and intimacy. Similarly, communal or workplace dining experiences enhance cohesion among colleagues, creating a sense of unity and belonging within communities or organizations.

(2) Food and Harmony

The divisions between *fan* and *cai*, *yin* and *yang* show the principle of balance and harmony. The cuisine philosophy of "five tastes in harmony (五味调和)" pursued by Chinese people emphasizes the harmonious balance of different colors, aroma, flavors, shapes and textures through varying the ingredients, cutting techniques, seasonings and cooking methods.

(3) Food and Health

Chinese people believe that they should not overindulge in certain foods and neglect others. Traditional Chinese cuisine uses more plant-based ingredients than meat, with grains as the staple food and other supplements. In this sense, Chinese cuisine is closely related to health, based on the philosophy that food and medicine have similar effects on the body in preventing and curing diseases.

◆ Text Comprehension

1. Judge whether the following statements are true (T) or false (F).

1) Enjoying delicious Chinese dishes is a treat for the tongue and an exploration of Chinese culinary culture and living philosophy.

2) The significance of banquets and meals lies in providing an opportunity for people to get together and share the happiness and sadness in life.

3) The staple mainly refers to a carbohydrate or starch—typically meats and vegetables.

4) A Chinese dish is usually made up of more than one ingredient in order to achieve a balance of contrast and harmony.

5) According to the *Huangdi Neijing*, all grain crops, serving as staple foods, provide enough nutrition for the body.

2. Answer the following questions.

1) How do Chinese usually evaluate a good dish?

2) How do Chinese maintain balance in their food?

3) What kind of meal is beneficial for health according to *Huangdi Neijing*?

10.2   Chinese Cuisine

There is a variety of cooking styles in China, each with its own distinct characteristics influenced by factors such as resource availability, climate, geography, history, cooking techniques and lifestyle. Despite these differences, Chinese cuisine can be broadly classified into four regional cuisines according to their distinct tastes and local characteristics: Shandong Cuisine (鲁菜), Huaiyang Cuisine (淮扬菜), Sichuan Cuisine (川菜) and Guangdong Cuisine (粤菜). These represent the northern school, eastern school, western school and southern school of Chinese cuisine respectively.

Shandong Cuisine

The Qi State, located in present-day Shandong Province, had a rich culinary history and advanced cooking techniques. These factors contributed to the development of Shandong Cuisine, which is considered China's earliest local cuisine. Its cooking tradition has greatly influenced the style of cuisine in the surrounding regions, especially to the north in Beijing and northeastern China. Accordingly, most of the documented early cuisine comes from the Shandong Province.

Shandong Cuisine is known for its wide variety of seafood and vegetable dishes, thanks to the abundant fresh water resources along the coast. The chefs have a special love for cooking meat and vegetables in a wok over a large, hot flame. They heat the oil to an extremely high temperature and quickly fry the ingredients, locking in their flavors without making them oily. Shandong people enjoy using spices from the onion family, such as green onions and garlic, in many of their dishes. Ginger is also commonly used, along with a touch of red pepper, although not as heavily as in Sichuan Cuisine. The use of spice is meant to enhance the flavors of the food. Vinegar and salt are both heavily used in Shandong Cuisine.

Huaiyang Cuisine

The embryonic form of Huaiyang (Jiangsu) Cuisine emerged after the Chu people unified the southeast of China and possessed abundant food ingredients. Blessed with the abundance of the Yangtze River and its tributaries, a subtropical climate, fertile soil and a coastline, the eastern area was known as "a land of fish and rice" in China. Therefore, Jiangsu Province boasts a grand variety of food ingredients, and the typical raw materials are fresh and live aquatic products. The flavor of Huaiyang Cuisine stresses freshness, exquisite workmanship, elegant presentation, and rich cultural traits.

Basic cooking techniques include stewing, braising, quick-frying, and stir-frying. Another popular cooking style exported to the rest of the world is red-stewing, in which meat is simmered slowly in dark soy sauce, sugar and spices. It's also worth noting that the Chinese vegetarian cuisine in this region has reached its peak due to both access to fresh ingredients and generations of specialized chefs. Typical Huaiyang dishes include deep-fried mandarin fish in sweet and sour sauce, boiled salted duck, and braised tortoise among many others.

Sichuan Cuisine

Sichuan Province, located in the southwest of China is known for its mild climate, fertile land and abundant resources. It is a basin surrounded by mountains, and the local cuisine features ingredients sourced from the mountains and rivers, resulting in delicious dishes. The Qin State conquered the Ba and Shu States, introducing the food culture of the Central Plains to these regions. One contributing factor to the exceptional cooking here is the presence of skillful chefs who were appointed as government officials by emperors during the Yuan, Ming and Qing dynasties. These chefs utilized indigenous ingredients to develop a cuisine that reflects the climatic and geographic characteristics of Sichuan Province.

Sichuan Cuisine is known for its spicy, hot and heavily seasoned flavors, which come from the generous use of garlic and chili peppers, as well as the unique flavor of Sichuan peppercorn. Peanuts, sesame paste and ginger are also prominent ingredients in Sichuan Cuisine. Sichuan Cuisine has a long history and is well-reputed home and abroad. In 2010, Chengdu was declared a "City of Gastronomy (美食之都)" by UNESCO Creative Cities Network.

Guangdong Cuisine

Guangdong Cuisine originates from Guangdong Province in south China. Located in the subtropics and tropics, this region is rich in greenery, making it naturally blessed with a wide variety of farming products, or in other words, ingredients for cooking. It is renowned for its skillful techniques of stir-frying, frying, stewing and braising. Special attention is paid to the heating temperature and duration to ensure that the dishes feature pure delicacy, freshness, tenderness, and crispness. The over-cooked or over-flavored dishes are not good in Cantonese chef's mind. Special care is taken to make sure that the tastes are light but not tasteless, tender but not raw.

Indeed, Guangdong Cuisine offers a greater variety of foods than any other place in the world. The southern school benefits from abundant ingredients and its choices are diverse and even exotic. When Marco Polo came to China in the Yuan Dynasty, he described "... they eat all sorts of flesh, including that of brute beasts and animals of every kind which Christians would not touch for anything in the world". In modern time, the Cantonese are said to make use of "anything with four legs excluding tables". Consequently, the southerners' exotic tastes have earned them a long-established reputation around China.

(Adapted from China Travel Guide and China Highlights websites.)

◆ Cultural Analysis

China, with its vast territory and rich history, has fostered a diverse food culture shaped by different landscapes and climates. As a result, China now boasts a sophisticated food culture and tradition that goes beyond just the food itself.

(1) The Influence of Cultural Evolution on Different Cuisines

The development of culinary culture mirrors the cultural evolution of Chinese society. Shandong Cuisine originated in the northern part of China alongside the development of Chinese civilization. Huaiyang Cuisine gained prominence through economic and cultural growth. Sichuan Cuisine acquired its unique flavor with the help of palace chefs, while Guangdong Cuisine developed by incorporating characteristics from foreign cuisines due to the special geographic position.

(2) The Impact of Geographic Characteristics on Different Cuisines

Different geographic environments not only provide distinct ingredients for dishes but also influence their flavors. For instance, Shandong Cuisine is characterized by its salty flavor, which is attributed to the region's cold climate, as salt is believed to help people endure lower temperatures. On the other hand, Sichuan Cuisine is distinguished by its hot and spicy tastes to cope with the humid climate of the region.

(3) The Target Markets for Different Cuisines

The different cuisines may be favored in different situations, Sichuan Cuisine is widely popular because it can be enjoyed both on high streets and in back lanes or prepared at home. Guangdong Cuisine is considered more expensive and is typically found in luxurious hotels. Many of the Chinese restaurants overseas offer Guangdong Cuisine, as their owners often come from the southern region of China.

◆ Text Comprehension

1. Judge whether the following statements are true (T) or false (F).

1) Chinese cuisine can be classified into three regional cuisines according to their distinct tastes and local characteristics.

2) Shandong people enjoy using spices from the onion family, such as green onions and garlic.

3) The flavor of Huaiyang Cuisine is light, fresh and sweet and its presentation is delicately elegant.

4) One contributing factor to the development of Sichuan cooking is that skillful chefs were brought to the district from the capital during the Song, Yuan, Ming and Qing dynasties.

5) An emphasis on preserving the natural flavor of the food is also a distinctive characteristic of Guangdong Cuisine.

2. Answer the following questions.

1) Why are there so many varieties of Chinese cuisine?

2) What makes Shandong Cuisine influential in Chinese cuisines?

3) How does Jiangsu Province highlight a grand variety of food ingredients?

4) What are the characteristics of Guangdong Cuisine?

10.3   Chinese Liquor

Liquor is an alcoholic beverage made from fermented sorghum, barley, rice, grapes or other grains and fruits. Regarding the origin of wine, there are mainly four legends: liquor making begins with God, an ape, Yidi（仪狄）, and Dukang（杜康）. These charming legends, filled with exaggeration and imagination, are all derived from the deep respect and admiration for liquor.

According to ancient beliefs, liquor was considered holy and regarded as a sacred liquid for sacrificial offerings to Heaven and Earth or to honor deceased ancestors. Following the Zhou Dynasty, liquor was deemed as one of the Nine Rites（九礼）, with each dynasty placing great emphasis on liquor production and its use in banquets. Later, along with the development of fermenting and brewing skills, liquor gradually became an ordinary drink. Thus, many Chinese customs are related to the use of liquor.

According to the brewing process, liquor can be classified into three types: brewed alcoholic beverage（发酵酒）, distilled liquor（蒸馏酒）, and blending type（配制酒）. Brewed alcoholic drinks are wines extracted or pressed from raw materials such as fermented fruit or grain. Usually, this kind of wine is not strong, with an alcohol content of no more than 15%, a mild pungency. Apart from alcohol, the raw materials also contain nutritional ingredients. Yellow rice wine, beer and grape wine all belong to brewed alcoholic drinks. Distilled liquor is made from fermented raw materials such as fruit or grain. It is usually quite strong, with an alcohol content of more than 30%. White liquor falls into this category. Blending wine is based on normal juice wine or distilled wine that is blended with alcohol or non-alcohol materials. After soaking and mixing, the blending wine is obtained. This type of wine offers the most abundant options with different edible values depending on the selected wine base and auxiliary materials chosen for blending.

Chinese drinking art has a long history accompanied by a set of customs and styles. As part of diet culture, drinking has had a series of etiquette that everyone should adhere to since ancient times. There are four procedures in drinking etiquette: *bai* (拜), *ji* (祭), *cui* (啐), and *zujue* (卒爵). First, a guest makes a courtesy call to express respect. Then, he spills a little liquor to the ground to thank the Earth for its virtue of breeding. Next, he tastes and praises the liquor to honor the host. Finally, he drains the whole glass.

Jiuling (酒令) is a game played in a banquet to make fun. Usually, one person is elected as the *Lingguan* (令官 , commander), and the others will follow his order to read poems, supply the antithesis to a given phrase or play other similar games. Those who disobey the orders or lose in the game must drink as punishment. This tradition of playing games and drink appeared in the Western Zhou Dynasty and developed in the Sui and Tang dynasties. To sum up, *Jiuling* is used to encourage people to drink, and the main purpose is to create a lively atmosphere during drinking.

The drinking vessels, which play an important role in the liquor culture, have evolved over time since the invention of liquor. Each dynasty in history had its own unique fashion and liquor culture, and this was reflected in the design and materials of the drinking vessels. The materials, shapes, designs, and making techniques varied from one dynasty to another. Chinese drinking vessels can be generally classified into pottery, bronze, lacquer, porcelain, and jade based on the materials used. These vessels were mainly used for storage, warming, and drinking purposes.

Liquor culture is not just about the act of drinking, but also about enriching our lives. When people drink, they not only enjoy the company of others, the time and place of drinking, but also incorporate poetry, art, traditions and games to elevate the experience of drinking into a refined pleasure. In daily life, liquor is used for celebrations, expressing gratitude, and easing sadness. It adds color to our lives which is why there are sayings like "no liquor, no banquet (无酒不成席)" and "no liquor, no folk custom (无酒不成俗)". Overall, liquor can uplift our spirits, keep us warm in cold weather, heal us when we're unwell, help us make friends, and provide comfort during difficult times.

(Adapted from Cchatty website.)

◆ Cultural Analysis

As a special cultural form, liquor culture holds a unique position in traditional Chinese culture, permeating every aspect of social life.

(1) Liquor and Social Communication

Liquor serves as a bridge for exchanging ideas and building friendships, and fostering greater closeness and acquaintance among people. Throughout history, wine has been widely used for offering sacrifices, celebrating, entertaining, encouraging, enjoying, and alleviating grief. Affection among people is enhanced when they propose a toast.

(2) Liquor and Chinese Literature

Liquor, known as the catalyst of intelligence and courage, has been a source of inspiration for numerous heroes, literati, and artists and has contributed to their achievements and works. Famous poets in China such as Li Bai, Meng Haoran（孟浩然）and Wang Wei（王维）were all known to enjoy wine and often wrote about it. Wang Xizhi（王羲之）, one of the greatest calligraphers in the Eastern Jin Dynasty, is known as the "sage of calligraphy". His masterpiece *Preface to the Poems Composed at the Orchid Pavilion*（《兰亭序》）was created when he was comfortably drunk and at ease.

(3) Liquor and Its Medicinal Effects

Liquor can be a remedy for treating a cold and refreshing oneself. According to Li Shizhen, an ancient medical scientist in the Ming Dynasty, liquor is considered one of the top medicines. Sensible drinking can help regulate the body's functions, stimulate secretion of saliva and gastric juice, promote primary digestion and absorption, and improve blood circulation. Liquor can also uplift spirits, provide refreshment, relieve stress and facilitate sleep.

◆ Text Comprehension

1. Judge whether the following statements are true (T) or false (F).

1) Liquor has been a product of fermentation techniques in Chinese history.

2) In ancient China, liquor was regarded as a sacred liquid used for sacrificial offerings to deceased emperors.

3) According to the brewing process, liquor can be classified into three types: brewed alcoholic beverage, distilled liquor, and blending type.

4) The drinking vessels have evolved over time since the invention of liquor.

5) Drinking plays a significant role in influencing Chinese interpersonal relationships.

2. Answer the following questions.

1) How is drinking connected with etiquette in ancient China?

2) What is *Jiuling* and what is the function of *Jiuling*?

3) What are the functions of drinking vessels?

◆ Exercises

1. Match the four major cuisines in China with their main features.

1) Shandong Cuisine	a) Preserving the natural flavor
	b) Salty flavor
2) Huaiyang Cuisine	c) Light, fresh and sweet
	d) Quickly fried in a wok over a large and hot flame
3) Sichuan Cuisine	e) Spicy and tongue-numbing
	f) The dishes feature pure delicacy, freshness, tenderness and crispness
4) Guangdong Cuisine	g) Heavily seasoned flavor
	h) Vegetarian cuisine has reached its peak

2. Choose the best answer to each of the following questions.

1) Which of the following statements is NOT true about the philosophy behind Chinese meals?

A. The bond of people at the family banquet is influenced by Confucianism.

B. Food and medicine are believed to have similar effects on preventing disease.

C. Taoism emphasizes the importance of nutrition in food and the art of cooking.

D. Chinese meals aim to provide a balance between *yin* and *yang* foods.

2) Which of the following practices is NOT recommended in Chinese meals?

A. Both staple food and accompanying food should be included.

B. Meat ingredients should be combined with non-meat ingredients.

C. The right spices should be added to stimulate appetite.

D. A variety of seasonings should be added to cover the natural taste.

3) Which of the following statements is NOT true about the geographic influence on cuisines?

A. Sichuan Cuisine primarily utilizes ingredients sourced from mountains and rivers.

B. Shandong Cuisine features a salty flavor because of the humid climate near the sea.

C. The exotic tastes of Guangdong Cuisine result from abundant ingredients in Guangdong Province.

D. In "a land of fish and rice", Huaiyang Cuisine uses fresh and live aquatic products.

4) Which of the following statements is true about the classification of wine?

A. Distilled liquor is not strong, with no more than 15% alcoholic degree.

B. Brewed alcoholic drinks contain raw materials with high nutrition.

C. Brewed alcoholic drinks offer the most abundant options with different edible values.

D. White wine belongs to blending wine, with more than 30% alcoholic degree.

5) Which of the following statements is NOT true about the effects of liquor drinking?

A. Liquor serves as a remedy for treating a cold and refreshing oneself.

B. According to Li Shizhen, liquor is considered one of the top medicines.

C. Wang Xizhi's masterpiece *Preface to the Poems Composed at the Orchid Pavilion* was created when he was comfortably drunk and at ease.

D. Excessive drinking can promote primary digestion and absorption, and improve blood circulation.

3. Translate the following sentences.

1) 品尝美味的中国菜不仅是舌尖的享受，也是对中国饮食文化和生活哲学的探索。

2) 宴会的意义在于为人们提供一个聚会的机会，一起分享生活中的喜怒哀乐。

3) 川菜广受欢迎，因为它既可以在大街小巷享用，也可以在家自制。

4) 酒是交流思想、建立友谊的桥梁，使人与人之间更亲密、更熟识。

5) 合理饮酒有助于调节身体机能，促进消化吸收，改善血液循环。

4. Discuss the following questions.

1) Can you use some examples to illustrate the relationship between geographic features and cuisine?

2) Can you list some poems about wine drinking?

3) Identify the differences between Chinese food and Western food and analyze the cultural differences.

5. Work in groups. Do research on the following dishes and fill in the table below. Then report your findings to the class.

Dishes	Ingredients	Stories Behind the Dishes
Dongpo Pork （东坡肉）		
Fotiaoqiang （佛跳墙）		
Panlongcai （蟠龙菜）		
Sliced Beef and Ox Tongue in Chili Sauce （夫妻肺片）		

◆ Extended Readings

Chinese Tea 中国茶

Tea is a beverage made by steeping in freshly boiled water the young leaves and leaf buds of the tea plant. According to legend, tea has been enjoyed in China since around 2700 BC. It was initially a medicinal beverage obtained by boiling fresh leaves in water, and it became a daily drink around the 3rd century AD, marking the beginning of tea cultivation and processing.

Historical records indicate that during the Shang Dynasty, ancient Chinese began to drink tea. It is well known that Shen Nong Shi (神农氏) was the oldest forefather and inventor of agriculture and medicine in China. Shen Nong Shi personally tasted hundreds of species of herbs and was exposed to 72 poisons in a single day. But he used a kind of tree leaves to ease his poisoning, and it turned out to be tea tree. This was recorded in a book named *Shen Nong's Herbal Classic* (《神农本草经》) written in the period of Qin and Han dynasties. This suggests that the beneficial effects of tea were already recognized by Chinese ancestors, making it possibly the first medicinal herb used by mankind. Tea also appeared in literature during the early Zhou Dynasty, mentioned in *The Book of Songs*.

The tradition of drinking tea for its medicinal benefits may have originated in the Yunnan region during the Shang Dynasty. In the Western Zhou Dynasty, tea was used as oblation. During the Spring and Autumn Period, tea was considered a kind of vegetable known as "bitter vegetable (苦菜)", and it was used as medicine to treat various illnesses during the Warring States Period in China. From the Han Dynasty to the Three Kingdoms Period, tea became a cherished and rare substance enjoyed by the aristocracy. It wasn't until the Tang Dynasty that tea became a popular beverage. Today, drinking tea has become an essential part of daily life in both rural and urban China, as well as in other parts of the world.

Chinese tea emerged as a key trade commodity between China and various foreign countries. In the early centuries, it was first introduced to Japan, accompanied by Chinese culture, art, and Buddhism. Gradually, the techniques for cultivating, processing, and enjoying tea were spread to East Asian countries and regions, aided by various trade routes, including the Silk Road. During the Tang Dynasty, the tradition of tea-drinking extended further to other Asian nations, such as Korea and Vietnam. Later, in the late 13th century, Marco Polo returned to Italy from his travels, bringing with him tea, silk, chinaware, and jewels.

Furthermore, during the Ming Dynasty, from approximately 1405 to 1433, Zheng He's seven voyages to the West significantly aided the dissemination of tea, silk, and porcelain through maritime trade routes. Additionally, border trade conducted by businessmen played a crucial role in spreading these goods and cultures. The Dutch East India Company then introduced tea to Holland in the early 17th century and eventually imported it to the rest of Europe by the mid-17th century. It wasn't until the late 17th century that tea began to be sold to the public in England. Following this introduction, the British developed a profound fondness for this delightful beverage. This affection for tea was further cemented when King Charles II married Portuguese Catherine of Braganza in 1662; she is rumored to have brought a small chest of *Qimen Maofeng* (祁门毛峰) tea as part of her dowry.

Tea art, an important cultural item and symbol in today's society, is a performing art that can be both simple and complex. It combines various elements such as people, tea, water, utensils, skills, and the environment to express the spiritual pursuit of both tea makers and drinkers. The tea ceremony (茶道) is practiced with the intention of promoting harmony among humanity, fostering unity with nature, disciplining the mind, calming the heart, and achieving enlightenment through purity of spirit. It represents the spiritual unity of man and nature as well as self-cultivation. Therefore, while primarily a mode of aesthetics, the tea ceremony also offers subtle insights into ethics and metaphysics while encouraging focus and concentration under the influence of delicious tea.

(Adapted from BioMed Central website.)

Eating Seasonal Foods According to the 24 Solar Terms 节气饮食

Chinese believe fruits and vegetables are at their best when they are in season. Eating seasonally is what the Solar Terms encourage us to do.

Start of Spring

The weather is getting warmer, so there are a lot of vegetables available. Fresh, seasonal vegetables are the main ingredients for dishes at this period. The most popular dish is Spring Roll (春卷), which is a thin sheet of dough rolled, stuffed and fried. The filling usually consists of carrots, cucumbers, chives and green bean sprouts. Another dish called *chunbing* (春饼), or spring crepe, is a similar version of Spring Roll but not fried. It is eaten directly after all the fillings are rolled in.

Rain Water

As its name implies, this term indicates an increase in rainfall. There is an ancient Chinese saying, "Rain during the spring time is as precious as oil," signifying the importance of rain to plants and farming. In Sichuan Province in southwestern China, local people stew pig hocks (猪肘) with beans and seaweed in an earthenware cooking pot. Many people in northern China make dumplings with pork and shepherd's purse (荠菜).

Spring Equinox

The Spring Equinox signals the equal length of the day and night time. On this day, Chinese people living in the countryside pick amaranth (苋菜) in the wild, and simply blanch it in boiling water and serve it with salt and soy sauce. Another seasonal delicacy is bamboo shoot, which can be prepared in dishes such as stir-fried eggs with shredded bamboo shoots or fried bamboo shoots with smoked bacon.

Start of Summer

It usually falls on 5th or 6th of May, marking the beginning of summer. All vegetation is in luxuriant growth. It's a crucial time for the harvest of wheat, canola (蓖麻) seed and other crops. The most popular dish during this time is salted duck egg; people believe it can provide them with the energy they need for tiring harvest work. Another seasonal food is a little red bean and pearl barley congee (红豆薏米粥). It helps to clear away heat, regulate the spleen and reduce inflammation.

Grain Buds

It is a time of humidity and heat. To keep healthy, Chinese people collect sow thistle (苦苣菜) from the wild and cook it as a dish. According to Traditional Chinese Medicine, eating bitter food in summer can help protect people's heart. Bitter gourd (苦瓜) is a seasonal food for the summer. It can be stir-fried with egg or pork, and in the Guilin area, the most popular dish is pork-stuffed bitter gourd soup (猪肉酿苦瓜汤).

Start of Autumn

In Beijing, people fatten up in autumn: eating meat on the day of Start of Autumn in order to replenish nutrition lost in summer and prepare for the cold weather. The seasonal vegetable is eggplant. As the air dries in autumn, the moisture in the human body also decreases; staying hydrated by drinking fluids and eating foods that promote moisture in the body is essential. There is a popular dish called white fungus, lotus seed, and lily bulb soup(银耳百合莲子羹), known for its ability to reduce dryness and moisturize your body inside and out.

Autumn Equinox

Most regions in China enjoy good cool weather with the arrival of the Autumn Equinox. This season brings forth the blooming of osmanthus (桂) and chrysanthemum (菊) flowers, as well as the peak days for hairy crabs (大闸蟹). The best place to have hairy crabs is in Shanghai, as it is close to Yangcheng Lake (阳澄湖) where the best hairy crabs are produced. Hairy crab is famous for its sweet meat and golden roe. It is very easy to cook, as it is typically steamed and served with sauce made from vinegar, ginger, and sugar. It is also customary to eat hairy crabs with yellow rice wine (黄酒).

Frost's Descent

After Frost's Descent, the weather gets even colder and sometimes there is a heavy frost. On the day of Frost's Descent, in order to combat the cold, Chinese people often eat persimmons (柿子). They can keep the body warm and the skin soft and moist, especially for the lips. Chinese radish is in season, and it is the most popular vegetable during this period. Chinese people believe that it can bring multiple health benefits, such as relieving a cough, reducing cholesterol and stabilizing blood pressure. In the south of China, many families cook beef brisket stew with radish (萝卜炖牛腩) on the day of Frost's Descent, as they believe this dish will help them fight against the cold weather .

Minor Snow

This period marks the arrival of the first light snowfall of winter, as temperatures in most parts of China drop below zero at night. During Minor Snow, people begin to stock up on supplies for the coming winter, and many choose to eat beef and mutton to help stay warm. Seasonal dishes like mutton soup and lamb hotpot are in huge demand during this time of the year. Traditional Chinese Medicine holds that mutton is warming in nature, which makes it a perfect food for the winter.

Major Cold

It is the coldest period of the year in most parts of China. On this day, Chinese eat sticky rice (糯米) with beans and meat. The sticky rice has warming effects, tastes mildly sweet, and it can help with spleen, stomach and digestion. Chinese people believe that it is good to eat the roots of plants in winter, and the Chinese yam root (山药) is in season. It has been an important and commonly used food remedy in Traditional Chinese Medicine for generations.

(Adapted from China Educational Tours website.)

Chapter Eleven

Chinese Arts and Crafts
中国工艺品

Chinese arts and crafts enjoy a long history. They were invented and fully developed by talented professional craftsmen, which has made them popular not only within the nation, but also around the world. Earthenware of the primitive society in the Neolithic Age is the earliest artistic work. The bronze ware of the Shang and Zhou dynasties, embroidery of the Song Dynasty, as well as cloisonne and porcelain of the Ming and Qing dynasties, have all enjoyed worldwide reputations for their exquisiteness and refinement. China's paper cutting, clay figurines, sugar painting, wood carving, kites and fans are all well known for their strong artistry and national flavor. They reflect the wisdom and perfect craftsmanship of the Chinese people.

11.1 Chinese Bronze Ware

Bronze is primarily an alloy of copper and tin, with sometimes the addition of lead. This alloy, invented 5,000 years ago, soon became widespread and led Chinese ancestors into a new stage—the Bronze Age. Generally speaking, the bronze culture underwent three stages: the forming period, the thriving period, and the transition period. The forming period began during the Longshan Culture (龙山文化), which existed 4,000 to 4,500 years ago in the Neolithic Age. During the thriving period from Xia, Shang to the Zhou dynasties, artistic achievements reached a high level: Bronze wares were widely used as musical instruments in sacrificial temples, weapons of war, and other vessels in court life. The transition period refers to the time from the end of the Warring States Period to the Qin and Han dynasties when bronze wares were gradually replaced by iron wares.

The earliest Chinese bronze wares were crafted using a method known as piece-mold casting (块范法)—as opposed to the lost-wax method (失蜡法) used in other Bronze Age cultures. In piece-mold casting, a model of the object to be cast is first made and then covered with an additional layer of clay. Once the clay dries, it is carefully cut into sections to remove the original model. The sections are then reassembled after firing to form the mold for casting. If the object being cast is a vessel, a core has to be placed inside the mold to create the vessel's cavity. The space between the core and the outer molds is then filled with molten bronze. The piece-mold method was likely the only one used in China until at least the end of the Shang Dynasty. One advantage of this rather cumbersome way of casting bronze was that decorative patterns could be carved or stamped directly onto the inner surface of the mold before firing. This technique enabled the bronze workers to achieve a high degree of sharpness and definition in even intricate designs. In the late Spring and Autumn Period, Chinese may have invented the lost-wax casting method. The bronze statues and plates unearthed from the Tomb of Marquis Yi of State Zeng（曾侯乙墓）in Sui County（随州）, Hubei Province are the earliest lost-wax castings found in China.

The majority of surviving ancient Chinese bronze artifacts are ritual products rather than practical tools or weapons. Weapons such as daggers and axes had a sacrificial meaning, symbolizing the divine power of the ruler. The strong religious associations of bronze objects led to the creation of numerous vessel types and shapes that were regarded as classic and totemic. These designs were copied, often in other mediums, such as Chinese porcelain, throughout subsequent periods of Chinese art.

The ancient ritual books of China detailed who was allowed to use specific sacrificial vessels and in what quantities. For example, the king of Zhou used 9 *dings*（鼎）and 8 *guis*（簋）, a duke was allowed 7 *dings* and 6 *guis*, a baron could use 5 *dings* and 3 *guis*, a nobleman could use 3 *dings* and 2 *guis*. According to actual archaeological finds, the tomb of Fu Hao（妇好）, an unusually powerful Shang queen, contained over two hundred ritual vessels—far more than the twenty-four vessels found in the tomb of a contemporary nobleman. It clearly indicated her higher status not only to her contemporaries but also, it was believed, to her ancestors. Simuwu Cauldron（司母戊鼎）, the largest and heaviest bronze vessel in China, was believed to have been commissioned by a king of the Shang Dynasty for worshiping his mother. It represented the highest artistic level. Many of the pieces were inscribed with posthumous forms of Fu Hao's name, indicating that they were made especially for burial in her tomb.

In the Spring and Autumn Period and the Warring States Period, military affairs relied heavily on weapons, so each state endeavored to craft practical bronze weapons. The famous Goujian Sword, forged by the King of the Yue（越）State, is adorned with intricate rhombus patterns. Though buried for more than 2,000 years, the sword shows no rust at all, and the sharp blade gleams with cold light as ever. It could slice through more than twenty layers of paper with a single cut.

In the Han Dynasty, bronze vessels were replaced by those made of jade, pottery, and iron. Afterwards, bronze was mostly used for mirrors in various shapes and patterns. However, the inscriptions on them are of high historical value.

The appreciation, creation and collection of Chinese bronze wares as pieces of art rather than just ritual items began in the Song Dynasty, and reached its peak in the Qing

Dynasty under the reign of Emperor Qianlong. The bronze ware is then categorized according to its use into sacrificial vessels (祭器), wine vessels, food vessels, water vessels, musical instruments, weapons, measuring containers, ancient money and others. The most highly prized are generally the sacrificial and wine vessels, which form the majority of most collections.

The decorative patterns of bronze ware were delicate and diverse. Among the popular patterns were the lines depicting beasts' faces, which seemed mysterious, and the depictions of dragons and phoenixes, which were believed to be mighty and auspicious. The *taotie* pattern (饕餮纹) was a popular bronze ware decorative design in the Shang Dynasty and the subsequent Zhou Dynasty. It was named by scholars of the Song Dynasty according to records in *Master Lü's Spring and Autumn Annals* (《吕氏春秋》). It features a full-face round-eyed animal head with sharp teeth and horns. In all these patterns, the eyes are always emphasized as they leave an awesome impression on viewers even from a distance. Gradually, people developed more complex methods for adorning their vessels. They inlaid jade, turquoise, iron or copper into the bronze vessels and their wisdom and creativity were admired by posterity.

(Adapted from Travel China Guide, The Metropolitan Museum of Act,

and Wikipedia websites.)

◆ Cultural Analysis

The Bronze Age in China marked a significant period of growth and maturity for the civilization, and the bronze ware is one of the most important works of ancient Chinese art.

(1) The Symbol of Human Progress

The invention of bronze stand as a milestone in the history of human civilization. It represents the first time that human beings used metal synthesis technology, which greatly enriched human life and accelerated the development of society. With its advantages of low melting point and good casting properties, bronze has played a crucial role in promoting manufacturing technology.

(2) The Manifestation of Patriarchal System and Ritual Music System

The bronze ware were mainly used for various ritual occasions such as sacrifices and feasts. Since rites were important for regulating social behavior and governing ancient

China, the nobles of all ranks were required to use appropriate ritual utensils and musical instruments based on their status, with violations considered a serious indecency or even a crime.

◆ Text Comprehension

1. Judge whether the following statements are true (T) or false (F).

1) The bronze culture thrived during the Xia, Shang and Zhou dynasties.

2) Chinese bronze wares were made by using the piece-mold casting method instead of the lost-wax method.

3) Bronze daggers and axes were usually used as weapons in the Shang Dynasty .

4) According to the ancient ritual books of China, only the king of Zhou had the right to use 9 *dings* and 8 *guis*.

5) During the Han Dynasty, bronze vessels were replaced by those made of jade, pottery, and iron.

2. Answer the following questions.

1) What is the advantage of using the piece-mold method in bronze casting?

2) What are the functions of bronze ware during its thriving period?

3) How were Chinese bronze wares usually decorated ?

11.2 Chinese Porcelain

Porcelain is a type of vitrified pottery with a white, fine-grained body that is usually translucent. It differs from earthenware, which is porous, opaque, and coarser in texture. In China, porcelain is defined as pottery that resonates when struck. In the West, it is a material that becomes translucent when held to the light. Over centuries, numerous new ceramic technologies and styles have been developed in China. Chinese porcelain is created by heating raw materials, typically *gaoling* clay (高岭土), in a kiln (窑) to temperatures between 1,200 and 1,400 °C. This porcelain has a wide range of applications including tableware, decorative figurines, as well as in technology and industry such as electrical insulators and laboratory ware.

The earliest Chinese pottery was earthenware, which continued to be produced for practical purposes throughout Chinese history. Pottery dating back to 10,000 years ago was found at the *Xianrendong* Cave（仙人洞）site in Jiangxi Province, making it one of the earliest known examples of pottery. During the middle and late Neolithic Age (about 5,000 to 1,500 BC), most of the larger archaeological cultures in China produced vessels that were often boldly painted or decorated by cutting or impressing. The decoration on pottery from the Banpo Culture（半坡文化）is abstract or features stylized animals such as fish, which are a specialty at the river settlement of Banpo. The distinctive Majiayao（马家窑）pottery, with its orange bodies and black paint, is characterized by fine paste textures, thin walls, and polished surfaces. The excavated pots were almost completely free of defects, suggesting that a high level of quality control was required during production.

The Han Dynasty marked a pivotal period in the development of porcelain in China. During this era, porcelain production underwent significant advancements, transitioning from simpler, more primitive forms to the creation of mature and refined pieces. Innovations in glazing techniques, firing processes, and shape design contributed to the production of a wide range of porcelain wares, including both functional items for daily use and decorative pieces. Additionally, porcelain from the Han Dynasty played a crucial role in cultural exchanges along the Silk Road, spreading Chinese craftsmanship and aesthetic ideas to distant lands. This period laid the foundation for the subsequent prosperity and diversity of Chinese porcelain, establishing it as an important art form with a rich cultural heritage.

The three-colored ware of the Tang Dynasty（唐三彩）is one of the most famous Chinese porcelain. It is named after the yellow, green and white glazes applied to the earthenware body, but other colors, such as blue, brown, and purple were also used. The wares were made not only in traditional forms like bowls and vases, but also in more exotic shapes of camels and Central Asian travelers, showing the influence of the Silk Road. Another popular type of ware at that time was *qingci*（青瓷）, known in the West as celadon. They featured a subtle bluish-green glaze and boasted simple, elegant shapes.

During the Song Dynasty, porcelain production flourished, achieving unprecedented levels of craftsmanship and creativity. Famous porcelain wares were often named after their places of production. Unique styles emerged from various kilns, each characterized by elegant glazes that exhibited a variety of colors and textures. The forms of the porcelain were often simple and archaic, reflecting a deep respect for tradition and history. Many decorative patterns drew inspiration from daily life and nature, capturing aesthetic sensibilities and cultural values of the Song Dynasty.

Blue-and-white porcelain（青花瓷）was first mass produced during the Yuan Dynasty. The potters of the subsequent Ming Dynasty perfected these blue-and-white wares, which soon came to represent the virtuosity of Chinese pottery. Jingdezhen（景德镇）, in Jiangxi Province, became the center of a porcelain industry that not only produced vast quantities of imperial wares but also exported products to distant places such as Turkey. The styles of decorative motifs and vessel shapes changed with each new Ming emperor, but the quality of the porcelain was indisputably superior to any other time period.

During the late Ming to early Qing Dynasty, porcelain was enriched with the innovation of five-colored porcelain（五彩瓷）. This involved applying a variety of over-glaze pigments to create decorative schemes of flower, landscape and figurative scenes. These wares gained great fame in the West. In the eighteenth century, inspired by techniques used in the decoration of metal ware, craftsmen painted enamel on porcelain to create vivid colors and stunning patterns. This technique became known as painted-enamel or *yangcai*（洋彩）.

Porcelain in Chinese culture is not only a functional object, but also regarded as an art form. Chinese porcelain is decorated with intricate designs that often include symbolic images and motifs, such as the popular lotus flower, which symbolizes purity and enlightenment. Even today, Chinese porcelain remains highly valued. Collectors around the world seek out rare and antique pieces, and contemporary artists continue to be inspired by the beauty and craftsmanship of Chinese porcelain. For centuries, this treasure of Chinese culture has captivated the world with its enduring beauty, inspiring new generations of artists and designers while remaining a cherished symbol of refinement and elegance.

(Adapted from Britannica, China Online Museum and Wikipedia websites.)

◆ Cultural Analysis

Chinese porcelain, renowned for its intricate designs, exquisite craftsmanship, and enduring quality, boasts a rich and extensive history. Its influence has extended beyond national boundaries, serving as a bridge for cultural exchange.

(1) The Symbol of China

The term "china" not only refers to the country of China, but also to its porcelain. This shows that in the eyes of Westerners, porcelain is synonymous with China. China is the birthplace of porcelain, and it stands as a unique contribution from ancient Chinese civilization to the world. The brilliance of porcelain has greatly enriched both our national culture and world art heritage.

(2) The Messenger of Culture

Porcelain, as a cultural symbol, has played an immeasurable role in the spread of Chinese culture in Europe. Since the 16th century, Chinese porcelain has been exported to Europe through new sea routes. The porcelain was not only valued for its practical use but also served as a carrier of China's splendid civilization. It is through porcelain that Westerners began to understand, appreciate and communicate with China. At the same time, Chinese porcelain has been influenced by European art and enriched by Western painting methods.

(3) The Embodiment of Artistic Value

Porcelains are famous at home and abroad for their crystal-clear delicacy, various decorations, rich and varied shapes, as well as elegant and gorgeous colors. Ceramic artists pay attention to the artistic effect achieved through the seamless integration of biscuit and external decoration. They also draw inspiration from the techniques and aesthetics of Chinese painting in order to enhance the overall beauty of their creations.

◆ Text Comprehension

I. Judge whether the following statements are true (T) or false (F).

1) In China, porcelain is defined as pottery that is resonant when struck.

2) The earliest Chinese pottery was earthenware, which continued to be produced for practical purposes throughout Chinese history.

3) The three-colored wares of the Tang Dynasty were made not only in traditional forms like bowls and vases, but also in more exotic shapes of camels and Persian travelers.

4) Famous porcelain wares were named after their production locations during the Song Dynasty.

5) Blue-and-white porcelain was first mass produced during the Yuan Dynasty.

2. Answer the following questions.

1) What are the differences between earthenware and porcelain?

2) How did porcelain develop in the Yuan Dynasty?

3) In what ways has porcelain gained popularity and appreciation in modern society?

11.3   Chinese Paper Cutting

The art of paper cutting in China can be traced back to the 2nd century AD, when paper was invented by Cai Lun (蔡伦), a court official of the Eastern Han Dynasty. As paper became more affordable, paper cutting became one of the most important forms of Chinese folk art. Over time, this art form spread to other parts of the world, with different regions developing their own cultural styles. These cut-outs are often used to decorate doors and windows, so they are also referred to as "window flowers" or "window paper cuttings". They are often glued to the exterior of windows, allowing light from inside to shine through the negative space of the cut-outs.

Traditionally, the paper artworks are made of red paper, as this colors is associated with festivities and happiness in Chinese culture. However, other colors are also used. Paper cutting is commonly featured on special occasions such as Chinese New Year, weddings and childbirth ceremonies, as it is considered to symbolize luck and happiness.

Chinese paper cutting originated from the practice of worshipping ancestors and immortals. According to archaeological records, a similar practice to paper cutting could be traced back to the Warring States Period, long before the invention of paper. At that time, people used other thin materials such as leaves, silver foil, silk and even leather to carve patterns. However, after the invention of paper, people realized that this material was easy to cut, store and discard, and it became the major material for this type of artwork.

Paper easily mildews and rots, especially in the rainy southeast of China. As a result, paper cutting art from previous centuries is hard to find in this region. In contrast, the dry weather in the northwest of China allows for the preservation of paper cutting art dating back to the Northern Dynasties in Turpan, Xinjiang (新疆吐鲁番).

During the Tang Dynasty, paper cutting had evolved into a mature art form, and it was not only considered a type of handicraft, but also a form of artwork. This is because ideas and concepts were expressed through the intricate patterns of paper cutting. In the Ming and Qing dynasties, paper cutting reached its peak in development. Folk paper cutting became more widespread among people, with expressive and abundant artistic expression.

The designs for paper cutting works vary widely, ranging from basic designs consisting of a single image to symmetrical designs formed by folding the paper into proportional sections before cutting out shapes. When unfolded, these shapes form symmetrical designs. Chinese paper cuttings are typically of the symmetrical variety and are usually folded an even number of times, such as twice or four times. When designed for windows, paper cutting is usually done in a free-form manner except for the flower pattern found in the corner. The themes of paper cutting window decorations vary widely; popular ones are based on stories from traditional Chinese opera while others depict farming, spinning, fishing, as well as various poultry-related activities, showcasing diverse aspects of life in their designs.

Today, paper cuttings are primarily used for decoration. They add a lively touch to walls, windows, doors, columns, mirrors, lamps and lanterns in homes and are also given as presents or gifts. Paper cuttings placed near entrances are believed to bring good luck and can also be used as patterns for embroidery and lacquer work. Young people use paper cutting artworks to decorate their bags and books.

Paper cutting also serves as a means of conveying cultural significance. Some designs convey wishes for a bountiful harvest or a prosperous life through imagery such as golden harvests, thriving domestic animals and plants, or the carp jumping over the dragon gate (鲤鱼跃龙门). Other designs feature legendary figures or scenes from traditional myths or stories, such as the meeting of Cowherd (牛郎) and Weaver Girl (织女) or the 24 stories of people's filial piety (二十四孝).

The most well-known Chinese characters depicted in paper cutting art are *fu* (福), which means lucky, and *xi* (囍), representing double happiness—both symbolizing people's gratitude towards life. *Fu* is commonly displayed during the Chinese New Year to wish for a fortunate year, while *xi* can often be seen at the windows or doors of newlyweds.

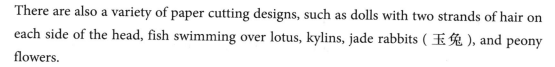

There are also a variety of paper cutting designs, such as dolls with two strands of hair on each side of the head, fish swimming over lotus, kylins, jade rabbits (玉兔), and peony flowers.

For over a thousand years, people have enjoyed creating paper cutting artworks as a leisure activity which has contributed to its enduring popularity as an artistic form.

(Adapted from Wikipedia website.)

◆ Cultural Analysis

Paper cutting is a traditional Chinese handicraft that involves creating intricate designs on paper using scissors or knives. It is a beloved art form rich in national characteristics.

(1) A Traditional Folk Art

Paper cutting is an indispensable artistic activity in Chinese folk art, reflecting the specific cultural traditions and everyday life of the people. For example, a big red paper character *xi* is traditionally placed on the newlywed's door, while the character *shou* (寿 , longevity) adds joy to celebrating a senior's birthday.

(2) Cultural and Artistic Value

There are many forms of paper cutting, and the motifs vividly depict the cultural traditions that are widely embraced by the general public. This not only reflects traditional cultural psychology, folk customs and aesthetic tastes, but also shows people's love for their lives and their pursuit of truth, goodness and beauty.

◆ Text Comprehension

I. Judge whether the following statements are true (T) or false (F).

1) Paper cutting decorations are often glued to the interior of windows, allowing the light from inside to shine through the negative space of the cut-outs.

2) Paper cutting can be made with various colored paper.

3) Chinese paper cutting originated from the practice of worshipping ancestors and immortals.

4) Paper cutting can be used as patterns for embroidery and lacquer work.

5) It is difficult to find paper cutting art works in the rainy southeast of China.

2. Answer the following questions.

1) What are the functions of paper cutting in folk activities?

2) What are the most popular paper cutting Chinese characters?

3) What are the common motifs found in paper cutting?

◆ Exercises

1. Fill in the table below with the types and features of porcelain of each dynasty.

A. five-colored porcelain

B. blue-and-white porcelain

C. three-colored porcelain

D. famous porcelain wares were named after their production locations

E. plain and elegant glazes of decorative patterns

F. exotic shapes of camels and Central Asian travelers

G. landscape and figurative scenes of over-glaze pigments

H. the purity of its body

Dynasties	Types	Features
Tang Dynasty		
Song Dynasty		
Yuan Dynasty		
late Ming and early Qing dynasties		

2. Choose the best answers to each of the following questions.

1) Which of the following statements is true about the method of piece-mold casting?

   A. It was invented in the late Spring and Autumn Period.

B. It could achieve a high degree of sharpness and definition.

C. It was used in all other Bronze Age cultures.

D. It allowed decorative patterns to be carved on the inner surface.

2) Which of the following statements is NOT true about the development of bronze?

A. Bronze was only used for mirrors in the Han Dynasty.

B. Bronze was made into weapons during the Warring States Period.

C. Most collections of bronze are sacrificial and wine vessels.

D. The appreciation of bronze as art reached its zenith in the Song Dynasty.

3) Which of the following statements is NOT true about porcelain in the West?

A. Chinese porcelain is enriched by Western painting methods.

B. The earliest pottery was made during the Palaeolithic Era.

C. Porcelain carried and spread China's culture to Europe.

D. Jingdezhen in Jiangxi Province exported porcelain to distant places such as Turkey.

4) Which of the following statements is true about the motif in paper cuttings?

A. Thriving domestic animals and plants express wishes for a bountiful harvest.

B. A carp jumping over a dragon gate symbolizes protection from evil spirits.

C. Designs featuring legendary figures are used during the Chinese New Year.

D. The most famous Chinese character depicted in paper cutting is the character *shou*.

5) Which of the following is NOT true about paper cuttings?

A. Chinese paper cutting originated from the practice of worshipping ancestors and immortals.

B. People used other materials to carve patterns before paper was invented.

C. People in the southeast typically did not engage in paper cutting art due to its hot climate.

    D. Paper cuttings can also be used as patterns for embroidery.

3. Translate the following sentences.

1) 青铜器的装饰图案通常精致多样。流行的图案包括兽脸、龙和凤。

2) 青铜器中的礼器和乐器主要用于祭祀、宴请等各种仪式场合。

3) 瓷器的辉煌在人类文明史上熠熠生辉，极大地丰富了民族文化和世界艺术的宝库。

4) 由于剪纸常用于装饰门窗，所以有时也被称为"窗花"或"窗花剪纸"。

5) 窗花剪纸的主题千差万别，其中最流行的是基于中国传统戏曲的故事。

4. Discuss the following questions.

1) What led to the substitution of bronze vessels with those made of jade, pottery, and iron in later times?

2) In what ways has porcelain served as a cultural messenger?

3) What is the significance of handicrafts in the development of culture?

5. Work in groups. Do research on the following Chinese handicrafts and fill in the table below. Then report your findings to the class.

Handicrafts	Origins	Characteristics	Major Themes
Clay figurine			
Sugar painting			
Wood carving			
Embroidery			

◆ Extended Readings

Lacquer Ware 漆器

In Chinese art, the term "lacquer" refers to a variety of decorative techniques used to coat wood, bamboo, metal or other surfaces with a hard and resinous finish. Originating during the Neolithic Era, lacquering was originally developed as a means of providing waterproof protection for wood and bamboo. However, it rapidly became a highly valued method of decorating fine objects.

Lacquer is the sap of a tree native to southern and central China—a natural polymer. When it dries, the sap is lightweight and strong, and it renders anything it covers nearly impervious to decay. The process of making lacquered objects starts with heating and purifying this sap. This can be an unpleasant task because the fumes are poisonous and may cause rashes on the skin. The fluid is then colored with carbon black, cinnabar red, or other pigments. Red designs on a black ground are characteristic of most lacquer wares. Application requires a hair brush, like a writing brush, and a steady hand capable of manipulating the stubborn, viscous medium. Lacquer is applied one coat at a time and then allowed to dry before sanding and application of another coat. Most objects have many thin layers of lacquer built up on their surfaces.

The oldest known lacquer object—a red wooden bowl—was discovered at the Hemudu (河姆渡) culture site and dates back to 5000 BC–4500 BC. However, it wasn't until the Shang Dynasty that more sophisticated methods of lacquering were developed. By the Warring States Period, lacquer had become a flourishing crafts industry. Because the whole process was labor-intensive lacquer vessels were more expensive than their equivalent bronze counterparts. As a result, they rivaled bronze ware as the most prestigious medium for making ceremonial or ancestral offerings. Later, during the four centuries of the Han Dynasty, numerous centres of lacquer production were established. As trade expanded, knowledge of the Chinese lacquer process spread to Korea, Japan, and Southeast Asia.

In the Han Dynasty, the process of lacquer production could be divided into several stages, and was performed by specialist artisans. The *sugong* (素工), for instance, would prepare the core to be lacquered, which might consist of wood, bamboo, cloth or even metal. After this, multiple layers of lacquer would be applied to the core by the *xiugong* (绣工). Once dry, the top layer would be applied and polished by the *shanggong* (上工), after which the *huagong* (画工)—specialist Chinese painters—would complete the decoration. Other craftsmen might be employed to add inlays or engravings, gilding, or inscriptions to complete the design.

An example of highly decorated Han lacquer can be seen in the set of four nested coffins（四层套棺）discovered in the tomb of a mid-level aristocrat at Mawangdui（马王堆）, which was said to take the equivalent of one million man hours to complete. Lavishly equipped, the well-preserved wooden tomb has several outer compartments holding some of the finest early Chinese silks, arranged around the lacquered coffins.

During the Tang Dynasty, Chinese lacquer workers began to cut sheets of silver or gold into animal, bird and flower shapes. These designs were then affixed onto the surface of the lacquered object. Afterward, the object was re-lacquered, rubbed and polished to reveal subtle traces of golden or silvery patterns. Other techniques, such as carving lacquer were also introduced. It was also during the Tang Dynasty that Chinese craftsmen passed on the gold and silver foil inlay method to the Japanese in the Nara Period（奈良时代，710–784）.

The goldsmithing art of adding inlaid gold and silver to lacquer was further developed by the Song people. They introduced new techniques, including *qiangjin*（戗金，engraving inlaid with gold), *diaotian*（雕填，inlaid with differently coloured lacquer), and *diaoqi*（雕漆，carved lacquer). The art of inlaying lacquer with mother-of-pearl was also enhanced during the Song Dynasty.

During the Yuan Dynasty, Chinese lacquer experts mastered the techniques of incising, engraving and filling in with gold foil or silver powder. They began to carve floral patterns, dragons, serpents and other images through a thick layer of red or (more rarely) black lacquer.

Lacquer carving continued to flourish during the Ming Dynasty, as well as the subsequent Qing Dynasty, in many different factories and production centres. It reached a particularly high level of craftsmanship under the Ming Emperor Yongle（永乐皇帝，1360–1424) and Emperor Xuande（宣德皇帝，1399–1435), renowned for its carved red lacquer dishes, trays, boxes, and cups. The decorative motifs included, landscapes with figures, as well as dragon, phoenix, and floral designs deeply carved against a typical yellow background. Later, under the Emperor Jiajing（嘉靖皇帝，1507–1567), more realistic designs appeared. These designs were characterized by a shallower, sharper style of carving, sometimes involving as many as nine coats of different colors against intricate floral or figurative backgrounds.

(Adapted from Visual Arts Encyclopedia website.)

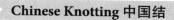

Chinese Knotting 中国结

Chinese knotting is a decorative handcraft art that originated as a form of Chinese folk art during the Tang and Song dynasties in China. They are usually arranged in a lanyard style, with two cords entering from the top of the knot and two cords exiting from the bottom. The knots are usually double-layered and symmetrical in design.

Archaeological studies indicate that the art of tying knots dates back to prehistoric times. Recent discoveries have revealed 100,000-year-old bone needles used for sewing and bodkins, which were used to untie knots. Some of the earliest evidence of knotting have been preserved on bronze vessels from the Warring States Period, Buddhist carvings from the Northern Dynasties period and silk paintings from the Western Han Dynasty.

Based on archaeological and literary evidence, it is believed that before 476 BC, knots in China served a specific purpose: as a method of recording and governing. According to the second volume of *Xici* in *the Book of Changes* (《周易·系辞》下), during the ancient rule of Bao Xi (包牺), knots were used for purposes other than just fishing. They were also utilized for recording and managing the community. The Eastern Han scholar Zheng Xuan (郑玄) annotated *The Book of Changes* by stating that "Significant events were recorded with intricate knots, while minor events were recorded with simpler knots (事大，大结其绳；事小，小结其绳)". Moreover, the chapter of Tubo (吐蕃) in the *New Book of Tang* (《新唐书》) mentioned that "the government would use tied cords to make agreements due to a lack of written characters (其吏治，无文字，结绳齿木为约)".

Simultaneously, additional to the use of recording and ruling, knots also became an ancient totem and belief motif. In ancient times, Chinese gave knots a lot of positive meanings from pictograms, quasi-sounds to totem worship. For example, a double coin knot pattern painted on the T-shape silk banner was discovered by archaeologists in Mawangdui Han Tomb (马王堆汉墓). The pattern depicts intertwined dragons as a double coin knot in the middle of the fabric painting. The upper part of the fabric painting illustrates the ancient deities Fuxi and Nüwa, who are also the initiators of marriage in China. This association has led to the meaning of love for double coin knots being reflected in many ancient poems. Tangible evidence has been discovered in the oracle bone script from Yin Ruins (殷墟甲骨文), indicating that 3,000 years ago knots were used as symbols rather than for functional purposes. Additionally, a three-row rattan knotting of a double coin knot was excavated from The Archaeological Ruins of Liangzhu City (良渚遗址), confirming the presence of decorative knots in China for at least 4,000 years.

The art of knotting gradually developed into a distinctive decorative form in China, particularly during the Spring and Autumn Period. The use of ribbon knotting and decorative knots on clothing became quite popular. In *Zuo Zhuan*, it was written: "The collar has an intersection, and the belt is tied as knots (衣有襘 , 带有结)." This marked the beginning of *Laozi* (络子) culture. The word *Lao* (络) refers to the ancient name for knots in China, and it became a tradition to tie a knot at the waist using silk or cotton ribbon. The peak of *Laozi* culture occurred during the Sui Dynasty and Tang Dynasty when basic knots such as Sauvastika knot (万字结) and round brocade knot (团锦结) gained popularity in both garments and common folk art found in palaces and homes. Therefore, knots were not only cherished as symbols and tools but also considered an essential part of everyday life for decorating and expressing thoughts and feelings.

During the Tang and Song dynasties, the love-based knot was a unique element that was evident in many poems, novels, and paintings. For instance, in Meng Yuanlao's (孟元老) memoir *Dongjing Meng Hua Lu* (《东京梦华录》), it was noted that a concentric knot (同心结) or a knot similar to a concentric knot was an essential part of the traditional wedding custom for the bride and groom to wear. Ancient poems also mentioned the concentric knot as a symbol of love, such as Luo Binwang's (骆宾王) poem: "Knot the ribbon as the concentric knot, interlock the love as the clothes (同心结缕带，连理织成衣)" and Huang Tingjian's (黄庭坚) poem: "We had a time knotting together, loving as the ribbon tied (曾共结，合欢罗带)". One of the most famous poems about the love knot was written by Meng Jiao (孟郊) titled "Knotting Love" (《结爱》).

The art of knot tying has steadily evolved over thousands of years, with the development of more sophisticated techniques and increasingly intricate woven patterns. During the Song and Yuan dynasties, the *Panchang* knot (盘长结), which is now one of the most recognizable Chinese knots, began to gain popularity. There are also numerous pieces of artwork that provide evidence of knots being used as clothing decorations during the Ming Dynasty. For example, in Tang Yin's (唐寅) beautiful paintings, intricately knotted ribbons are clearly depicted.

During the Qing Dynasty, knotting finally broke free from its pure folklore status and became an esteemed art form in Chinese society, reaching the pinnacle of its success. The culture of *Laozi* experienced a resurgence during this period as well. Basic knots were widely used to adorn objects such as *ruyi* (襦衣), sachets (香袋), wallets, fan tassels (流苏), spectacle cases, and rosaries (念珠) in daily life. This era also saw the expansion of single knot techniques into more intricate designs. According to the Chinese classical novel *Dream of the Red Chamber*, *Laozi* was embraced and popularized among middle and upper-class society members as a means to express love and luck between family members, lovers, and friends during the Qing Dynasty.

In the 1980s, Lydia Chen (陈夏生), who generously funded the Chinese Knotting Promotion Centre, collaborated with *ECHO of Things Chinese* (《汉声杂志》) to locate and document the remaining practitioners of the knotting tradition. Their work was featured in a series of articles and books. She named these traditional crafts "Chinese knots" and created practical manuals to share the art of Chinese knotting with a wider audience. As a result, Chinese knotting has become a popular symbol and souvenir at festivals and markets today.

(Adapted from Wikipedia website.)

Chapter Twelve

Traditional Chinese Medicine
中国传统医学

Traditional Chinese Medicine (TCM) originated in China several thousand years ago and is a valuable part of the country's precious cultural and scientific heritage. TCM follows the ancient principles of *yin* and *yang*, believing that people's existence, growth, behavior and death are inseparable from nature. By adhering to the laws of nature, revering life, and balancing *yin* and *yang*, TCM has developed various forms of treatment, such as herbal medicine, acupuncture and moxibustion, massage, cupping, *qigong*, and food therapy—all with the aim of restoring or maintaining good health.

12.1　TCM Theory

Traditional Chinese Medicine is characterized by holism and treatment based on syndrome differentiation. The concept of holism views the body as a whole, where the five *zang* organs（五脏）, nine orifices（九窍）, limbs and bones function through a system of meridians. Additionally, TCM focuses on the close relationship between man and nature. Treatment based on syndrome differentiation is the basic principle under which TCM understands and treats diseases—analyzing, inducing and synthesizing the clinical data obtained through the four methods of examination: observation（望诊）, auscultation（闻诊）, interrogation（问诊）, and palpation（切诊）. Through this process, TCM practitioners are able to identify symptoms and signs to determine proper treatments.

The fundamental TCM theories involve a scientific understanding of life, health, and diseases. They can be categorized into four parts: the philosophical foundation of TCM, which includes the *yin-yang* theory, the five-element theory, and essential-*qi* theory; detailed knowledge of the human body, including the functional activities of the *zang* and *fu* organs（脏腑）, *qi*, blood, body fluids and meridians and the mechanisms of life activities; comprehensive knowledge of disease causes and pathogenesis; principles of life cultivation and disease prevention and cure.

The *yin-yang* theory is based on the ancient Chinese philosophical concept of two opposite yet interrelated things or phenomena. It describes how things in the universe develop and change in relation to each other. In this system, everything is interconnected, and no entity can exist in isolation. The opposition and balance of *yin* and *yang* are inherent in all things.

Yin and *yang* are always subtly transforming into each other under certain circumstances, or in extreme situations. The transformation of *yin* and *yang* may occur in a relationship when they become extremely unbalanced. For instance, in some cases of acute hot diseases, the vitality of the body is greatly consumed and damaged due to an excessive accumulation of heat. Therefore, if there is high fever and profuse sweating, a sudden collapse of *yang-qi* (阳气) may occur and the patient's temperature will drop suddenly, his/her complexion will become pale and his/her four limbs will feel cold. This represents a transformation from a *yang* syndrome to a *yin* syndrome.

In TCM, the theory of *yin* and *yang* is used to explain physiological and pathological phenomena of the body. It is also a principle used in diagnosing and treating diseases.

TCM identifies five *zang* organs, six *fu* organs and six extraordinary *fu* organs based on their shapes and functions. It is acknowledged that the earth represents *yin*, nurturing all living organisms. This is exactly what the *yin* organs or *zang* organs—the heart, liver, spleen, lung, and kidney set out to do—Deeply situated in the body, they play a vital role in producing, transforming, regulating and storing fundamental substances—*qi* (气), blood (血), *jin* (津) and fluids (液). On the other hand, *fu* organs are considered to be *yang* organs. Heaven represents *yang*, symbolizing a sense of magnanimity and boundlessness. The *yang* organs or *fu* organs—the stomach, small intestine, large intestine, gallbladder, bladder and triple energizer—all perform similar functions. Located closer to the external places of the body, they can receive, break down and absorb food to transform it into fundamental substances. They can also excrete waste matters and sweat.

The extraordinary *fu* organs, such as the brain, marrow, bone, blood vessels, gallbladder and the uterus, are similar to *zang* organs in function but similar to *fu* organs in shape. Because they do not fit into either category, they are called "extraordinary *fu* organs".

Each organ has its own specific duties. For example, the heart occupies the first place among the five *zang* organs and governs the life activities of the whole body. This is why it is referred to as "the monarch organ" in *The Inner Canon of the Yellow Emperor*. The function of the heart in controlling the mind is known as the "heart storing spirit". It means the heart governs mental activities. It is thus clear that in TCM the concept of the heart includes certain functions of the brain. The heart also regulates blood flow. A sufficient supply of heart-blood guarantees a normal and ruddy complexion, hence "the heart's brilliance manifests on the face".

Zang and *fu* organs belong to different categories and play distinct roles. However, their functions are interdependent and mutually supportive at all times. Wherever the *fu* organs' influence reaches, it finds a ready echo in the *zang* organs, providing the body with a desirable and congenial environment.

(Selected and adapted from *English for Traditional Chinese Medicine.*)

◆ Cultural Analysis

(1) The Concept of Microcosm-Macrocosm

In TCM, the human being is considered a microcosm (small world) that corresponds rigorously to the macrocosm (large world); the body reflects the plan of the cosmos. For example, according to ancient Chinese thought, *qi* is the fundamental substance constituting the universe and all phenomena are produced by the changes and movement of *qi*. *Qi* in the human body moves in different ways to support life. Once it stops, life comes to an end.

(2) The Harmony Between Man and Nature

TCM emphasizes the close correlation between man and nature. In TCM, the concepts of structure, function and pathology of the human body do not merely refer to what is observed within the human body itself, but also relate to astronomy, geography, philosophy, and even ethics. According to TCM principles, people get sick due to disharmony caused by changes in certain factors such as environment, emotion, or the patients' lifestyle.

◆ Text Comprehension

l. Judge whether the following statements are true (T) or false (F).

1) In the whole body system, the five *zang* orifices, nine organs, limbs and bones function through a system of meridians.

2) Human beings cannot be separated from their *yin* and *yang* aspects in TCM.

3) *Yin-yang* theory is based on the ancient philosophical concept of two opposite yet interrelated things or phenomena.

4) The heart is referred to as "the monarch organ" by Li Shizhen.

5) When *qi* stops, we have to see a doctor to avoid life-threatening consequences.

2. Answer the following questions.

1) What is the relationship between *yin* and *yang*? How is the *yin-yang* theory applied in the TCM?

2) What are the five *zang* organs and six *fu* organs? What is the relationship between them in TCM?

3) How do you understand the concept of *qi* in nature and in the human body?

12.2   Chinese Materia Medica

Chinese materia medica, an important component of traditional Chinese medicine, is the study of the basic theory of Chinese medicines and their origins, collection, processing, attribute and clinical applications. The number of recognized Chinese medicines has gradually increased to a total of 8,000 different kinds of species and materials, among which 500 are commonly used in clinical practice. Because traditional Chinese medicines mostly come from natural resources (mainly plants, some from animals or minerals), they are also called "green medicines". They have been used for several thousand years and continued to gain recognition from many countries around the world.

The initial knowledge of Chinese materia medica was formed gradually as our remote ancestors consciously tested and observed the properties of herbs over a long period. It is recorded in ancient books that Shen Nong "tasted hundreds of herbs and came across toxicants about seventy times in one day", vividly showing the hardship suffered by our remote ancestors to understand Chinese materia medica. *Shen Nong's Herbal Classic* (《神农本草经》) is the earliest ancient medical book extant in China. It recorded 365 medicines and classified them into three grades: high, middle and low grades. It also discussed the four attributes and five flavors, as well as the compatibility of Chinese medicines, which established a foundation for the development of Chinese materia medica. In the Ming Dynasty, the great medical scientist Li Shizhen summarized and synthesized ancient herbology throughout his life. Over 27 years, he edited the *Compendium of Materia Medica* (《本草纲目》) which contained 1,892 medicines and more than 11,000 prescriptions. In this book, the pictures of medicine were drawn, former errors were corrected, and the medicines were classified into 16 major categories and 60 types according to their natural properties and ecological conditions. Li Shizhen made outstanding contributions to the development of Chinese materia medica and is recognized as one of the greatest scientists in the world.

The theory of the properties of Chinese medicines is the basic theory of Chinese materia medica, which includes the four attributes, and the five flavors. The four different attributes are cold, hot, warm and cool. Generally speaking, Chinese medicines with a cold or cool attribute are good for clearing heat, purging fire, cooling the blood and removing toxic substances. They can alleviate or relieve *yang* heat syndromes. Chinese medicines with a hot or warm attribute have the effects of warming the interior, dispersing cold, restoring collapsed *yang-qi*, warming the meridians, activating the collaterals, supplementing fire and supporting *yang*. They can alleviate or relieve *yin* cold syndromes.

The five flavors of Chinese medicines are acrid, sweet, sour, bitter and salty. They are determined by the actual tastes and effects of the medicines. In general, acrid medicines have the function of dispersing and promoting *qi* and blood circulation. Sweet medicines are used for tonifying, regulating the middle-*jiao* (中焦) and relieve spasms. Sour medicines have the effects of astringing and arresting discharge. Bitter medicines are used to purge, dry dampness and fortify *yin*. Salty medicines can soften a mass and disperse stagnation. They are also used as purgatives, which promote defecation and suppress excessive *yang*.

Peiwu (配伍 , the compatibility of medicines) is an important principle in prescribing. Each prescription typically consists of four to eight ingredients on average. It usually includes the monarch herb, which is the chief herb and main ingredient; the minister herb, which augments and promotes the function of the main ingredient; the assistant herb, which reduces side effects of the monarch herb; and the envoy herb, which harmonizes and coordinates the actions of all other herbs.

(Selected and adapted from *English for Traditional Chinese Medicine*.)

◆ Cultural Analysis

(1) Neutralization and Harmony

The concept of "neutralization and harmony" is rooted in Confucian philosophy. In the context of pharmacology, it not only refers to the appropriate combination of different herbs in appropriate proportions, but also emphasizes a state of harmony, balance and unity. The idea of "neutralization" attaches importance to the coordination and balance of the advantages and disadvantages of traditional Chinese medicines, as well as using medication according to people's physique, timing, and environment.

(2) Balance and Compatibility

The *peiwu* framework, consisting of the monarch, minister, assistant, and envoy, draws from the ancient structure of state officials. Originally referring to four types of people, it later came to represent the different functions of each medicine in traditional Chinese medicine prescriptions. This metaphor serves to distinguish between the various functions of each component and emphasizes the collective strength of all the medicines working together.

◆ Text Comprehension

1. Judge whether the following statements are true (T) or false (F).

1) Minerals can also be used in traditional Chinese medicine therapies.

2) The *Compendium of Materia Medica* lists 1,892 distinct herbs, and more than 11,000 prescriptions.

3) The *Compendium of Materia Medica* states that Shen Nong "tasted hundreds of herbs and came across toxicants about seventy times in one day".

4) The four different attributes of Chinese medicines are cold, hot, warm and cool.

5) The five flavors of Chinese medicines are determined solely by the actual tastes.

2. Answer the following questions.

1) What are the characteristics of Chinese materia medica?

2) What are the four different attributes and the five flavors of Chinese medicines? What is their drug efficacy respectively?

3) How do you understand *peiwu*?

12.3　Contrast Between TCM and Western Medicine

TCM is a culmination of the extensive experience of the Chinese people in their enduring battle against disease. Over thousands of years, influenced and guided by ancient Chinese philosophy, TCM has evolved into a discipline with a unique theoretical framework and diverse methods for diagnosis, treatment, and health maintenance. These have been acquired through the long-term accumulation of medical practice and integration with other fields of study.

The concept of TCM treatment is known for its holistic approach and treatment based on syndrome differentiation, while Western Medicine focuses on identifying the cause of a disease and then using appropriate medicine according to the human body's physiological systems. For example, TCM does not recognize the concept of a nervous system, but it has been proven effective in treating neurological diseases. Similarly, Western Medicine does not consider wind as a pathogenic factor, yet it can effectively treat conditions such as wind rash (rubella) and wind arthralgia as identified by TCM. While the underlying theories of these two medical systems differ, both have demonstrated success in treating the same diseases.

In the two theoretical systems of medicine, doctors approach clinical diagnosis and treatment with different logic and thinking. In Western Medicine, understanding a disease means perceiving it as a distinct entity that can be isolated from the patient's body. The Western physician begins by identifying clinical symptoms and then conducts thorough check-ups and laboratory examinations to uncover the underlying mechanism—a precise cause for a specific disease—before formulating an exact, quantifiable prescription for the disease. In TCM, understanding a disease means finding correlations between all the patient's symptoms and signs. It is necessary to integrate the symptoms with other aspects of the patient's life and behavior in order to determine the disease. The Chinese physician carefully observes and organizes symptoms and signs that may not be noticed by Western physicians.

Observation is a crucial aspect of the Chinese physician's diagnosis. Every detail about the individual is carefully observed: their tongue, eyes, skin color, hearing, pulse, age, weight, body type, voice, hair, posture, and body odor. The TCM physician gathers all relevant information including symptoms and other factors related to the patient, such as living environment, weather, habits and moods, and integrates them into what TCM refers to as a "pattern of disharmony". This pattern essentially describes the imbalance in the patient's body and a prescription is provided to regulate this imbalance.

In terms of diagnosis and treatment, a doctor of Western Medicine may diagnose several patients with the same stomach pain, attributing it to peptic ulcers caused by a certain bacteria. From the perspective of this Western doctor, all these patients are suffering from the same disorder. However, a doctor of TCM may conclude that they have different patterns of disharmony based on their unique symptoms and signs, complexions, affects, tongue properties and coatings, pulses, etc. For example, one patient may be characterized as having the pattern of disharmony called "deficiency of *yang* of spleen and stomach"; another may be said to have the "deficiency of *yin* of stomach" —a disharmony that is quite different from the first patient. Additionally, another patient's condition may be characterized as "damp-heat of spleen". In TCM, this concept is referred to as "identical diseases with different symptoms" and "treating the same disease with different methods".

(Selected and adapted from *English for Traditional Chinese Medicine*.)

◆ Cultural Analysis

(1) Clinical Medicine vs. Laboratory Medicine

In TCM theory, diagnosis and treatment have been summarized and developed mainly on the basis of observation and practice over a long period of time. However, Western Medicine initially developed in the laboratory before moving to clinical applications. With the development of science, it continues to progress towards refinement and specialization.

(2) Natural Medicine vs. Compounds Medicine

The medicines used in TCM are derived entirely from nature. Many of these medicines have a dual regulatory effect, with their function not necessarily stemming from the main ingredient. Their effectiveness is supported by human trials. TCM also acknowledges that certain poisonous drugs can be used to treat diseases. In contrast, the medicines used in Western Medicine are laboratory-produced compounds tested on animals such as rats.

◆ Text Comprehension

1. Judge whether the following statements are true (T) or false (F).

1) In the two theoretical systems of medicine, doctors approach clinical diagnosis and treatment with different logic and thinking.

2) Western physicians perceive a disease as a distinct entity that can be isolated from the patient's body.

3) The underlying theories of the two medical systems are different, so Western Medicine can't cure the same disease as TCM.

4) The effectiveness of TCM is supported by animal trials.

5) The Western physician observes and organizes symptoms and signs that may not be noticed by Chinese physicians.

2. Answer the following questions.

1) How do Western Medicine and TCM diagnose patients with stomach pain?

2) What specific details do Chinese physicians observe in their diagnosis of a patient?

3) What are the differences between TCM and Western Medicine ?

◆ Exercises

1. Provide descriptions of the following terms.

Terms	Descriptions
The *yin-yang* theory	
Zang and *fu* organs	
Peiwu	

2. Choose the best answer to each of the following questions.

1) The philosophic foundation of TCM includes the *yin-yang* theory, the five-element theory, and _____.

   A. observation, auscultation, interrogation, palpation

   B. *zang-fu* theory

   C. essential-*qi* theory

   D. none of above

2) TCM recognizes _____ *zang* organs, _____ *fu* organs and _____ extraordinary *fu* organs based on their shapes and functions.

   A. 3, 5, 12

   B. 3, 6, 12

   C. 5, 6, 6

   D. 5, 6, 12

3) Chinese medicines come from natural resources, including _____, animals and minerals.

   A. plants

   B. compounds

   C. seafood

   D. all of the above

4) The five flavors of Chinese medicines are _____.

   A. hot, cold, sweet, salty and sour

   B. hot, cold, acrid, bitter and salty

   C. acrid, sweet, sour, warm and cool

   D. acrid, sweet, sour, bitter and salty

5) Observation plays an essential part in the Chinese physician's diagnosis. The physician needs to observe: _____.

A. tongue, eyes, skin color and hearing

B. pulse, age, weight and body type

C. voice, hair, posture and body odor

D. all of the above

3. Translate the following sentences.

1) 中国人很早就懂得用医药来治病疗伤，保障自己的健康。

2) 中药的来源主要是植物，也有一些来自动物或矿物质。

3) 中医认为人体是一个以脏腑经络为内在联系的有机整体，同时这个整体与自然界又是统一的。

4) 阴阳学说广泛应用于中医，以解释人体的组织结构、生理功能和病理变化，用来作为治疗诊断的指南。

5) 现代中国也有很多中医名家，他们努力攻克医学难关，为民造福。

4. Discuss the following questions.

1) What is the basic theory of TCM?

2) In which aspects do you think TCM can complement Western Medicine?

3) What is the relationship between Chinese philosophy and TCM?

5. Work in groups. Do research on the following Chinese herbs and fill in the table below. Then report your findings to the class.

Chinese Herbs	Folk Stories	Riddles	Poems
Angelica root （当归）			
Quisqualis indica （使君子）			
Chinese pulsatilla root （白头翁）			
Chinese thorowax root （柴胡）			

◆ Extended Readings

Acupuncture and Moxibustion 针灸

Acupuncture and moxibustion are important components of TCM. These practices can prevent and treat diseases by stimulating certain acupoints（穴位）on the body with metal needles, or applying heat with ignited moxa wool. Chinese acupuncture and moxibustion have gained great popularity due to their special methods and amazing curative effects.

The origin of acupuncture and moxibustion can be traced back to the clan commune period of Chinese primitive society 4,000 years ago. According to historical records, acupuncture instruments were originally made of stone named *bian* stone（砭石）. The use of *bian* stone needles for treatment first appeared in the east coast of China, where the inhabitants depended on fishing for their livelihood. On the other hand, moxibustion originated in the north of China, where people subsisted on animal husbandry. Through the accumulation of clinical experience in both regions, acupuncture and moxibustion therapy was developed.

The science of acupuncture and moxibustion is based on the TCM theories, especially those related to the *jingluo*（经络, meridians and collaterals）. According to TCM, the *jingluo* are pathways through which the *qi* and blood of the human body circulate. They are connected to the internal *zangfu* organs and extend externally throughout the body, forming a network that links tissues and organs into an organic whole. This network transports *qi* and blood to nourish the *zangfu* organs, skin, muscles, tendons and bones, and regulate the balance between *yin* and *yang* of the whole body. It consists of meridians and collaterals with the twelve regular meridians serving as the major trunks of this system. Each regular meridian is named after its corresponding organ among the twelve *zangfu* organs respectively.

Acupoints are not only the locations where the *qi* and blood of *zangfu* and *jingluo* flow to the surface of the body, but they are also the reaction points for certain diseases. The therapy of acupuncture and moxibustion requires the stimulation of certain acupoints on the human body to activate the meridians and collaterals, and regulate the function of internal organs, *qi* and blood. Among the 361 acupoints, those along the fourteen meridians are distributed along the twelve regular meridians, as well as *du*（督, governor vessel）and *ren*（任, conception vessel）meridians. All points in this category can be used to treat disorders related to their respective meridians and collaterals. They are commonly used points that make up a significant portion of all acupoints.

The invention of acupuncture instruments is closely related to the development of human productivity. Originally made of stone or bone in remote antiquity, the needles were later replaced by metal ones made from copper, gold or silver. Nowadays, stainless steel instruments are commonly used. In addition to needles, traditional Chinese acupuncture and moxibustion also use moxa in cigar or small pyramid shapes to blister or warm the skin.

Acupuncture and moxibustion have been proven through modern medical experiments to have a positive effect on more than 300 diseases, including internal, external, gynecological, pediatric, and eye, ear, nose and throat conditions. They are particularly effective in treating certain syndromes such as pain, wind stroke, facial paralysis and insomnia. Chinese acupuncture and moxibustion are easy to apply and cost-effective. They are widely preferred and valued in medical therapy worldwide.

(Selected and adapted from *English for Traditional Chinese Medicine*.)

A Legendary Story of *Gegen* 葛根的传说

Hidden within the great treasure house of TCM and the healing practices of rural China are pearls of folk wisdom. One form of this wisdom is found in folk tales about the origins of plant names or how a plant came to be used as medicine—perhaps by chance discovery, invention by immortal beings, or simply by observing a diseased animal eating a plant and then returning to a healthy state. For centuries, storytellers have passed down the tales from one generation to the next. This rich oral tradition conveys much about Chinese culture, folk customs, social habits, history, medical knowledge, mythology, and wisdom.

The following story is about *gegen* (kudzu vine root). It is used to treat a condition termed "superficial syndrome", which occurs when a disease manifests under the surface of the skin (such as measles without skin eruptions) but is not yet severe. This condition is often accompanied by fever, thirst, a lack of sweating, and headache. It is also used to treat diarrhea and dysentery. Since ancient times before written history, this medicinal herb has been known as *gegen* in TCM. It is first mentioned in the middle class of herbs in *Shen Nong's Herbal Classic*.

Once upon a time, an old man spent his days digging medicinal roots on a great mountain covered in a dense forest. One day, he heard men shouting and horses neighing from the mountainside below. He did not know what was wrong, so he peered out from behind some trees to see what was happening. A few minutes later, a young man about fourteen or fifteen years old was frantically running across the sharp mountain stones and scurrying around trees. The boy caught sight of the old man and ran to him. Then, in a most respectful way, the boy threw himself to his knees before the feet of the old man.

"Why do you bow on the ground before me in such a respectful way?" asked the bewildered root-digger.

"Grandfather, grandfather, help me! Help me! They want to kill me!" pleaded the boy.

"Who are you?" asked the old man.

"I am the son of the gentleman Mr. Ge," replied the boy.

"Who wants to kill you?" asked the old man.

"In the court, there is a treacherous official," explained the boy as he gasped to catch a breath. "He falsely accuses my father of having a private army and says he stations troops and conspires to rebel against the Emperor. The Emperor believes this is true, so he ordered his officials to lead an army to surround my home and kill everyone in the family. My father said to me, 'You are the only hope for continuing our family line.' He told me to run away and to avenge when I grow up. But the officials have found me and followed me here! Grandfather, please save me! If you save me, you save entire Ge family."

The old man firmly stroked the ends of his long silvery mustache, deep in thought. After a moment, he said aloud, "I know the gentleman Ge, and he is very loyal. In fact, his family has been loyal to the Emperors for several generations."

As the soldiers following the boy drew closer, the old root-digger and the frightened boy could hear the horses breaking through the forest. The old man looked towards the backside of the mountain and had an idea.

"Follow me quickly," he commanded, leading them into a thicket of trees.

The boy followed him deep into the mountain forest where they found refuge in a well-hidden stone cave. They stayed there for several days while the army searched in vain for three days before finally calling off their pursuit.

When it was safe to leave their hiding place, the old man asked, "Where do you want to go?"

The boy cried and said, "All of my family members were caught and exterminated along with my eight relative families."

"Grandfather, you saved me," the boy cried with deep gratitude, "I want to serve you for my whole life. After your death, I will wear hemp clothes and mourn for you. But, I don't know if you would accept me."

The old man considered the boy's offer and replied, "You may live here with me, but my home is in this forest. I spend my time collecting herbs and medicinal plants, every day climbing one mountain after another. It is not as comfortable or easy as your previous lifestyle."

"I am happy just to be alive. You have saved me and the Ge family," the boy replied. "If you will adopt me, I am willing to do the hard work."

From then on, the boy followed the old herb gatherer, collecting herbs and roots every day. The old person always dug a particular herb with a very large tuberous root, which was highly sought after for treating fever, thirst, and diarrhea.

Several years later, the old man died, but he had passed on his knowledge of herbs to the boy as if he were his own son. Like the old herb gatherer, the boy specialized in digging herbs with the large tuberous roots. He used them to successfully treat many sick people. However, the herb did not have a name.

One day someone asked, "What is the name of the herb?" The son of the gentlemen Ge looked back on his life experience and replied, "I am the only one left in the Ge family, like a root for my family, so I will call this herb *gegen*."

In China, when a man dies, he leaves behind a root—the new generation—called *gen*. Today, the medicinal herb derived from the root of kudzu is still called *gegen*.

(Adapted from ABC Herbalgram website.)

References

常俊跃，霍跃红，王焱．2016.中国文化（英文版）（第2版）．北京：北京大学
　　出版社．

崔进．新编旅游英语．2007.武汉：武汉大学出版社．

《大学英语选修课·学科课程系列教材》项目组．2011.中国文化概论．北京：
　　高等教育出版社．

冯桂冰．2007.中医英语．北京：高等教育出版社．

辜正坤．2007.西方学术精华概论．北京：高等教育出版社．

国务院侨务办公室，国家汉语国际推广领导小组办公室．2007.中国文化常识．
　　北京：高等教育出版社．

候香浪，何明霞．2015.中国文化英语教程．武汉：武汉大学出版社．

金元浦．1999.中国文化概论．北京：首都师范大学出版社．

廖华英．2015.中国文化概况．北京：外语教学与研究出版社．

李小重．1998.饭店英语．武汉：武汉测绘科技大学出版社．

林玮生．中西文化范式发生的神话学研究．2017.广州：中山大学出版社．

钱穆．2015.民族与文化．北京：九州出版社．

［美］塞缪尔·亨廷顿著．周琪，刘绯，张立平等译．文明的冲突与世界秩序的
　　重建．2009.北京：新华出版社．

束定芳．2016.中国文化英语教程．上海：上海外语教育出版社．

［美］孙隆基．2015.中国文化的深层结构．北京：中信出版社．

唐正秋，林琳．2013.中国文化．大连：大连理工大学出版社．

王志茹，陆晓丽．2017.英语畅谈中国文化．北京：外语教学与研究出版社．

王会昌．1992.中国文化地理．武汉：华中师范大学出版社．

徐日辉．2021.会说话的青铜器．武汉：华中科技大学出版社．

许渊冲．2021.许渊冲译陶渊明诗选．北京：中译出版社．

薛荣．2011.中国文化教程（英文版）．南京：南京大学出版社．

杨汉瑜，冯雪燕 . 2015. 中国文化概论 . 北京：新华出版社 .

叶朗 . 2010. 中国文化英语教程 . 北京：外语教学与研究出版社 .

祝吉芳 . 2016. 冲突、碰撞与趋同下的中西文化 . 北京：北京大学出版社 .

周仪 . 2011. 中国文化概论 . 重庆：重庆大学出版社 .

［美］朱利安·斯图尔德著 . 谭卫华，罗康隆译 . 杨庭硕校译 . 2013. 文化变迁论 . 贵阳：贵州人民出版社 .

Lv, Y. 2018. Existence and development: The value attribution of Mozi's educational thought. *Advances in Social Science, Education and Humanities Research, 290*, 245–248.

Ebrey, P. B. 1993. *Chinese Civilization*, New York: The Free Press.

Thorp, R. L. & Vinograd, R. E. 2001. *Chinese Art & Culture*. Englewood Cliffs: Prentice Hall.

Owen, S. 1996. *Anthology of Chinese Literature*. New York: W. W. Norton & Company.

Lee, W. Y. 1995. Women's education in traditional and modern China. *Women's History Review,* 4(3): 345–367.

Zhao, J. H. 2022. Similarities and differences between Chinese and Western ancient education. *Advances in Social Science, Education and Humanities Research, 653*: 55–59.

Si, C. M. & Si, Y. C. 2011. *Introduction to Chinese Culture*. Beijing: Peking University Press.

Appendix

A Chronology of Chinese History
中国历史编年表

3000 BC—2100 BC	Yellow Emperor（黄帝）& Yan Emperor（炎帝）	
	Yao（尧）	
	Shun（舜）	
	Yu（禹）	
2070 BC—1600 BC	The Xia Dynasty（夏）	
1600 BC—1046 BC	The Shang Dynasty（商）	
1046 BC—771 BC	The Zhou Dynasty（周）	The Western Zhou Dynasty（西周）
770 BC—221 BC		The Eastern Zhou Dynasty（东周）
770 BC—476 BC		The Spring and Autumn Period（春秋）
475 BC—221 BC		The Warring States Period（战国）
221 BC—206 BC	The Qin Dynasty（秦）	
206 BC—24 AD	The Han Dynasty（汉）	The Western Han Dynasty（西汉）
25—220		The Eastern Han Dynasty（东汉）
220—265	The Three Kingdoms（三国）	The Kingdom of Wei（魏）
221—263		The Kingdom of Shu Han（蜀汉）
222—280		The Kingdom of Wu（吴）
265—316	The Western Jin Dynasty（西晋）	

317—420	The Eastern Jin Dynasty（东晋）	
420—479	The Southern Dynasties（南朝）	The Song Dynasty（宋）
479—502		The Qi Dynasty（齐）
502—557		The Liang Dynasty（梁）
557—589		The Chen Dynasty（陈）
386—534	The Northern Dynasties（北朝）	The Northern Wei Dynasty（北魏）
534—550		The Eastern Wei Dynasty（东魏）
550—577		The Northern Qi Dynasty（北齐）
535—556		The Western Wei Dynasty（西魏）
557—581		The Northern Zhou Dynasty（北周）
581—618	The Sui Dynasty（隋）	
618—907	The Tang Dynasty（唐）	
907—923	The Five Dynasties（五代）	The Later Liang Dynasty（后梁）
923—936		The Later Tang Dynasty（后唐）
936—946		The Later Jin Dynasty（后晋）
947—950		The Later Han Dynasty（后汉）
951—960		The Later Zhou Dynasty（后周）
960—1127	The Song Dynasty（宋）	The Northern Song Dynasty（北宋）
1127—1279		The Southern Song Dynasty（南宋）
916—1125	The Liao Dynasty（辽）	
1115—1234	The Jin Dynasty（金）	
1271—1368	The Yuan Dynasty（元）	
1368—1644	The Ming Dynasty（明）	
1644—1911	The Qing Dynasty（清）	
1912—1949	The Republic of China（中华民国）	
1949—	The People's Republic of China（中华人民共和国）	